x71M1XDC

THE FUNDAMENTALS OF PSYCHOLOGY

THE FUNDAMENTALS OF
PSYCHOLOGY

ANA MONTANO

95 Merrick Way, Suite 700 Miami, FL 33134

Library of Congress Control Number: 2014937969
ISBN: 978-0-9961036-0-2

Editor: Dr. Beth Lagaron

ABOUT THE AUTHOR

ANA MONTANO has worked in the field of psychology for almost a decade. She obtained a bachelor's degree in psychology and one in criminology from the University of Florida in Gainesville, FL. She went on to obtain her master's degree in the field at American University in Washington, DC. She has extensive research experience, particularly in the areas of social psychology, child psychology, cognitive psychology and clinical psychology, and has worked on a variety of research projects involving decision making, stereotyping, treatments for ADHD, attractiveness and body image, among others. She currently resides in Miami, FL, where she teaches and works as Psychology Program Director at Dade Medical College.

ACKNOWLEDGEMENTS

THE SUCCESSFUL COMPLETION of this text can be traced back to the wonderful faculty of UF and AU, many of whom acted as great mentors in my inquisitive exploration of psychological research and allowed me to gain considerable insight in the field. Without the mentorship of Dr. Catherine Cottrell, Dr. Clara Cheng, Dr. Anthony Ahrens, Dr. Michele Carter, and Dr. David Haaga, I would hardly be where I am today.

I'd like to thank my colleagues at Dade Medical College for their endless support and for keeping my work life relatively stress-free while I completed this project, particularly Michelle Oses, Aeilyng Pereira, Dr. Beth Lagaron, Sara Hekmat, Ariel Espinosa, Diana Bustos, and the entire Gen Ed and Education Department. Extra thanks are due to Beth for meticulously editing this book. I also owe a special thanks to Bill Cruz and Jaxanna Martinez, of the Marketing and Design Department, without whom I would have never been able to see this through.

On a personal note, I'd like to thank my parents, Jose and Maria Fabre, and my closest friends, Lauren Cruz, Leilani Diaz, Lis Mesa,Yamille Hernandez, Raquel Duenas, Irella Casco, James Sallee and Ellen Knezevich, for believing that I could do this before I did.

Finally, I'd like to give my sincerest thanks to Ernesto Perez, Jr., who inspired and pushed me to write this book until I succeeded. Without his backing, this certainly would not be in print.

This text is humbly dedicated to all my students, past and present, for showing me that the greatest joy in psychology is to teach it.

TABLE OF CONTENTS

About the Author .... *v*

Acknowledgements .... *vi*

Chapter 1: The Foundations of Psychology 1

Greek Philosophers 1

The Beginnings of the Science of Psychology 2

Contemporary Psychological Theories 3

Biological Perspective 3

Psychodynamic Perspective 4

Behavioral Perspective 5

Cognitive Perspective 6

Humanistic Perspective 7

Evolutionary Perspective 8

Sociocultural Perspective 9

The Enduring Issues of Psychology 10

The Science of Psychology 12

Sampling 13

Research Methods 15

Ethical Guidelines 22

Chapter 1 Review Questions 24

Chapter 2: Biological Psychology 27

The Nervous System ... 28

Neurons ... 28

The Divisions of the Nervous System ... 31

The Central Nervous System ... 35

The Peripheral Nervous System ... 43

The Endocrine System ... 45

How Genes Affect Behavior ... 47

Animal and Human Studies ... 48

Evolutionary Psychology ... 50

Chapter 2 Review Questions ... 52

Chapter 3: Sensation and Perception 55

Sensation ... 56

Vision ... 57

Hearing ... 61

Olfaction ... 64

Taste ... 64

Somatosensory System ... 66

Perception ... 68

Perceptual Constancies ... 70

Distance and Depth ... 71

Individual Differences in Perception ... 74

Chapter 3 Review Questions ... 77

Chapter 4: Consciousness 79

Sleep 80
Stages of Sleep 82
Sleep Disorders 84
Dreams 87
Drug-Altered States of Consciousness 90
Depressants 91
Stimulants 93
Hallucinogens 95
Substance Use Disorder 96
Other Types of Consciousness 98
Chapter 4 Review Questions 100

Chapter 5: Psychology of Learning 103

Behavioral Perspective of Learning 104
Classical Conditioning 104
Operant Conditioning 109
Extinction and Spontaneous Recovery 116
Generalization in Conditioning 117
Similarities and Differences 119
Cognitive Perspective on Learning 120
Latent Learning 120
Insight Learning 122
Learning Sets 122
Social Learning 123
Chapter 5 Review Questions 126

Chapter 6: Memory 129

Sensory Memory 130

Short-Term Memory 132

Long-Term Memory 134

Serial Position Effect 137

Types of Long-Term Memory 138

Forgetting 142

Interference and Errors of Reconstruction 143

Special Types of Memory 146

Flashbulb Memories 146

Exceptional Memories 147

Recovered Memories 148

Chapter 6 Review Questions 150

Chapter 7: Intelligence and Cognitive Abilities 153

Contemporary Theories of Intelligence 154

Intelligence Testing 155

Ranges of IQ 156

Criticisms of IQ Testing 158

Heredity and Environment 160

Cognition 161

Language 162

Images and Concepts 165

Problem Solving 165

Problem Solving Barriers 167

Decision Making 168

Decision Making Heuristics 169

Chapter 7 Review Questions 173

Chapter 8: Motivation and Emotion 177

Understanding Motivation 178

Instinct Theory 178

Drive Reduction Theory 178

Incentive Theory 179

Maslow's Hierarchical Theory 180

Motivation of Hunger 181

Biological Factors 182

Environmental Factors 183

Eating Disorders 184

Sexual Motivation 186

Sexual Orientation 188

Social Motivations 189

Love and Belonging 189

Achievement 190

Emotion 191

Theories of Emotion 191

Universality of Emotion 193

Communicating Emotion 195

Gender Differences in Emotion 196

Cultural Differences in Emotion 197

Chapter 8 Review Questions 198

Chapter 9: Development Through the Life Span 201

Studying Development 201

Prenatal Development 203

Development in Infancy and Childhood 204

Cognitive Development 206

Social Development 209

Erikson's Stages of Psychosocial Development 212

Adolescence 214

Social Development 215

Moral Development 217

Adulthood 217

Young Adulthood 218

Middle Adulthood 218

Late Adulthood 219

Cognition in Adulthood 220

Facing Death 221

Chapter 9 Review Questions 223

Chapter 10: Personality 227

Psychodynamic Perspective 228

Freud's Personality Structure 229

Personality Development According to Freud 232

Neo-Freudian Psychodynamic Theorists 235

Behavioral and Social Cognitive Perspective 236

Reciprocal Determinism and Self-Efficacy 237

Locus of Control 239
Humanistic Perspective 241
Criticisms of the Humanistic Perspective 242
Trait Perspective 243
Assessment of Personality 246
Chapter 10 Review Questions 250

Chapter 11: Social Psychology 253

Social Influence 254
Conformity 254
Compliance 256
Obedience 258
Social Cognition 261
Attitudes 261
Forming Impressions 262
Stereotypes 267
Attributions of Behavior 267
Social Interaction 270
Prejudice and Discrimination 271
The Rules of Attraction 272
Helping Behavior 274
Chapter 11 Review Questions 277

Chapter 12: Abnormal Psychology 281

Defining Abnormality 282
Perspectives of Psychological Disorders 283

Contemporary Models of Abnormality 284
Classifying Mental Disorders 286
Depressive Disorders 287
Bipolar and Related Disorders 289
Anxiety Disorders 290
Generalized Anxiety Disorder 290
Panic Disorder and Agoraphobia 291
Phobic Disorders 292
Obsessive-Compulsive Disorders 293
Somatic Symptom and Related Disorders 296
Dissociative Disorders 296
Sexual Dysfunctions and Paraphilic Disorders 298
Gender Dysphoria 299
Schizophrenia 300
Personality Disorders 301
Neurodevelopmental Disorders 303
Chapter 12 Review Questions 306

Chapter 13: Stress and Health 309

What is Stress? 310
Stress and Personality 313
How Stress Affects the Body 315
Sources of Major Stress 319
Stress-Related Psychological Disorders 320
Coping With Stress 321
Defensive Coping 322

Direct and Constructive Coping ... 325
Chapter 13 Review Questions ... 327

Chapter 14: Psychological Therapies 331

Historical Perspective ... 332
Psychoanalysis ... 333
Humanistic Therapy ... 335
Roger's Client-Centered Therapy ... 335
Gestalt Therapy ... 336
Behavior Therapies ... 337
Therapies Based on Classical Conditioning ... 338
Therapies Based on Operant conditioning ... 341
Cognitive Therapies ... 342
Rational-Emotive behavior Therapy (REBT) ... 343
Stress-Inoculation Therapy ... 343
Group Therapies ... 344
Does Therapy Work? ... 346
Biomedical Therapies ... 347
Drug Therapies ... 348
Other Biomedical Therapies ... 349
Chapter 14 Review Questions ... 351

Glossary ... *355*
References ... *383*
Index ... *411*
Image Credits ... *433*

CHAPTER 1

THE FOUNDATIONS OF PSYCHOLOGY

THE FIELD OF **PSYCHOLOGY** has evolved over the years to what we know it to be today: the scientific study of mental functions and behavior.

GREEK PHILOSOPHERS

Though psychology is a relatively new science, its roots date back to the time of Greek philosophers. Long before Freud, Pavlov and Beck, there were Socrates, Plato and Aristotle. Despite lacking the scientific tools and research guidelines we employ today, many great thinkers began to wonder how and why we think and behave the way we do. One of the earliest known philosophers to do so was Socrates (470-399 BC).

Socrates believed that we are born with knowledge and that we use reasoning to access it when needed. He also believed in the concept of **dualism**, which is the idea that the abstract world of the mind is separate from our physical world, where our bodies and real objects exist. Socrates's student, Plato, championed many of his ideas, including the concept of dualism. Plato (428-347 BC) also put forth the idea that we use reason to balance our desires and our emotions – a concept that would later be explored by Sigmund Freud.

Early philosophers' ideas have greatly influenced contemporary psychology.

Aristotle (384-322 BC), a student of Plato, disagreed with Socrates and Plato's idea of innate knowledge. Instead, he believed we acquire knowledge by using logic and reasoning to observe the world around us. This idea of observation and reasoning predates our modern day scientific method which relies on the same basic principles to make sense of the world.

THE BEGINNINGS OF THE SCIENCE OF PSYCHOLOGY

Though Greek philosophers had many fresh ideas about the inner workings of the mind that would stand the test of time, they did very little in the way of scientifically proving these ideas. The true birth of scientific psychology came with Wilhelm Wundt (1832-1920). Wundt believed that thinking could be studied objectively and scientifically, the way all natural events are. Memory was one of his main research interests and he opened up the first psychological research lab at the University of Leipzig in Germany to explore the subject.

Many of his students took their experience in his lab to universities in other countries in Europe and to the United States. Emerging shortly thereafter was William James (1842-1910), who studied various different sciences alongside psychology. He believed that psychology was the point where philosophy and physiology met. He, too, began doing psychological experiments at Harvard and based on his research, he wrote the book, *The Principles of Psychology* (1890). One of his biggest contributions to the field was his theory of **functionalism**. This theory explores how we use our mental abilities to function in our environment.

Along with Wilhelm Wundt, William James helped bring psychology to the forefront of scientific research. More and more students became interested in exploring and explaining human thought and behavior.

CONTEMPORARY PSYCHOLOGICAL THEORIES

While the study of psychology has been more or less defined over the years as the way we study our behavior and mental states, these psychological methods can vary greatly from one psychologist to another. Many different approaches exist in contemporary psychology and each one demonstrates a unique perspective used to analyze the same psychological phenomena.

BIOLOGICAL PERSPECTIVE

Physiological psychologists believe that biological processes underlie our behavior and our mental processes. This is the approach favored by many psychiatrists and clinical psychologists who aim to find the explanation of psychological phenomena in the structures and functions of our brain and different systems in the body. The focus of this approach can range from genetics to biochemistry to neuropharmacology and encompasses the complex relationship between the mind and body.

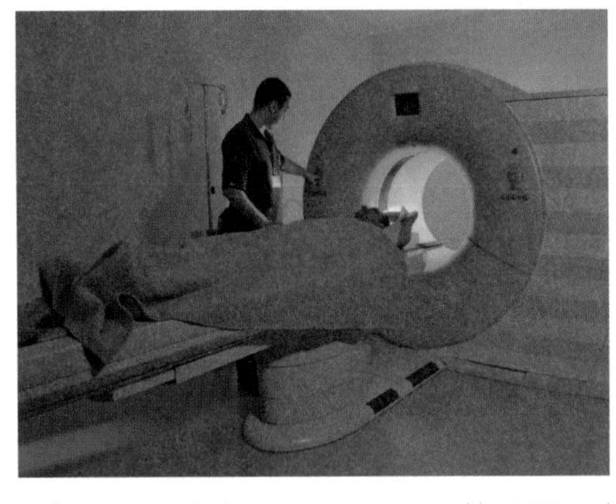

Biological psychologists use measures like MRI and EEG, among others, to examine physiological activity in the body and apply that to psychology.

One psychologist may be interested in studying whether schizophrenia has a genetic component, while another researches the effect of cocaine on the brain. Both of these are starkly different topics, but both fall under the biological perspective umbrella.

PSYCHODYNAMIC PERSPECTIVE

Sigmund Freud (1856-1939), undoubtedly one of the most famous and polarizing figures in psychology, is known as the founding father of the psychodynamic approach to psychology. His approach emphasized the way in which we are motivated by a combination of our primitive and forbidden desires, our sexual drives, our primal fears and wishes, and traumatic experiences from our childhood. All of these make up what he called the *unconscious*. According to Freud, the unconscious exists as a separate part of our brain from that which is consciously aware. For example, the memory of a traumatic accident in childhood might be repressed, or forgotten, but it would still underlie and influence the way a person feels, behaves, and thinks. This theory suggests that humans are largely unaware of their true motivations and are not always in control of their behavior and thoughts.

Many of his theories have been criticized because they are impossible to test scientifically. Nonetheless, contemporary versions of his theories are still applied in psychology today and have laid the groundwork for the study of personality and psychological disorders.

BEHAVIORAL PERSPECTIVE

As the field of psychology progressed, new perspectives began to emerge. Beginning with the work of Russian physiologist Ivan Pavlov (1849-1936), **behaviorism** began to gain popularity among psychologists. The central tenet of behaviorism and the behavioral perspective is that psychology should study only observable behavior. In one of the most well-known psychological experiments, Ivan Pavlov observed that dogs had an anticipatory drooling response prior to being fed, simply when hearing the sound of their feeder. Based on this observation, he decided to see whether the dogs could be taught to salivate to the sound of a ringing bell, even when there was no food present. His experiment was a success and the dogs' learned response to this change in the environment created the foundation on which behaviorism was built (Pavlov, 1927).

In the mid-twentieth century, John B. Watson (1878-1958) and B. F. Skinner (1904-1990) became proponents of the behaviorist perspective. They did not believe in the idea of consciousness. They believed that only measurable and observable behavior should be studied. In successful experiments with animals and human subjects, they found that behavior could be changed in response to changes in

Ivan Pavlov and his staff demonstrating the conditioning phenomenon with a dog.

the environment. Their work in the field provided great advancements in our understanding of learning.

COGNITIVE PERSPECTIVE

The interest in behaviorism began to wane in the 1960s when new questions were raised about perception, development, and interpersonal relations that behaviorists had ignored or could not explain with their theories of observable behavior. From these issues rose the answer to these questions: the cognitive approach to psychology. Contrary to behaviorists, cognitive psychologists believe that mental processes can be studied scientifically even if the inner workings of our brain cannot be observed directly. They believe that we can make inferences about the thoughts and cognitive processes that underlie behavior. Similar to how Wundt had studied memory in the beginnings of scientific psychology, cognitive psychologists can analyze recall of information systematically to deduce the mental processes involved in human memory.

Technological advances have allowed cognitive psychologists to explore the neurological mechanisms by which we think, learn, remember and feel, thus leading to the expansion of the field of cognitive neuroscience. Cognitive psychology has also been very successful in combination with behavioral psychology in the field of psychological therapies. Therapies merging the two approaches have been successful in treating psychological disorders by changing the way people behave along with the way people think.

HUMANISTIC PERSPECTIVE

The humanistic approach to psychology became prominent in the mid-20th century, in response to the more traditional approaches to psychology. Humanistic theory heavily emphasizes human beings' inherent drive toward **self-actualization**, which is the force within

The humanistic perspective emphasizes the realization of creative drives, like painting.

an individual to reach their highest potential. While many other approaches are focused on explaining mental illness, this approach focuses on the study of positive psychology; devoting more effort to human potential, self-expression, creativity, self-esteem, and altruism, among other topics.

This approach is popular with psychologists who believe that we have overemphasized the negative aspects of human psychology while dismissing mental wellness and human strengths. However, because many of the theories in humanistic psychology are not easily studied scientifically, it has not been totally accepted into mainstream psychology. Still, many well-known humanistic psychologists, like Abraham Maslow (1908-1970) and Carl Rogers (1902-1987) have made excellent contributions to the field of psychology as a whole and have changed the way psychotherapy is practiced.

EVOLUTIONARY PERSPECTIVE

The evolutionary psychological perspective dates back to Darwin (1809-1882) and his theory of evolution. According to Darwin, the behaviors that are beneficial to a species' survival are the ones that will be passed down through generations, while behaviors that are disadvantageous to survival will tend to die out over time. Similarly, psychologists with an evolutionary perspective seek to identify the psychological traits and behaviors that have evolved over time. These psychologists analyze the roots of our behavior to explain their function.

Similar to the other psychological perspectives, researchers in this area study many different topics from anger, fear and aggression to sexual attraction and happiness. While a psychodynamic psychologist might want to identify what childhood experiences may have led to a fear of snakes, an evolutionary psychologist might instead want to identify how fear of snakes has been adaptive to human beings over time.

According to Darwin's theory, all organisms are descended from a common ancestor and have evolved over long periods of time. This theory suggests that there is a link between us and modern day apes.

SOCIOCULTURAL PERSPECTIVE

Sociocultural psychology is a relatively new approach that has emerged in response to the fact that for the greater part of the twentieth century, psychological investigators did very little research on cultural and racial differences or gender. In reality, much of the research done in the field since its inception was conducted by white males on white male college students. Though large strides were made in the field during these times, the psychological experiences of women and racial and socioeconomic minorities were excluded from consideration.

The sociocultural perspective has sought to change all that. It focuses on how interactions with others in society affect our thought patterns and behaviors. Essentially, it aims to explain how culture, gender, age, and ethnic differences shape us. How similar is a middle-aged Hispanic woman living in a predominantly Hispanic neighborhood to a college-aged African American male living in the suburbs of an affluent community? A sociocultural psychologist would want to know.

These psychological approaches are not always competing perspectives. More and more, in contemporary psychology, researchers and professionals have brought them together to create a large patchwork encompassing all of these. Together, they all contribute to our understanding of the mind and the psychological experience.

THE ENDURING ISSUES OF PSYCHOLOGY

Throughout the development and growth of psychology, several issues have been identified as topics of great debate and sources of research (Blake, 1995). These "Enduring Issues" stem directly from questions you've probably had yourself from time to time. They are usually present in some form in the discussion of any topic in psychology and they will be discussed further in subsequent chapters of this book.

- Person-Situation

Someone cuts you off at high speed on the highway: is it because they are inconsiderate and reckless or because they might be having an emergency and need to get to a hospital?

We do not often consider the perspective of others when explaining behavior. A high speed driver could be driving fast for any number of reasons unrelated to internal factors.

The field of social psychology focuses on identifying the nature of the primary influences on our behavior — how much of the behavior is a reflection of internal motivations, thoughts, and feelings, and how much of it is influenced by other people, circumstances, or incentives?

- Nature-Nurture

Bobby has his father's bad temper: is it a product of a hereditary trait or was it learned throughout his upbringing from observing his father?

This question arises frequently in the study of development, intelligence, personality, and psychological disorders. A debate that has been raging for millennia; it seeks to explain whether we are a product of our innate, inherited tendencies or whether we are molded by our learned experiences.

- Stability-Change

Once a cheater, always a cheater?

An oft-heard question in bad relationships: can people change? Many psychologists' best research ideas come from questions we all have from time to time. This particular debate has interested many developmental psychologists, as well as personality and abnormal psychologists. Is our behavior fixed throughout our lifetime or does it change over time as we grow older due to our experiences?

- Diversity-Universality

Achmed is a teenager living in the slums of a poor neighborhood in Morocco. Amy is a Caucasian neurophysicist living in a large urban metropolis. How similar or how different is their psychology?

Many psychologists and non-psychologists alike believe that, on a basic level, we are all very similar – we're human, after all. However, research has shown over time that a person's way of thinking and behaving can vary greatly depending on his or her culture, religion, race, age, and gender. How similar are we really? Which psychological traits are universal and which vary depending on individual characteristics? These questions might be of interest to sociocultural psychologists or a psychologist of any discipline who wants to see how a particular theory applies to different social groups.

- Mind-Body

Michael takes mood-altering drugs prescribed by his therapist. How does the drug's effect on his biological processes affect his psychological experience?

Exactly how are the mind and body connected and how does a change in one affect the other? Biological psychologists and neuropsychologists are interested in exploring the biological basis of our behavior and how our bodies affect our perceptions of the world around us. The direction of this relationship may be interchangeable. For instance:

How would the course of a life-threatening illness be affected by positive thinking and feeling?

How would emotions and thoughts be affected by the development of a life-threatening illness?

Each might be uniquely different depending on the person. As with all the enduring issues, there is no "right" answer and the truth probably lies somewhere in the middle.

THE SCIENCE OF PSYCHOLOGY

What differentiates psychology from the early philosophers theorizing about how the mind works is the use of the **scientific method**. Psychologists rely on the scientific method to answer the questions that many of us wonder about ourselves and other people. This method involves creating theories based on observations and collecting data to test the theories. Researchers then interpret their findings to see if their theories are correct. The ultimate goal of research is to accurately describe a phenomenon, explain why it occurs, and be able to predict when it will occur. Finally, researchers also hope to be able to control what they study.

If a team of psychologists wanted to study a pattern of anxious behavior, first they would attempt to *describe* what the presenting symptoms are. The process of describing a phenomenon might involve officially identifying it as a disorder. For instance, a particular pattern of anxious behavior could represent what we now know as Generalized Anxiety Disorder (GAD). Further, researchers might want to *explain* why and how people come to suffer from GAD. With enough research, they might be able to accurately *predict* when GAD will surface and thus, be able to prevent it. As with any other anxiety disorder, psychologists would then want to find a therapy or medication that would *control* the symptoms of the illness.

The findings of a psychological study stand as a **theory**, a substantiated explanation of a phenomenon in nature. Theories are based on the empirical study of a specific topic and allow researchers to further **hypothesize**, or make predictions, about the topic being studied. For example, research has shown that authoritative parenting styles lead to happier, more successful, and more capable children (Maccoby, 1992). Based on this theory, one might hypothesize that authoritative parenting styles are correlated with intelligence. This hypothesis could be further tested and become a theory in its own right.

SAMPLING

Before a hypothesis can be tested, regardless of the research method being used, one must first choose the participants, or the subjects, that will take part in the study. Obviously, one cannot possibly research every person on the planet in order to learn how people on average think and behave. Instead, scientists are limited to studying a **sample**, or a small section of the population, to learn about people at large.

Sampling is an important factor, because with improper sampling methods, the results of an experiment can be skewed and inaccurate. Imagine, for example, that your psychology instructor wanted to devise a study to gather information on the eating habits of students at your college. Your college would be the population, so she would have to take a sample from it. Suppose that she decided to choose a morning English course, which is comprised of only nursing students, as her sample. Would this be an appropriate sample of your college as a whole? Probably not. For one, by choosing only the morning class, she is excluding a big part of the population of the college from participating: the students that attend school in the evenings or online. Who else is being excluded? Students from programs other than nursing. Perhaps nursing students, who may also work in hospitals outside of going to school, exhibit more irregular eating because of their grueling schedules. Does that mean that on average all students at your college have irregular eating patterns? If the sample had included students that were in other programs or ones taking English online, you would probably find that the answer is no.

This example illustrates two important requisites for adequate sampling. The first is that sampling must be **random**, meaning that every member of the population should have an equal chance of being in the study. The sample in this hypothetical example was one that was convenient to test, but it was not selected at random. It is also not a **representative sample**, or one that closely represents the larger group it is drawn from. For one, less than half of the college's students attend school in the mornings, so the sample does not represent the students that attend school in the evenings or online at all. In addition, it is only representative of students in one program and does not take into account those that are in other programs.

A better way to conduct this study might be to randomly select students from a list of all students enrolled at the school, regardless of program and class section. This would ensure that all students at the school are better represented in the sample. This is one of the first crucial steps of research. Once a random, representative sample has been chosen, we are ready to test our hypothesis on the selected participants.

Research should be conducted on samples that are selected totally at random – the way lottery numbers are chosen from a pool of numbers.

RESEARCH METHODS

The way in which psychologists actually test their predictions can vary considerably depending on the question being researched. Several different methods are employed to test psychological theories, including case studies, experiments, and naturalistic observations. Each of these methods has its own strengths and weaknesses that are important to consider when designing a study.

DESCRIPTIVE METHODS

Descriptive methods of research are useful when one aims to simply describe a behavior or phenomenon without necessarily explaining why it occurs and without making any attempts to predict or change it.

- Naturalistic Observation

Laboratory studies can be a rich source of information, but they may alter the way participants behave simply because they are "out of their element." **Naturalistic observation** studies allow researchers to observe behavior in the context in which it occurs in real life, without interference. For instance, one might want to study the incidence of red light-running on a busy intersection. One could employ a survey to ask participants how often they run red lights at that intersection or bring participants onto a driving course that mimics the conditions of said intersection, but researchers are not likely to get truthful, accurate data from either of these methods. On the other hand, a researcher using naturalistic observation could gather data by sitting for several hours or days at that intersection and noting when someone runs the red light.

The main advantage of this method is that it allows you to see more natural behavior as it actually occurs in everyday life, as opposed to the kind of data you might gather under artificial conditions. However, the method also has disadvantages. For one, psychologists must not interfere with observed behavior, which might mean missing important information or opportunities to study an interesting activity in more detail. They must observe the behavior as it occurs naturally, as fleeting or brief as it may be. Similarly, psychologists are limited in the generalizations that they are able to make from this data, since many unknown factors may be influencing behavior.

Other issues arising from naturalistic observation come from human error. Psychologists may fail to record or observe important information either due to oversight or because they perceive the event to be irrelevant. **Observer bias** also plays a large role in the interpretation of natural, spontaneous behavior. This is the idea that a researcher's perspective may be distorted due to previously conceived expectations or biases. Using multiple observers or using videotaped interactions that can be analyzed by many different researchers can help reduce the effect of observer bias and similar issues. Whenever possible, the person analyzing and scoring the observation should be left unaware about the purpose and hypothesis of the study as prior knowledge or vested interest may influence observer perceptions.

- Case Studies

A case study is another descriptive method of research that is used to study a person or a small group in great detail. It typically involves various methods of data collection including surveys, interviews, historical data, and observations, among others. The aim of the case study is to identify the patterns and causes for the behavior of the research subject or subjects.

Take the study of language, for example. Pierre Paul Broca (1824-1880) studied language in the brain of two patients that were unable to produce meaningful words or phrases after a brain injury. Using this method, he was able to pinpoint the part of the brain linked to speech production, now known as Broca's area (Dronkers et al, 2007). Researchers may not have easy access to others with brain injuries resulting in such clear-cut cognitive deficits, but the case study method allows them to glean important information based on the cases that are available. One of the most famous case studies in the field is that of Phineas Gage, who survived an accident in which a large iron rod pierced through his head (Campbell, 1851). His miraculous experience led psychologists to identify the part of the brain that controls emotion and the planning and execution of tasks, which were affected in Gage after the accident.

While the case study can be a source of rich and detailed data, it, too, is not without its disadvantages. Like naturalistic observation, observer bias can play a role in the interpretation of information. In addition, because case studies typically study a very small number of people, one cannot assume that these

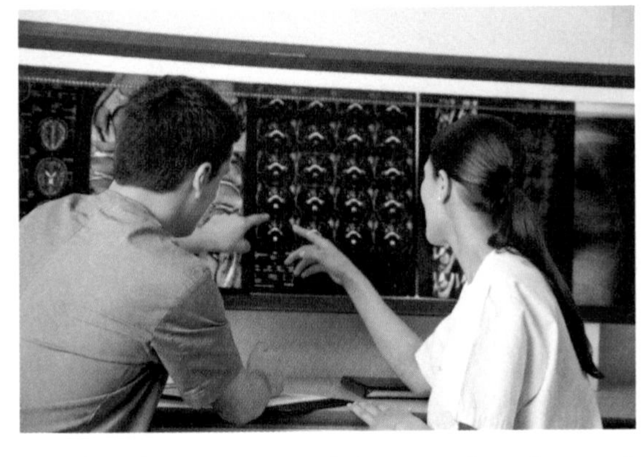

Data from brain scans can help researchers distinguish unique or abnormal patterns of brain activity compared to normal samples.

conclusions generalize to the population as a whole. In the end, research aims to explain phenomena in a way that applies to as many people as possible. The findings of case studies limit one's ability to draw general conclusions. Nonetheless, case studies are important in identifying and describing psychological phenomena for further research.

- Surveys

Surveys are one of the most common ways in which psychologists gather data about the general population. In the past few months, you've probably been asked to participate in a survey at least once. Help lines want to know what you thought of their customer service. Advertisers want to know what you think of their new product. And psychologists are interested in all kinds of questions about your behavior, thoughts, and feelings. Surveys usually take the form of in-person or phone interviews, or pen-and-paper and online questionnaires. They all involve asking participants a series of pre-determined questions. The major advantages of the survey method are that it can reach a large number of people at the same time and it is relatively cost-effective. With one e-mailed survey, a researcher may garner thousands of responses.

The downside to surveys is that researchers must rely on the honesty and self-awareness of participants to answer truthfully. Often, research in psychology is based on questions of a sensitive nature that participants might be hesitant to answer openly. In order to elicit honest responses, questions should be carefully written, and participants should

Surveys can gather plenty of useful information from many people at once. The U. S. Census would be an example of a survey you have likely taken.

be assured that their responses will remain confidential.

CORRELATIONAL RESEARCH

The descriptive methods of research described above are essential to the study of psychology, but they are not designed to assist in making predictions or explaining behavior. For these purposes, psychologists use correlational research. That is, they attempt to find underlying associations, or **correlations,** between two variables. For example, a psychologist might be interested in seeing whether having more close interpersonal relationships is correlated with better physical health. She might do this by surveying people on their families, romantic and platonic relationships, and by measuring their overall health using simple physical examinations. The findings of this type of study could have very important implications for interpersonal and health psychology.

Despite its utility, the researchers of correlational studies would not be able to determine the direction of the relationship. The question, "Do close interpersonal relationships *cause* good health or does good health *cause* better interpersonal relationships?" would remain unanswered. In other words, correlation does not necessarily mean causality. Further research might indicate that one causes the other or vice versa. Some third variable may actually be the cause for the correlation between these two variables. Based on the findings of a correlational study, one would not be able to say which is truly the case.

Much of the research you will read about in this book and that you hear about in the news is based on correlational research. This includes any and all research related to gender, age, or race because those variables cannot be manipulated in a research study. One can only study how these variables are associated with other variables. It is true that artificial sweeteners may be associated with cancer in humans (Lim et al., 2006). However, it does not necessarily mean they *cause* cancer. While still somewhat limited, this level of research allows psychologists to make predictions, a characteristic that other research methods lack. Based on correlational data, you might be able to accurately predict the development of cancer after years of eating foods that are artificially sweetened.

EXPERIMENTAL RESEARCH

The only way to determine causality is to use the experimental research method. This is the most frequently used method for psychologists that want to uncover the causes of behavior. The difference between this method and all the aforementioned methods is that, in an experiment, a researcher manipulates a variable. That allows him or her to be able to assume causality.

Suppose a team of psychologists is interested in how caffeine affects reaction time, and they want to design an experiment to answer this question. A reasonable hypothesis might be that it would decrease your reaction time – that is, you would be faster to react when influenced by caffeine. In order to test this, researchers would first select the people to participate in the study, known as participants or subjects. Then they would divide the participant pool into two or more groups. One group might be given 30 mg of caffeine, the amount contained in a can of soda. This group would be considered the **experimental group**, because they are the ones exposed to the manipulated variable (caffeine). The researchers would then place that group in a reaction time task to test their hypothesis. Another group of participants, the **control group**, might be given no caffeine and also placed in the reaction time task in order to truly see the difference in performance between people that have caffeine in their system and people that do not.

In this example, there are two variables: caffeine and reaction time. Caffeine would be an example of an **independent variable**, because it is manipulated by the researchers. In any given experiment, there may be different levels of an independent variable. For example, 30 mg of caffeine might be one level. Another level could be 60 mg. Reaction time, on the other hand, is a **dependent variable**. It is not manipulated by researchers, only observed, and if the hypothesis is correct, its variation *depends* on the independent variable. The experimental group would be the one that is exposed to the independent variable, or the ones that consumed caffeine. If multiple levels of the independent variable were being tested – i.e. 30 mg versus 60 mg – a second experimental group would be created. The control group, on the other hand, would not be exposed to any level of the independent variable. It acts as a baseline, which allows researchers to really see the difference between reaction time with and without caffeine.

You may be wondering, why is a control group necessary if they are not exposed to the variable being tested? The reason is to prevent false results that are caused by a third, unforeseen variable. Suppose that exercise also decreased reaction time and unbeknownst to the researchers, the majority of their participants had just come from the gym before participating in the study. If there were only an experimental group, one would see fast reaction times and attribute them to the caffeine; when, in reality, they had nothing to do with the caffeine and were mostly due to the exercise. Having a control group decreases the possibility of this happening. The researcher would be able to see that both the control and experimental groups had faster reaction times, and since the control group had no caffeine, they would not be able to confidently say that caffeine has an effect on reaction time.

In this way, the experimental research method attempts to hold all other variables constant and test only the independent variable of interest. This makes it a very important tool for psychological researchers, but it is not without its drawbacks. For one, the nature of a controlled experiment is artificial. This may mean that participants are not acting naturally the way they would in a real-life situation, which somewhat limits its generalizability to the real world. There is also the risk of **experimenter bias**, which, similar to observer bias, may influence the way a researcher interprets the results of an experiment.

- The importance of replication

Often, many different research methods are used by researchers to explore the same topic. This is because research builds on itself. One research study may use a descriptive method of research to do an exploratory analysis of a behavior or phenomenon. Further questions regarding the same topic could be answered using more stringent methods of research such as correlational or experimental methods. As with many accepted psychological theorems, the research has been replicated many times and analyzed using different methods to ensure that results confirm original findings. This is why research studies include a step-by-step method of how the study was conducted; so that other researchers may replicate the procedure.

When a study is replicated many times using multiple different methods of research and the findings are the same, one can be more confident that those results accurately represent some real-life phenomenon. On the other hand, if the findings of subsequent research studies do not match those of the original, it calls into question the validity of said findings. Further research may be required to arrive at a more appropriate theory.

ETHICAL GUIDELINES

The matter of using animal and human subjects in research is very sensitive. To ensure that participants and their rights are adequately protected from research that may be harmful, guidelines have been put in place that must be strictly adhered to when conducting research (American Psychological Association, 2003).

For one, research may not be conducted until documented **informed consent** is given. Informed consent ensures that the participant understands possible risks, side effects, and what is expected of them as part of the research study. Participants should be informed of the nature of the research and any aspects of the research that might influence their decision to participate, including unpleasant experiences and possible harm. Participation in research must be voluntary, even if it is compensated. For example, a researcher would not be able to make research participation a mandatory part of a course grade. The incentive to participate, monetary or otherwise, must not be great enough that it might constitute coercion. Participants must be aware that their privacy is protected and that all records and documents relating to the research will be kept confidential. In addition to these guidelines set forth by the (APA), researchers must follow the U.S. Code of Federal Regulations.

Researchers must take careful measures to maintain confidentiality. They should ensure that data is inaccessible to those who are not involved in the research and that information that could identify a participant is removed from their experimental results.

The issue of consent is also heavily addressed in the American Psychological Association (APA) guidelines, since anyone participating in research must be competent and knowledgeable of the research in order to consent to participate in it. For this reason, special populations like children, the elderly, and disordered individuals are given extra consideration when carrying out a research study. Animals are also offered special protection to ensure that they are comfortable, healthy, and treated humanely.

Rats are often used in psychological research because their behavior and physiology can be used to infer a lot about human behavior and physiology.

CHAPTER 1 REVIEW QUESTIONS

1. Socrates argued that our thoughts and ideas are separate from the physical world. This is a concept referred to as ____________________________.

2. A psychologist believes that people are heavily driven by their innermost desires and traumas from their childhood. She probably agrees with the ________________________________ perspective in psychology.

    a. Cognitive

    b. Biological

    c. Psychodynamic

    d. Behavioral

3. "Psychology is the study of the mental processes that go on in our brains." Which psychologist would be most likely to disagree with that statement?

    a. Sigmund Freud

    b. B. F. Skinner

    c. Carl Rogers

    d. Wilhelm Wundt

4. A psychologist heavily interested in the way culture affects human behavior would be considered to have a ______________________ perspective.

    a. Sociocultural

    b. Cognitive

    c. Biological

    d. Evolutionary

5. Match each enduring issue with the proposed research question.

a. Person-Situation ___ Does intelligence increase over our lifetime?

b. Nature-Nurture ___ Is aggression learned or inborn?

c. Stability-Change ___ Do women experience more anxiety than men?

d. Diversity-Universality ___How does color blindness affect perception?

e. Mind-Body ___ Are medical professionals more altruistic?

6. Dr. Knezevich is studying the factors that attract people to one another. She wants to test the idea that people that are perceived as intelligent are also more attractive. This is an example of a ____________________.

7. A psychologist is studying a miraculous child who became fluent in 10 languages by the age of 13 using intelligence tests and other tasks. This is an example of:

a. Naturalistic observation

b. A case study

c. A survey

d. Experimental research

8. Which is the only research method in which one manipulates a variable? ______________________________

9. In a study of helping behavior, a psychologist wants to find whether fear decreases the likelihood of helping in an emergency. In this study, the helping behavior would be the:

    a. Independent variable

    b. Dependent variable

10. According to ethical guidelines, participants in research should have ____________________________________ before they agree to participate in a study.

CHAPTER 2

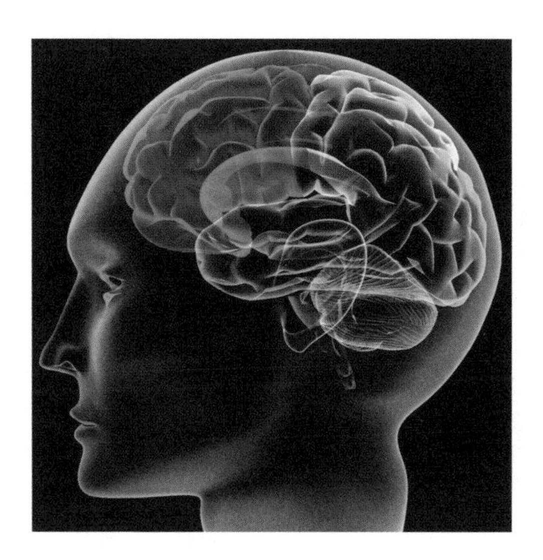

BIOLOGICAL PSYCHOLOGY

MANY PSYCHOLOGISTS, especially those with a strong biological perspective, believe that biological factors, such as the nervous system, endocrine system, and genetics play a big role in the way we think and behave. This branch of psychology is known as **biological psychology** or **psychobiology**, and it is the study of cognitive functioning and behavior in relation to our biological processes. Even psychologists without a strong biological perspective can agree that certain systems in the body have a major effect on how we feel. In this chapter, we will discuss how these systems work together to create your psychological experience.

THE NERVOUS SYSTEM

The human nervous system plays a large role in our behaviors, thoughts, emotions, and sensations. Think of the nervous system as a vast network of roads that all take you somewhere important. In order for your body to function as it does, information is constantly being passed throughout this network from one place to another, where it can be processed. This system is divided into several parts depending on their function and they work in tandem with other systems of the body. To understand how information is transmitted, we must look at the system from a microscopic perspective before moving on to the big picture. The cells that make up every part of the nervous system are called **neurons**, or nerve cells, and they transmit information through electrical and chemical signals throughout the body.

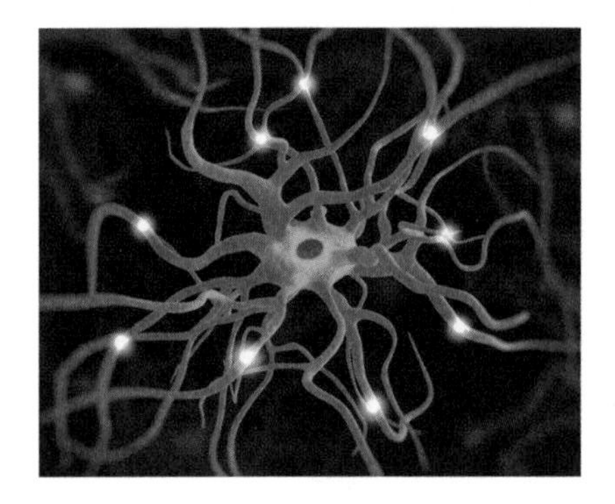

Neurons communicate with each other through chemical and electrical impulses.

NEURONS

Neurons act in the body as messengers and their form matches their function. Like other cells in the body, they have a cell nucleus which is surrounded by a cell membrane. However, unlike other cells, neurons have specialized fibers that extend out of the cell body that enable them to transmit messages from one place to another.

A typical neuron has many thin structures branching out of the cell body, called **dendrites**. In addition to the dendrites, neurons have an **axon**, a long fiber that extends out from the cell body. Messages from the cell body of each neuron travel down the axon and are transmitted to other nearby neurons. The dendrites of a

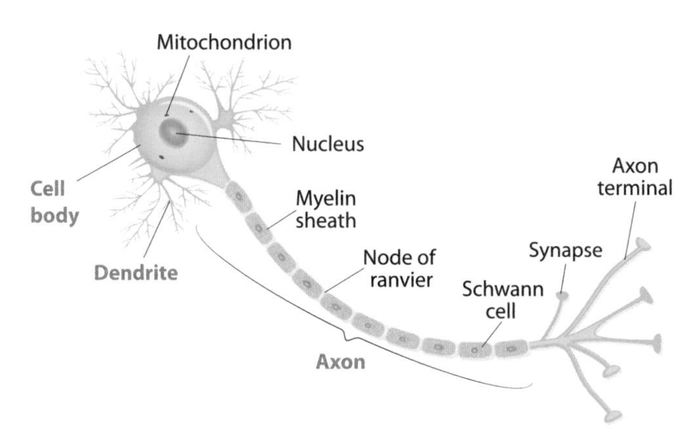

Anatomy of a typical neuron.

neuron act as the input; they receive messages from other neurons and transmit it to the cell body of the neuron. If it weren't for these structures, the transmitted message would never reach the cell body. The axon has the opposite function; it transmits messages from the cell body out to nearby neurons.

Our nervous system is made up of billions of these neurons, which are present everywhere from our brains to all parts of our peripheral nervous system. These neurons use electrical and chemical signals to communicate with one another and send messages from one part of the nervous system to the other. How they do this is through the **synapse,** the area where neurons communicate using electrochemical signals. This area includes the axon terminal of one neuron, the dendrites of another neuron, and the space between them. Though many of these cells occupy the same space, they are not directly connected. Instead, they are separated by a synaptic gap, or a tiny space. Imagine dozens of people all floating in a pool without coming into contact with each other. Though they are all occupying the same space, they are not touching directly. The water between each person represents the synaptic gap. If you were in that pool and you wanted to pass a toy ducky to someone else in the pool, you could float it over with a little push. That energy from the push is the equivalent of an **action potential**. In the synapse, all communication between neurons begins with an action potential. At the cellular level, it is a bit more complex than a simple push.

- Action potentials

At any given moment, a neuron is either at rest or it is activated by an **action potential**. When a neuron is at rest, it is not transmitting a message. Neurons at rest have a more negative charge inside the cell relative to the outside of the cell, because there are more negative **ions**, or negatively charged atoms, inside the cell. A neuron in this state is simply not stimulated to act.

STRUCTURE OF A TYPICAL CHEMICAL SYNAPSE

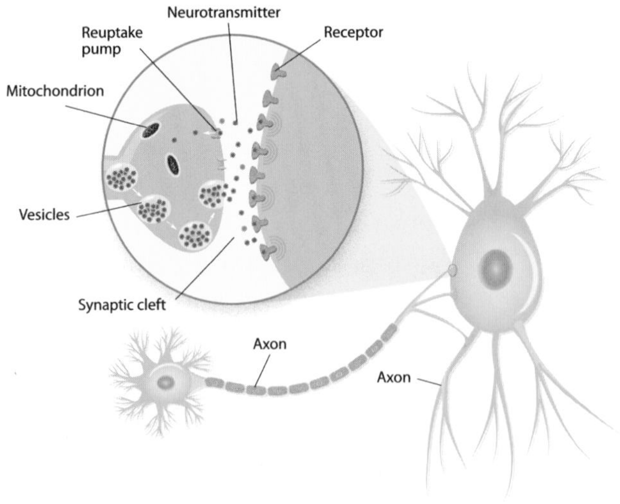

When an electrical impulse reaches the terminal of one neuron, neurotransmitters held in the synaptic vesicles are released. They are able to cross the synaptic gap and bind to receptors in adjacent neurons. This is how signals are passed from one neuron to another.

When a neuron is stimulated, the cell membrane allows an influx of positively charged ions into the cell. The change in the electrical charge of the membrane sets off a chain reaction that allows the neural impulse, or action potential, to travel down the axon of the neuron, or "fire." At the ends of the axon – the axon terminals – there are special sacs that contain chemicals called **neurotransmitters**. When the electrical impulse reaches the end of the axon, the sacs open and the neurotransmitters are released into the synaptic space.

These neurotransmitters bind to areas on the dendrites of nearby neurons, propagating the same reaction in those nearby neurons. This binding reaction is very specific, and not all neurotransmitters "fit" in all receptor sites. To visualize this, think of the pegs you used to play with as a child. The square peg fits in the square hole, and so forth. A "square" neurotransmitter would not be able to fit in a "round" receptor site. This ensures that nervous system reactions are only propagated in appropriate neurons. For example, serotonin and dopamine, both heavily implicated in psychological functioning and disorders, are two different neurotransmitters. So the neural pathway for each one would be separate from the other. This means that dopamine would not bind to a receptor site for serotonin and vice versa.

Normally, single impulses – meaning a single neuron being stimulated – do not make adjacent neurons fire. Many repeated impulses from one or more neighboring neurons are required to trigger the action potential. After the neurotransmitters have bound to adjacent neurons, they detach and are usually reabsorbed into the axon terminals where they can be reused or disposed of and the neuron returns to its resting state. Neurotransmitters that did not bind to any site are also reabsorbed for future use.

THE DIVISIONS OF THE NERVOUS SYSTEM

Every neuron in our bodies is connected to other neurons through action potentials, and using this mechanism, messages are constantly being transmitted throughout the nervous system. The larger organizational framework of the nervous system depends on the specific functions of the neurons (Figure 2.1). The nervous system is divided into two major parts: the **central nervous system (CNS)** and the **peripheral nervous system (PNS).** The central nervous system is made up of the brain and spinal cord. It receives sensory information and coordinates decisions and actions. The peripheral nervous system is responsible for relaying information from the senses and for carrying out the actions of the central nervous system. For example, a large corporation typically has a headquarters and many smaller satellite offices or franchises. The franchises carry out the work of the company as a whole. They sell a product and transmit the profits to the headquarters, but ultimately the headquarters has all the decision-making power. The nervous system works exactly the same way, with the central nervous system division integrating information from the

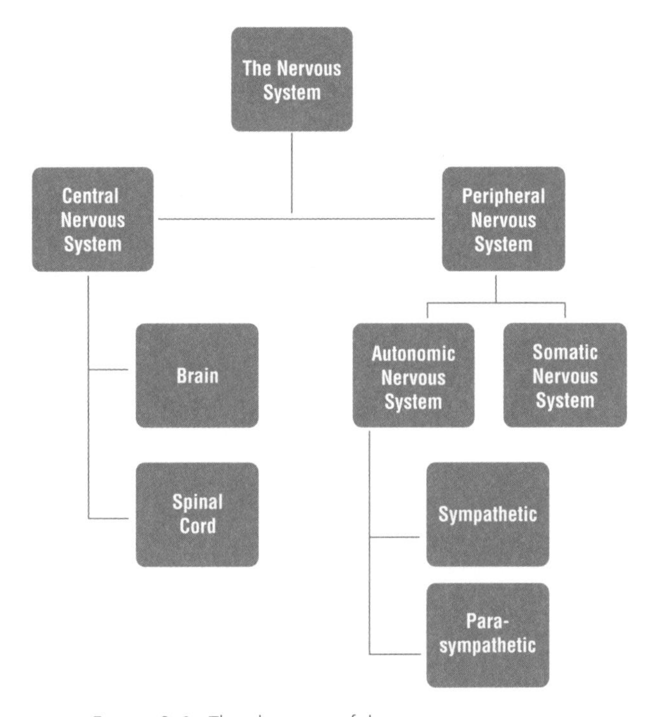

Figure 2.1: The divisions of the nervous system.

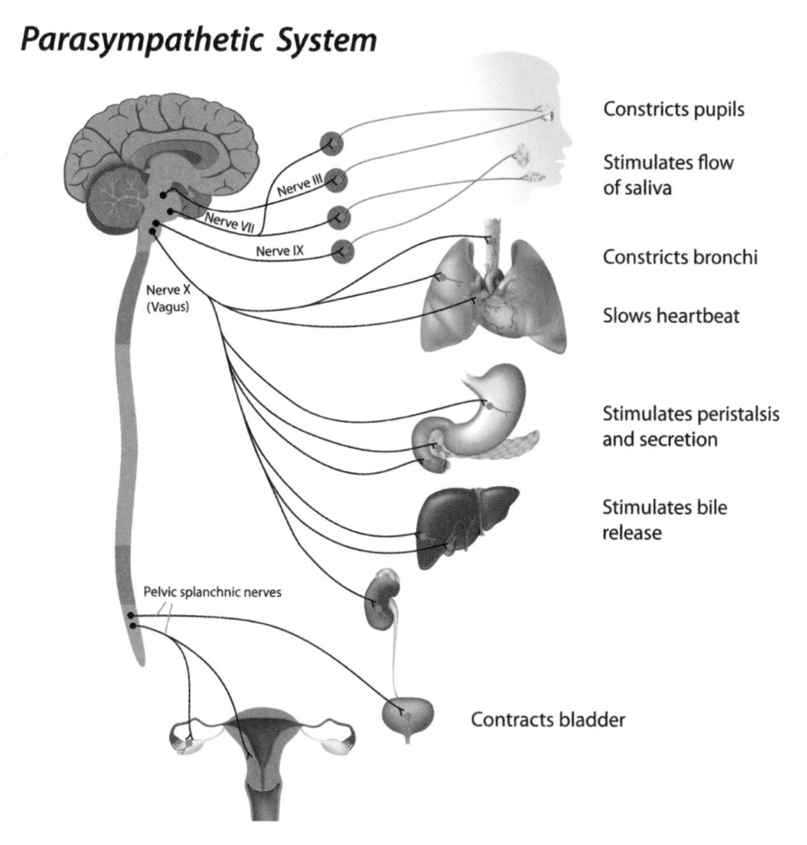

The parasympathetic pathway of the Autonomic Nervous System.

peripheral nervous system and making decisions on behavior that will be carried out by the peripheral nervous system.

The peripheral nervous system is divided into two parts: the **somatic nervous system** and the **autonomic nervous system.** The somatic nervous system deals with voluntary control of body movements and the transmission of information from the senses to the central nervous system. The autonomic nervous system is involuntary, and it controls essential internal life functions such as heart rate, digestion, respiratory rate, salivation, perspiration, and sexual arousal. You do not have to consciously process digestion or respiration. That is constantly going on behind the scenes "automatically" through the work of the *auto*nomic nervous system.

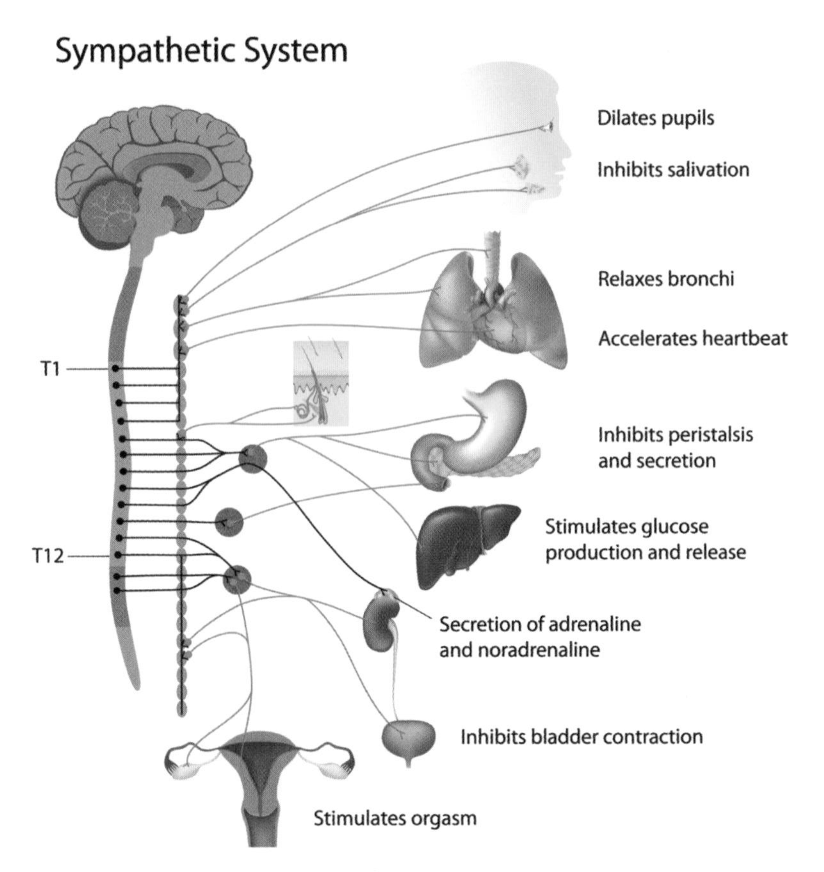

The sympathetic pathway of the Autonomic Nervous System.

The autonomic nervous system is further divided into the **sympathetic** and **parasympathetic** divisions, and the actions of each are opposite from one another. The sympathetic division of the nervous system mobilizes the body for anything we perceive to be a threat. This is what is known as the **fight-or-flight** response. The name of this response comes from the fact that when presented with a danger, such as a large, aggressive black bear, you would either fight for your life by attacking it or flee to safety. In a situation like this, your physiological response may include increased heartbeat, dilated pupils, rapid breathing, and perspiration. As we will discuss later on, hormones like norepinephrine and cortisol are released during this process, to give you the rush of adrenaline you need to handle such situations.

The parasympathetic division, on the other hand, is responsible for the activities that occur when the body is at rest, like digestion and sexual arousal. When the body is at rest, the heartbeat and breathing are typically at normal levels, allowing the body's normal daily functions to take place. The two divisions work together to maintain the body's nervous system in balance.

THE CENTRAL NERVOUS SYSTEM

As we discussed before, the central nervous system is the body's control center. It is responsible for processing the information it receives from the peripheral nervous system, and it coordinates the activities of the body. It is made up of the brain and the spinal cord, which together contain the majority of neurons in the nervous system.

THE BRAIN

The brain is the executive part of the central nervous system that exerts control over other parts of the body. It is where learning and decision making take place and where our memories are stored. It is divided into three basic parts: the hindbrain, the midbrain and the forebrain.

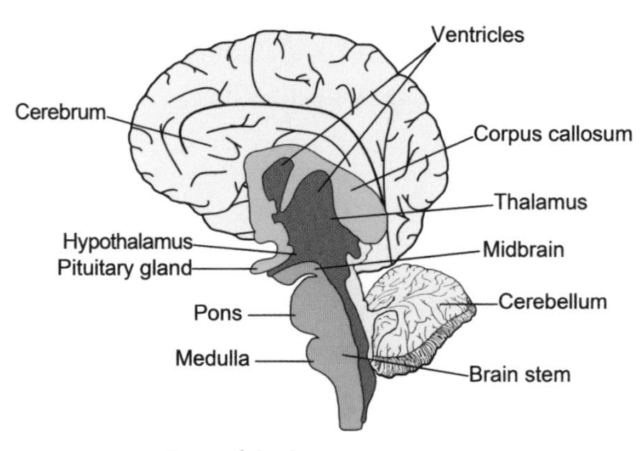

Parts of the brain.

- The hindbrain

The **hindbrain** is the part of the brain closest to the spinal cord that supports vital bodily functions. It is made up of the medulla, the pons, and the cerebellum. The **medulla** is the long, narrow structure directly above the spinal cord that makes up the lower half of the brain stem. It is involved in functions such as breathing, heart rate, and blood pressure. The **pons** is a structure located on the brain stem that carries signals to and from the forebrain. It is also involved with sleep, respiration, swallowing, posture, and facial expressions, among other functions.

Behind the brain stem sits the **cerebellum**, which means "little brain" in Latin. It plays an important part in motor control and has been found to have some involvement in cognitive functions, such as attention and language. Even though it does not generate movement, it is responsible for coordination and balance when executing movements. Recent research studies have found that dysfunction in the cerebellum may be associated with schizophrenia and attention deficit disorder (Tamminga & Vogel, 2005). In the case of schizophrenia, as with attention deficit disorder, attention may be affected, causing disorganization of thought and speech. In some cases of schizophrenia, motor control abilities suffer as well, leading to rigid or bizarre movements characteristic of catatonia.

- The midbrain

The **midbrain** is the part of the brain associated with vision and hearing. It is also involved in sleeping and alertness. It helps relay sensory information to the forebrain and it is one of the places in the brain where the sensation of pain is processed.

- The forebrain

The **forebrain** is the largest and top-most part of the brain, containing the cerebrum, as well as other important structures, like the thalamus and the limbic system.

The **thalamus** is a structure in the brain that relays information to and from the cerebral cortex and regulates consciousness, sleep, and alertness. All sensory information is passed through this structure on its way to be processed in different parts of the brain. The thalamus is surrounded by a set of brain structures known as the **limbic system**, including the hypothalamus, amygdala, and hippocampus. This system supports many different functions crucial to the study of psychology (Figure 2.2).

Your amygdala would be the structure involved in your emotional response when you watch a scary movie that makes you jump with fear.

The *hypothalamus* is heavily involved in the activities of the autonomic nervous system, including controlling our stress response and linking the nervous and endocrine systems, allowing them to work together. It controls basic metabolic processes like body temperature, hunger, thirst, sexual drive, and our sleep-wake rhythms. When you feel hungry, thirsty, sleepy, or sexually aroused, the hypothalamus is stimulated in your brain. The *amygdala* is another part of the limbic system that is involved in motivation and emotion, particularly fear and self-preservation. Together with the hippocampus, it is involved in the formation of new emotional memories. The *hippocampus* is essential to forming new memories. Damage to this area can affect one's ability to form new long-term memories.

Hypothalamus	Amygdala	Hippocampus
• Regulates the stress response • Involved in emotional behavior • Hunger, thirst, sexual drive, body temperature	• Involved in motivation and emotion • Especially fear and self-preservation • Aids in the formation of emotional memories	• Essential for the formation of long-term memories • Particularly episodic and semantic memories

Figure 2.2: The structures of the limbic system and their functions.

Finally, the forebrain also includes the **cerebrum**, which controls all voluntary actions in the body. This is the large ridge-covered part of the brain that surrounds the brain stem – what most of us visualize when we think of the "brain." The cerebrum processes our thoughts and sensory information, produces language and emotion, and houses our memories. The cerebrum is divided into two equal hemispheres – left and right – and it is covered by the **cerebral cortex**, a layer of thin tissue. This layer is grooved and folded, and is more developed in humans than other animals.

The two hemispheres of the brain are connected by a wide, flat bundle of nerve fibers known as the **corpus callosum**. This structure ensures that communication between the two sides of the brain is coordinated and seamless, even when the activity in each hemisphere is quite different. Some research has suggested that the left hemisphere is better at logical, analytical tasks (Kingstone, Enns, Mangun, & Gazzaniga, 1995), whereas the right hemisphere is better at visuospatial tasks, music, facial recognition, and problems that involve creative solutions (Bowden & Jung-Beeman, 2003). However, it is important to remember that the complex functions of the brain cannot be simplified

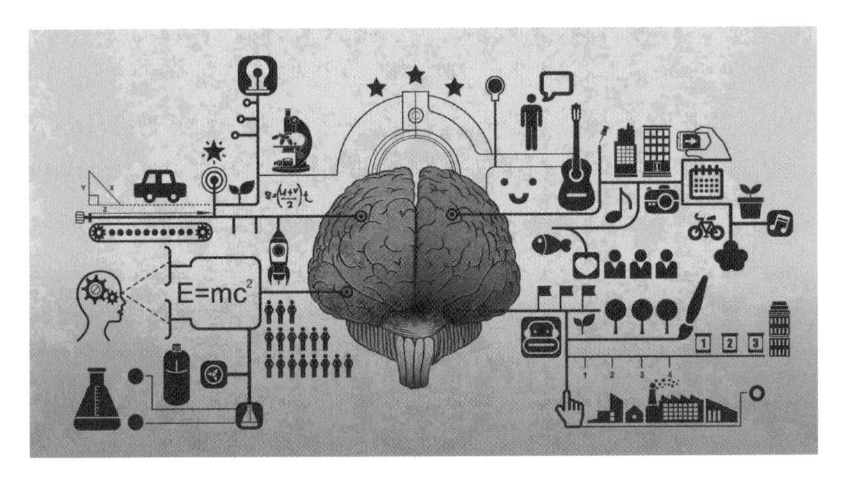

The right hemisphere would be more involved in logical and analytical tasks while the left hemisphere would be involved in creative and visuospatial tasks.

to the differences between the left and right brain. As we have already seen, there are many parts of the brain that are involved in several of the same processes. The left and right hemispheres are constantly exchanging information and working together.

The two hemispheres of the brain can be divided into four lobes that are specialized for different functions. They are the frontal lobe, the parietal lobe, the temporal lobe, and the occipital lobe.

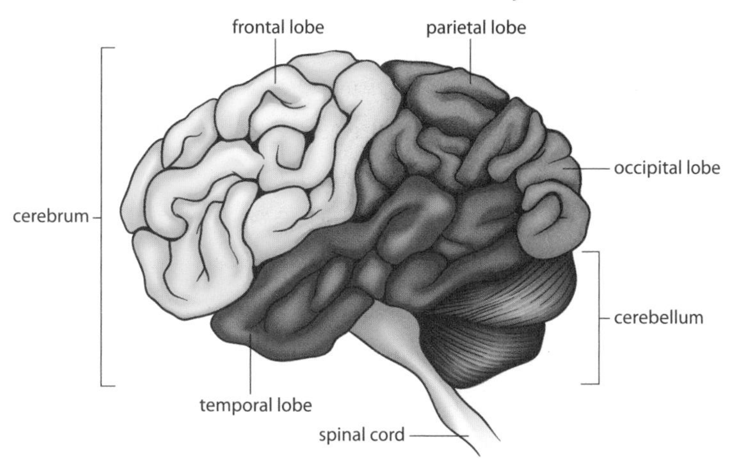

The lobes of the brain.

- The **frontal lobe** is the part of the cerebral cortex right behind the forehead. This part of the brain is involved in the planning and execution of tasks. It includes decision making, morality, emotional control, concentration, and other goal-oriented behaviors. If you are trying to decide what topic you want to write your term paper on, the frontal lobe would be involved in imagining how difficult or enjoyable different options might be and in doing so, would come to a final decision.

- Behind the frontal lobe is the **parietal lobe**, taking up the top half of each brain hemisphere. The parietal lobe integrates sensory information from all over the body and oversees spatial abilities, like the ability to read a map. It would also be involved in your hand-eye coordination when catching a baseball.

- At the very back of the head, above the cerebellum, is the **occipital lobe**, which processes visual information. Damage to the occipital lobe can lead to partial or complete blindness (Schacter, Gilbert, & Wegner, 2009). The sensory information from vision is processed here, as though your eyes were projecting images directly onto the back of your head.

- Located in front of the occipital lobe and below the parietal lobe, parallel with the temples, is the **temporal lobe**. The temporal lobe processes auditory information, including the comprehension of language. It is also involved in balance and equilibrium, the regulation of emotion and motivation, and some complex visual tasks such as facial recognition. Much of what is processed here comes from receptor cells in the ear, which transmit information about sound and balance.

STUDYING THE BRAIN

Psychologists use many different techniques to study the working brain. Historically, scientists relied on observations of people who had undergone brain surgery or had a brain injury to see how their psychological experience was changed. Obviously, it would be highly unethical to damage the brain of a person in the name of science, so scientists usually used case studies like these to understand the brain. With technological advances, psychologists have other options available to them.

For example, the *electroencephalograph* (EEG) is used to study the neural activity in different parts of the brain, using electrodes that are taped to the scalp. The information gathered by the EEG is translated into waves that can give psychologists an idea of the strength of neural activity in different parts of the brain. The brain waves are created as a result of the changing electrical charges caused by neural action potentials.

The EEG electrodes attached to this boy's head would allow researchers to observe his neural activity.

Newer imaging techniques such as *computerized axial tomography* (CAT) scans and *magnetic resonance imaging* (MRI) allow scientists to see three-dimensional images of the inner brain on a computer without having to perform surgery. Functional imaging methods such as fMRI (functional magnetic resonance imaging) are able to do more than just produce an image of the brain's structure; they can track the movement of blood in the brain and this blood flow indicates what areas in the brain are experiencing increased neural activity. This makes it possible for scientists to see specific sites of neural activity in response to different stimuli. Psychobiologists and neuropsychologists rely on methods like these to explore how memory, learning, and emotion take place in the brain.

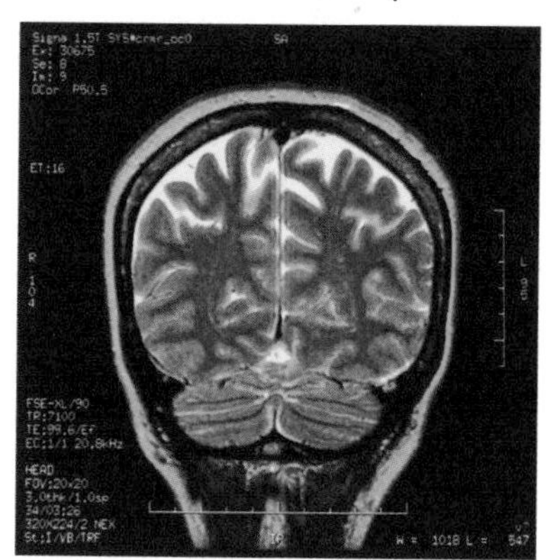

MRI scans show activity in the brain.

THE SPINAL CORD

Though the brain is the largest and most intricate part of the nervous system, the other half of the central nervous system, the spinal cord, has several crucial functions. The **spinal cord** is made up of long axons and connects the brain to the rest of the body. The long, uninterrupted connection from the peripheral nervous system to the brain also allows for much faster processing. If the nervous system is a complex roadway, then the spinal cord would be the highway. Without this fast and important connection, we would no longer experience sensations from other parts of the body and we would not be able to control our body movements.

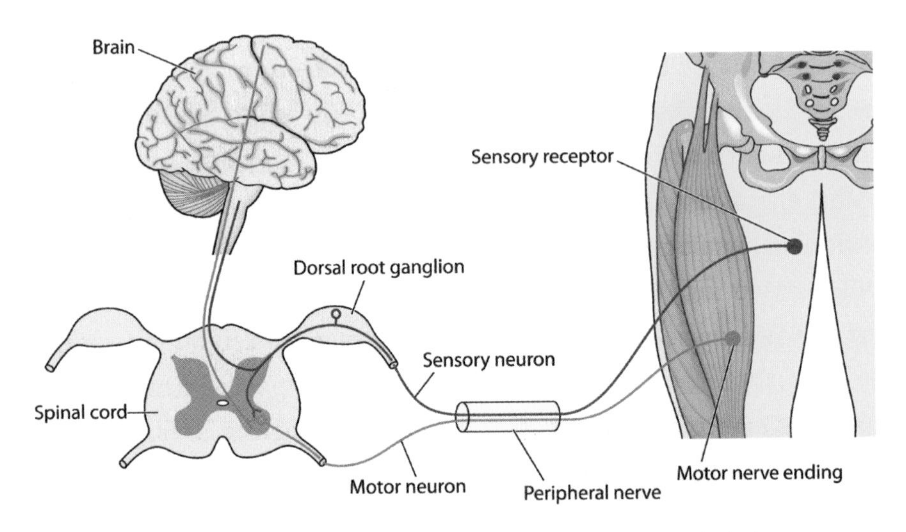

The brain transmits motor movement commands to the spinal cord, which then transmits those messages to our motor nerve endings, causing movement. Sensation from our sensory receptors transmit messages about what we sense to our brain through the same pathway.

In addition to this very important task, the spinal cord also allows for reflex movements. When you touch something hot, for example, you immediately respond so as not to burn yourself. This is a reflexive movement, and it is possible because of the spinal cord. The mechanism by which this works involves a series of neurons in the spinal cord called **interneurons**, or association neurons. Their job is to quickly connect messages from **motor neurons** and **sensory neurons**. From our sensory neurons, we are able to transmit information from our senses – the things we see, hear, feel, smell, and taste – to the central nervous system. Our motor neurons run in the other direction and transmit information from the brain and spinal cord to our muscles. When we sense something painful, our sensory neurons carry the message to the spinal cord. There, interneurons transfer the message directly to the motor neurons in order for us to have a quick response that we do not have to process in the brain; the response is reflexive.

This response is very useful and geared toward survival. It would take a lot longer for you to remove your hand from a hot stove if the pain signal was sent all the way to the brain for you to ponder whether or not the heat is strong enough to be potentially damaging. This reflexive mechanism prevents the passing of valuable time, during which you may be incurring third degree burns on your fingertips.

THE PERIPHERAL NERVOUS SYSTEM

The peripheral nervous system (PNS) transmits information to and from the central nervous system (CNS), the brain and the spinal cord. This allows sensory information from the outside world to be processed and allows for our voluntary movements to be carried out.

As we already discussed, the somatic nervous system includes sensory neurons that process all the information we register through the senses, as well as the motor neurons that transmit messages from the central nervous system to our muscles for movement. So if you were playing an instrument, such as a hand drum, the sound and the sensations of your fingers striking the surface of the drum would be transmitted to the brain through the somatic system. The motor command to move your hands to play the drum to the beat would also be carried out through the somatic system, only in the other direction, using motor neurons instead of sensory neurons.

The autonomic part of the peripheral nervous system coordinates messages to and from the CNS and our internal organs. This part of the system regulates vital functions like heart rate and breathing.

Specifically, the sympathetic nervous system is active when we are physiologically aroused, and the parasympathetic nervous system is responsible for our physiological responses when we are resting.

Imagine this scenario: you are home alone late in the evening, and you hear the sound of your front door knob rattling. Then you hear the breaking of wood and the door swinging open. What are you experiencing? Most people in this situation would feel fear. More specifically, they would experience an increased heart rate, rapid breathing, sweating, and perhaps some shaking. This response is caused by your sympathetic nervous system. It would also cause less noticeable effects in your body, like pupil enlargement, relaxation of the bladder, constriction of the blood vessels, and inhibition of the digestive system. The body also begins to free up sources of energy and more blood flows into the muscles to allow you to spring to action. This system also alerts your endocrine system to release specific hormones that aid in this fight-or-flight response. These changes allow you to focus your energy on the situation, increase strength and stamina, and increase the speed and accuracy of your response time.

The other key part of the autonomic nervous system, the parasympathetic division, has the opposite effect on the body. It slows down the heart to its normal resting rate, resumes digestion, slows breathing, and contracts the pupils to their normal size. After an emergency has passed, this system would take over and relax the body. So if you were out on your terrace enjoying the warm breeze and a cold lemonade, your parasympathetic nervous system would be working behind the scenes to ensure that your body systems are in balance and that you are properly digesting what you drink and eat, leading to regular urination and defecation. Unlike the sympathetic system, this division conserves as much energy as possible. The two systems work complementary to each other to maximize the effectiveness of your body's resources.

THE ENDOCRINE SYSTEM

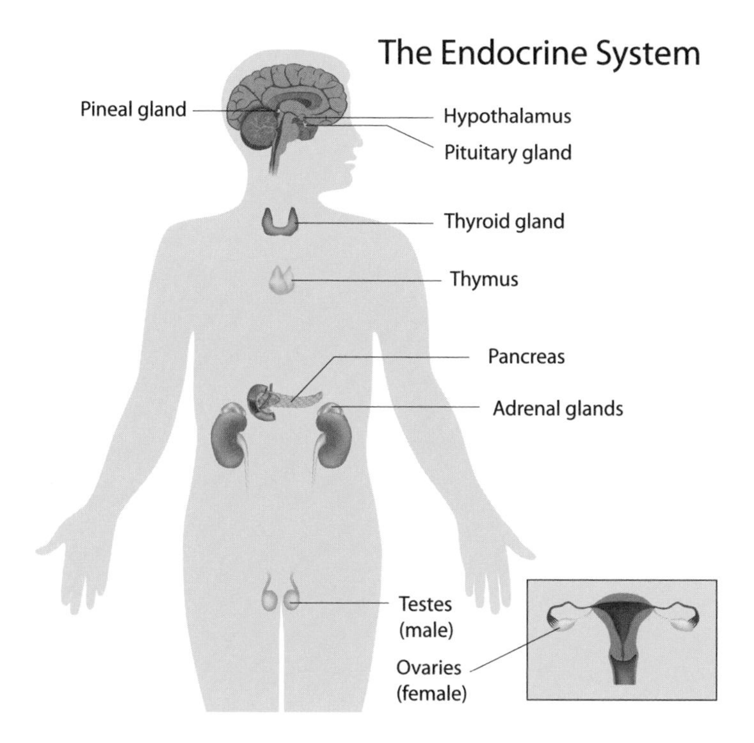

The endocrine glands distributed throughout the body have unique and vital functions.

The endocrine system works closely with the nervous system, as discussed above, to cause changes to the body. It is made up of several organs known collectively as **endocrine glands**, which are responsible for releasing specific chemicals, called **hormones**, into the bloodstream. In this way, the endocrine system is responsible for various effects on the body depending on the hormone being released. Different hormones can influence alertness, mood, stress reaction, sexual behavior, and concentration. Imbalances in some hormones can also lead to psychological disorders, such as depression or anxiety (Arborelius, Owens, Plotsky, & Nemeroff, 1999).

The major endocrine glands are spread out throughout the body, and each has a specific function. One of the most important glands is the **pituitary gland**, which sits at the base of the brain and controls the activities of the other glands in the endocrine system. It does so by releasing important hormones that affect the other glands in the system and stimulating them to release a variety of different hormones as needed in the body.

The **thyroid gland** is another important and well-known gland in the endocrine system. It is located in the neck and is responsible for regulating the body's metabolism; that is, the rate at which the body uses energy to maintain itself. This gland also affects one's degree of attention and alertness and can affect a person's day-to-day levels of energy. You've probably heard of this gland in relation to chronic weight problems. People with a thyroid that does not adequately produce thyroid hormones struggle with abnormal weight gain. The reverse is true for people with an overactive thyroid who might experience excessive weight loss, along with restlessness and problems sleeping.

Above the kidneys lie two other endocrine glands, the **adrenal glands**. They are responsible for releasing a variety of hormones in response to stress that cause the changes in the body that we need to react quickly to an emergency or possible injury. One of these hormones is *epinephrine*, which is also commonly known as adrenaline. When people talk about an "adrenaline rush," they're referring, in part, to this valuable hormone. Epinephrine activates the sympathetic nervous system, which works to mobilize the body and focus all its energy on getting through a situation that is perceived as an emergency. The hormone *norepinephrine* is also released by the adrenal glands when the body's survival mode is activated. It works in a similar fashion to epinephrine and boosts your alertness and focus. The adrenal glands also secrete *cortisol*, which is slower-acting than the other two, and works to increase blood pressure and give you more energy. As we will see when we tackle the topic of stress, elevated levels of cortisol can be very unhealthy because the hormone also decreases the activity of the immune system – it inhibits your body's ability to fight off disease and infection (Segerstrom & Miller, 2004). These glands play an important role in the physiological sensations you experience when you feel fear, anxiety, and stress.

The **gonads** – testes in males and ovaries in females – are the endocrine glands that secrete masculine and feminine hormones that are responsible for our sex characteristics. At puberty, the gonads will secrete androgens, which are predominantly masculine, and estrogens, which are predominantly feminine, in different levels in both sexes. These hormones are responsible for the gender-specific sex characteristics that develop at this stage, including breasts in females and facial hair in males. When sexual maturity is reached, the gonads produce reproductive cells for men and women – the sperm and the egg, respectively.

These glands all work with each other and with other systems in the body to create complex physical and psychological reactions that sustain and promote life.

HOW GENES AFFECT BEHAVIOR

Any discussion on the biological basis of behavior is not complete without mentioning genetics. **Genetics** is the study of how different traits are passed down in living organisms. This field is closely tied to biological psychology and to any discussion regarding nature versus nurture, which is why it is so important to the field of psychology. After all, one of the oldest and most persistent debates in the area revolves around this very topic. Are we a product of our upbringing or our inherited traits?

The field of **behavioral genetics** attempts to answer that question. This sub-division of psychology deals with the way our inherited **genes,** or the units of heredity, affect our behavior. Behavioral geneticists are concerned with identifying what characteristics – including intelligence, talents, temperament, and personality, among others – are passed down from one generation to another. They also seek to identify genes that may be responsible for predispositions to psychological or medical disorders. So how can we obtain this information?

When a crime is committed, prosecutors rely confidently on genetic material left behind at the scene of the crime, whether it comes from hair, skin cells, blood, or saliva. This is because every single cell in our bodies contains genetic material, in the form of **chromosomes**.

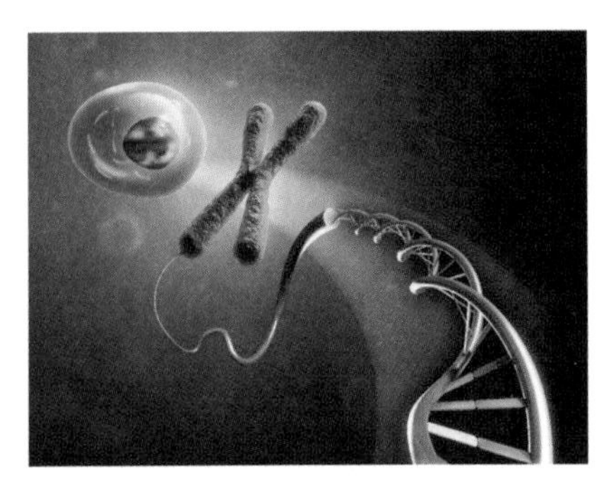

Chromosomes containing DNA make up every cell in the body.

Chromosomes are organized structures of genetic material that we inherit from our parents. Each parent contributes 23 chromosomes totaling 46 in each cell. Chromosomes contain many genes, which are composed of deoxyribonucleic acid, more commonly known as DNA. The information contained in these genes can determine anything from height to eye color. Of course, behavioral geneticists are not interested in those factors; they are interested in psychological factors.

ANIMAL AND HUMAN STUDIES

The study of animals is very important to this field because it allows psychologists to perform experiments that cannot be conducted on humans. One such type of study is called a **strain study**. In a typical strain study, animals are inbred over many generations to create genetically similar animals. These animals are then raised together with animals from different strains to allow researchers to see the differences that appear as a result of genetic variances when the environment is the same. In **selection studies**, animals with certain desirable traits are inbred to produce offspring with more of those traits. Outside of research, these kinds of genetic selections are performed with pets, leading to desirable mixed breeds like the "Labradoodle," which is a mix between a Labrador retriever and a Poodle.

Labradoodle: the result of genetic selection.

Obviously, researchers cannot ethically perform these types of studies with human subjects. Instead, researchers studying humans rely on naturally-occurring genetic phenomena that can give some insight into the hereditary basis for human psychology. **Family studies** are one type of investigation that assumes that if a gene is responsible for a trait, family members should exhibit more of that trait than non-family members because they have more genes in common. For example, if depression has a genetic influence, it stands to reason that relatives of people with depression would exhibit greater rates of depression than the general population.

Identical twins are an asset to psychological research.

By the same logic, twins are also invaluable to the study of nature versus nurture, because twins have identical genetic make-up. Any psychological differences between them must be due to different experiences. Similarly, if twins are raised in separate environments and some trait is pronounced in both, it supports the idea that this trait might be influenced by genetics. The study of separated twins has led researchers to conclude that genetics does, indeed, play a role in intellectual disability, schizophrenia, depression, reading skills, and intelligence (Bouchard, 1984, 1996; Johnson, Bouchard, Segal & Samuel, 2005). **Twin studies** such as these can help determine which traits are genetically influenced and which are unchanged by genetics.

Adoption studies follow a similar procedure; they involve comparing the traits of children that were adopted at birth and brought up by parents that are not genetically related to see if they are more similar to their biological parents or their adoptive parents. Like some twin studies, adoption studies are able to isolate the genetic component from the environmental component, which in most children is deeply interwoven. Often, this is the only way for researchers to separate nature and nurture in humans, allowing them to see the significant contributions of each one.

EVOLUTIONARY PSYCHOLOGY

Evolutionary psychologists take another approach to the study of the biological roots of our psychological traits. Unlike many psychologists that focus on the individual, evolutionary psychologists study the species as a whole. They are interested in finding ways in which our behavior promotes our survival. Evolutionary psychology has its foundations in Darwin's principle of **natural selection**, which proposed that organisms that are best adapted to the environment are more likely to survive and reproduce than those that are not well adapted; thus passing on those evolutionary adaptations to other generations (Darwin, 1859). On the other hand, organisms without said adaptive traits would be more likely to die off before reproducing, which would make their genetic traits die off as well.

Evolutionary psychologists base their theories and research on these principles as they apply to psychological traits. They believe that human behavior is the result of psychological adaptations that have evolved in response to recurrent problems. They further argue that the behaviors and traits that are universal to all cultures have strong evolutionary bases. These traits include helpfulness and cooperation, the ability to identify and prefer healthier mates, language ability, and the ability to communicate non-verbally.

This theoretical perspective is relatively new compared to more established and empirically tested perspectives in the field. However, it contributes to an understanding of our psychology as a species and how it has evolved from our human ancestors.

CHAPTER 2 REVIEW QUESTIONS

1. Which of these is not part of a neuron?
    a. Dendrite
    b. Axon
    c. Cell body
    d. Corpus callosum

2. T/F. The spinal cord is part of the peripheral nervous system.

3. When a neuron fires, ________________ is released into the synaptic gap.

4. Which neurons are responsible for the transmission of information from your eyes and ears?
    a. Motor neurons
    b. Central nervous system neurons
    c. Sensory neurons
    d. Autonomic nervous system neurons

5. The ________________________ of the endocrine system regulate(s) the body's stress response.

6. Which part of the limbic system is responsible for the

formation of new memories?

a. Hypothalamus

b. Amygdala

c. Hippocampus

d. Thalamus

7. The lobe in the cerebral cortex that is primarily responsible for decision making is the:

   a. Frontal lobe

   b. Occipital lobe

   c. Temporal lobe

   d. Parietal lobe

8. T/F. It is impossible to study the genetic versus environmentally-learned differences in humans.

9. The part of the brain that connects the left and right hemisphere is called the ____________________.

10. Which are the ways in which the brain's structure and function can be studied? ______________________________

    ____

    ____

    ____

CHAPTER 3

SENSATION AND PERCEPTION

THINK FOR A MOMENT about all the things you are sensing right now. Do you feel the texture and tightness of your clothes on you? Do you hear ambient noises from your surroundings? What can you see and smell around you?

At any given moment, our senses are bombarded with a constant stream of information from our environment. The process of seeing, hearing, and feeling is two-fold; it involves the stage of **sensation**, which is the neurological process that occurs when energy from the environment stimulates our sensory organs. It also involves perception, which is the mental process that occurs when we interpret this sensory information.

SENSATION

For sensation to occur, an external or internal stimuli must be present to stimulate a **receptor cell** in one of the sense organs. Each receptor cell is specialized to receive information from specific types of energy. For example, the receptor cells in your eyes respond only to light and not sound waves. Likewise, light would have no effect on the receptor cells in the ear, which respond to sound waves.

When this energy is strong enough, it stimulates the receptor cell, which then sends electrochemical signals to the brain to be interpreted. This process is called **transduction** and it is the link between sensation and perception. Like any other action potential in the nervous system, many neurons must fire in order for the stimuli to be sensed. The stronger a stimuli is, the more neurons fire in response to it. Very weak stimuli might not be sensed at all or set off a very slow firing sequence in sensory neurons. So how strong does energy have to be to produce sensation?

To answer this question, we must understand the concept of sensory thresholds. Any sensation requires a minimum amount of intensity in order to be sensed. Think back to the last time you had a hearing test. A short beep is played through headphones in each ear. You are instructed to press a button every time you hear something. This test is designed to ascertain your **absolute threshold.** The absolute threshold represents the smallest amount of energy that one will sense. How bright does a light have to be for you to see the light at all? How loud does a sound have to be for you to hear it? As you might have already guessed, the answer to these questions is, it depends. The absolute threshold for sound for someone with great hearing would be lower than someone with mediocre hearing.

Meaning, the former would still be able to detect a much lower amount of energy. Other factors, such as environmental conditions, also affect absolute threshold from one person to another and even the same person's threshold under different conditions.

A standard hearing assessment would test how well you can hear sounds of different intensities.

Psychologists also study the **difference threshold** of sensations, also known as the just-noticeable difference. This is the smallest amount of change in the strength of a stimulus that one would be able to notice. If you were listening to the radio in your friend's car and your friend started slowly raising the volume, at what point would you notice that the radio is louder? That is your difference threshold. As with the absolute threshold, every sense has a difference threshold that varies by individual. Whether it is the diminishing amount of light available when the sun is setting or the spiciness of one bite of chili compared to the next, when there is a difference in the strength of a stimulus, at some point you notice the change.

VISION

The visual sense is arguably the most important for humans and has a received a lot of attention from psychologists interested in sensation and perception.

THE VISUAL PROCESS

The sensation of visual stimuli begins when light stimulates receptor cells in the eye. In order to do so, light must first pass the **cornea**, which is the transparent outer layer of the eye. Then it enters the eye through the **pupil**, the opening in the center of the colored part of your eye. The

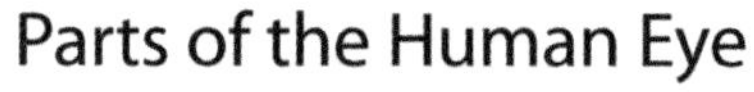

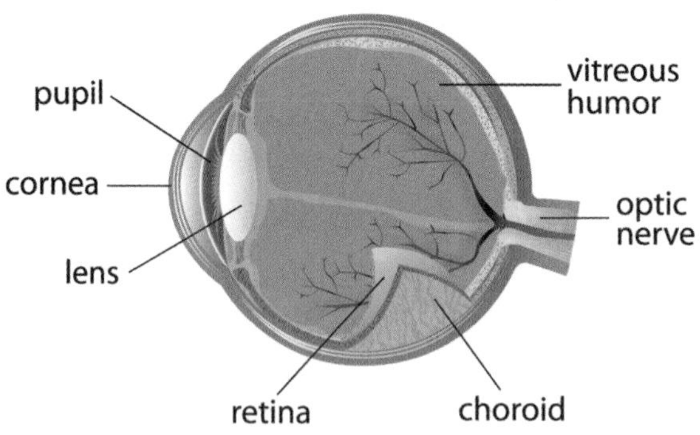

pupil controls the amount of light being let into the eye at any given time. When it is very bright, the pupil constricts, or gets smaller, to protect the eye from overstimulation. When it is very dim, the pupil dilates, or gets bigger, to allow as much light as possible into the eye to help us see in these conditions. This is an example of the process of **adaptation**. Each of our senses adjusts to sensory stimuli so as to not overload our senses.

Once light enters the eye, it passes the **lens**, a clear structure in the eye that helps focus the light onto the retina. The **retina** lines the back part of the eye and contains the receptor cells for vision. Our visual focus is a point in the retina called the **fovea**. This point can be identified as a small indentation on the otherwise smooth retina. Though your visual field is vast and encompasses everything that you see in your peripheral vision, your visual focus is very small and images striking this area are clearer and sharper than images striking any other part of the retina.

The receptor cells responsible for vision are rods and cones, which are named after their shapes. *Rods* respond to varying amounts of light, processing light and dark. *Cones*, on the other hand, are responsible for color vision and function better in brighter light, compared to rods, which work better in dim light.

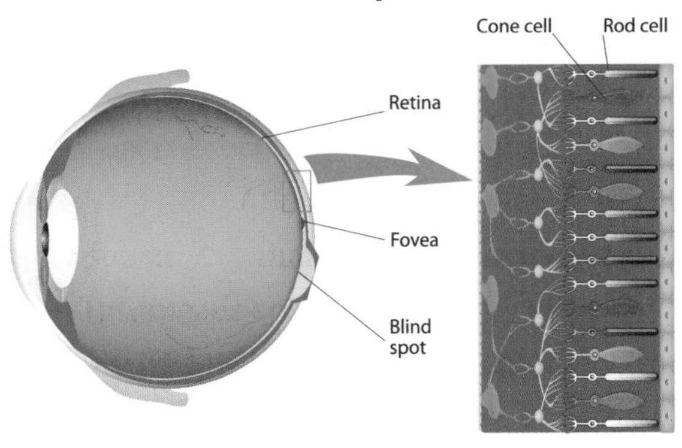

Rods and cones, the receptor cells for vision, are in the retina, lining the rear part of the eye.

The information received by the rods and cones is transmitted through the **optic nerve** to the brain. The optic nerve is a thick collection of neural fibers – similar to the way many individual threads create rope – that connects the eyes to the brain. Through the process of transduction, this information is turned into electrochemical codes that the brain can interpret. If you recall from the previous chapter, the part of the brain that is responsible for this processing is the occipital lobe.

- Adaptation

As mentioned above, our senses adapt quite well to changes in the environment. In vision, there are two types of adaptation. The first is called **dark adaptation** which occurs when you go from an environment with a lot of light, like the outdoors in the middle of a sunny day, to one with very little light, like a dark theater. Your eyes, at first, take some time to be able to see inside this new darkened environment; but after a while, you're able to see shapes in greater detail. What is occurring is that the rods and cones are becoming more and more sensitive to light the longer you stay in poor lighting conditions in order to help you see.

The second type of visual adaptation is the opposite process, called **light adaptation**. When there is a lot of light available, our rods and cones become less sensitive to light. This occurs for the same reason that we squint at the ballpark when it is very sunny, to protect us from damaging our visual systems as a result of overexposure to light.

• Color Vision

If you walked through a blooming garden in the springtime, you would be surrounded by a vast array of colors. The human eye is capable of seeing a wide spectrum of colors. So what is color? And how do we sense it?

Every color you can see has three distinct properties: hue, saturation and brightness. A *hue* is the attribute that makes it discernible as red, green, yellow, or blue. *Saturation* refers to how pure a color is. Royal blue would be considered a very saturated blue, whereas baby blue would not, because it is far more diluted by white. Finally, *brightness* refers to the extent to which a color appears to be reflecting light. Varying the hue, brightness, and saturation can affect the color you see.

Several theories exist to explain exactly how it is that we process these different colors physiologically. One of the earliest known theories of color vision is Young and Helmholtz's **trichromatic theory** of color. This theory holds that three types of receptors, or cones, are responsible for the perception of color: one sensitive to red light, one sensitive to green light, and one sensitive to blue-violet light (Wooten and Miller, 1997). The other colors that we perceive are be created by mixing the signals from these three receptors.

According to the trichromatic theory of color, the broad spectrum of colors we can see is created by mixing signals from blue-violet, red, and green receptors.

This theory does not fully explain several phenomena in vision, such as why some people who are colorblind see only reds and greens or blues and yellows. A German scientist, Ewald Hering (1834-1918) came up with a complementary theory called the **opponent-process theory**. This theory supposes that we have three pairs of color receptors: yellow-blue, red-green, responsible for the hues we see, and black-white, which determine the brightness of the colors we see (Hering, 1964). These receptors are able to detect each of these hues but not at the same time, which explains why people do not see yellowish blues or reddish greens. This theory also explains the phenomenon of *afterimages*, which is what happens when you stare at an image for several moments, and then you see the reverse colors upon closing your eyes or looking at a plain white background.

An afterimage looks like a negative of a photo, reversing the colors you actually see with its opponent pair.

These two theories have coexisted since they were proposed, and psychologists tend to agree that both of these are correct and reflect different aspects of the visual system. Some cones in the retina process the three different kinds of color, while others that are deeper in the visual pathway to the brain are pairs of receptors.

HEARING

Sounds are the psychological experience that our brains create in response to physical energy from the environment. Your auditory system transmits this energy, which is in the form of sound waves, to your brain, where it is processed as the sounds you hear – crying babies, cars honking, music, or birds chirping.

Sound waves are oscillating changes in air pressure that are transmitted through air or water and are interpreted by the brain as sound. They have two characteristics that determine the type of sound we hear: frequency and amplitude. A sound wave's *frequency*, or cycles per second, determines the pitch of the sound. A high pitched shriek would have a higher frequency than the rumble of a car engine. The *amplitude* of a sound, or how high the sound wave is, determines the volume of a sound. Sound waves that are very high, like those that might be produced by a foghorn or the guitar at a concert, would be perceived as louder than the sound waves of a whisper, which would have a smaller amplitude.

A Sound Wave

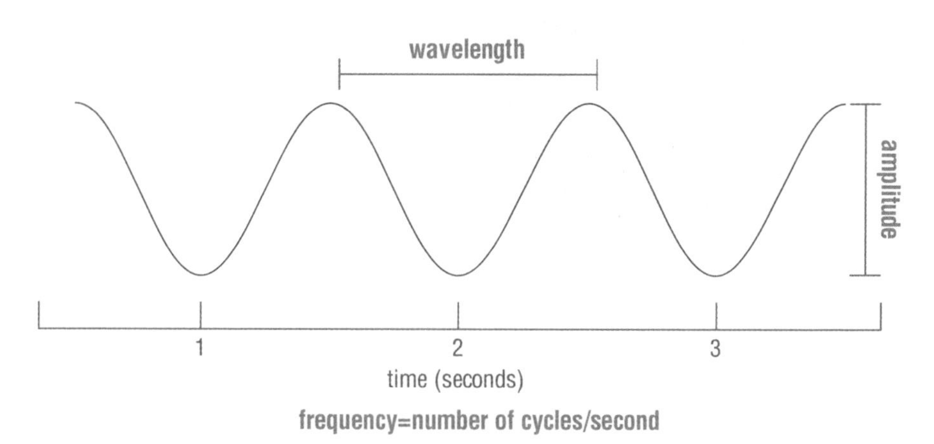

As in vision, our auditory sense adapts to the environment, as one might, for instance, after growing accustomed to the chatter and music in a loud bar that was deafening at first.

THE AUDITORY PROCESS

In order to hear a sound, the sound waves must enter the ear and be processed by the auditory system. First, a sound is funneled into the inner ear by the outer ear. The sound waves set off a series of vibrations in the inner ear starting with the *eardrum*. The movement of the eardrum causes three bones of the middle ear to move in sequence. They are the hammer, anvil, and stirrup. These vibrations are amplified by the movement of these tiny bones, carrying the vibrations to a membrane called the *oval window*. These vibrations then create undulations in the fluid contained in a snail-shaped structure called the *cochlea*. When the fluid in the cochlea begins to ripple, the *basilar membrane* is stimulated. This is a stiff structure that separates the cochlea in two. Atop the basilar membrane is the *organ of Corti*. This is where the receptor cells for hearing are located.

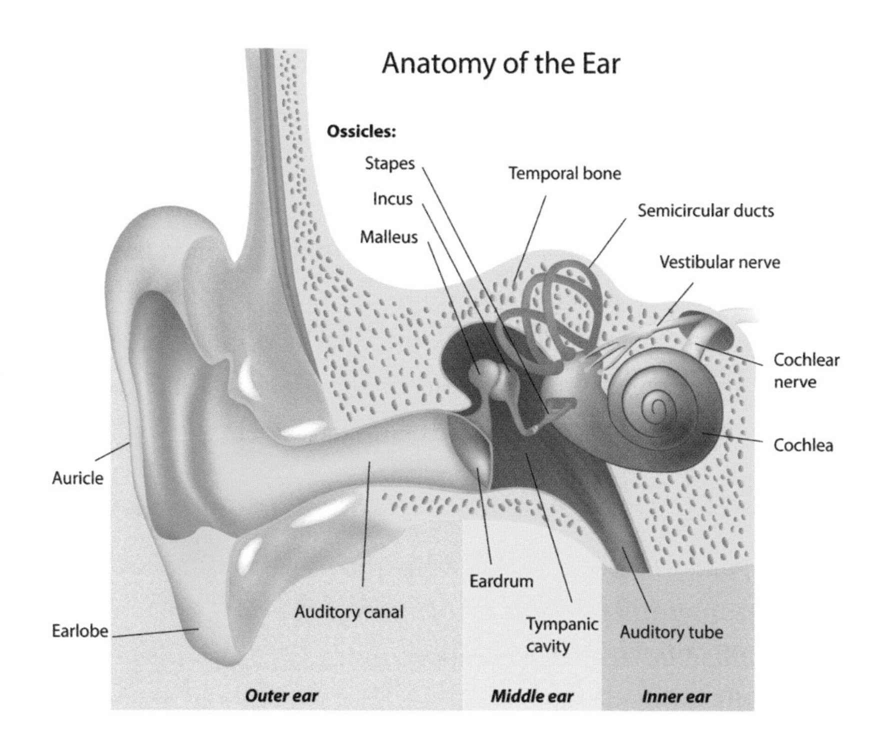

The organ of Corti is full of tiny **hair cells**, which are the receptor cells for hearing. The fibers on the hair cells move in response to the vibrations of the inner ear. This movement is translated into a signal that is sent through the **auditory nerve** to the brain. Like the optical nerve, the auditory nerve is a bundle of neurons that carries information from each of the ears to different parts of the brain. If you recall from the previous chapter, the temporal lobe of the brain is the one that interprets auditory information. The signals also pass through the medulla where they are redirected to other parts of the brain.

OLFACTION

Olfaction, or simply, our sense of smell, is another one of our basic senses, though it may not be as crucial to survival for humans as it is for animals that need it to sniff out predators, prey, as well as mates. This sense is mediated by receptor cells in the nasal cavity. Anything that has an odor, from your morning coffee to a chlorinated pool, transmits airborne molecules that enter the nose and activate our receptor cells for smell. These receptor cells are also sensitive to **pheromones**, which are chemicals that can affect behavior such as sexual behavior.

The information received from the receptor cells is transmitted to the **olfactory bulb** in each cerebral hemisphere to be processed. This part of the brain perceives different odors. Our sense of smell also adapts and with long enough exposure to odors, even strong ones, our receptor cells become less sensitive to them.

TASTE

Our sense of taste, or **gustatory perception**, is another important sensory system. Taste is the sensation we experience when a substance in the mouth activates our taste receptors. These receptor cells are contained in sensory organs commonly known as **taste buds**, and they are located on the tongue. There are five basic taste qualities: sweet, sour, salty, bitter, and umami. Umami is a savory taste that induces salivation. Different parts of the tongue are more sensitive to each of these taste qualities. The tip of the tongue is most sensitive to sweet and salty tastes. The back of the tongue is more sensitive to bitterness, and the sides to sourness.

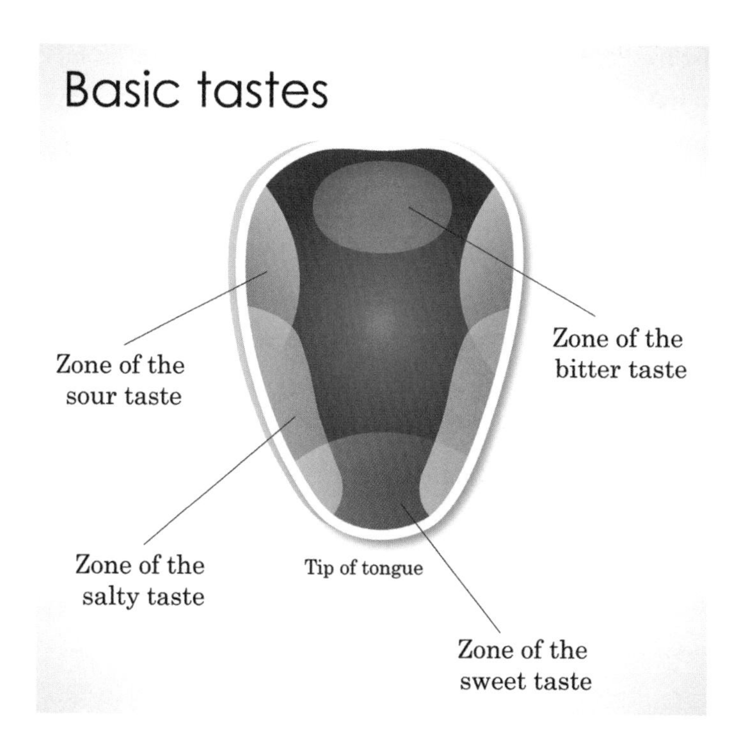

Have you ever wondered why you can feel the sides of your jaw after eating sour candy? It is because your taste buds on the back sides of your tongue are more sensitive to sour tastes.

You are probably thinking about these taste qualities and thinking about the way a banana tastes compared to a taco or a beer. It is important to distinguish these basic taste qualities from flavor, which is what you are likely imagining. Flavor is determined not only by these basic taste qualities but by olfaction, which is why food does not taste as good when you are sick and your nose is stuffy. These senses interact to create the flavor of food.

When you eat something, the chemical substances in the food stimulate the receptor cells in your taste buds to send signals to the parietal lobe of your brain and the limbic system, where the sensation of taste is processed. This process can also lead to adaptation, which is why, for example, the sweetness of yogurt may decline with time

(Theunissen, Polet, Kroeze, & Schifferstein, 2000). Previous exposure to one substance may also alter the taste of another, explaining why most people do not like to drink orange juice after brushing their teeth.

SOMATOSENSORY SYSTEM

The **somatosensory system** is a broad sensory system that encompasses the sensation of touch, temperature, body position, and pain. Our **tactile perception**, or sense of touch, is created from several different types of information gathered by receptor cells in our skin. Since we are covered in it, our skin has the distinction of being our largest sense organ. Our skin can detect a variety of sensations including pressure, temperature, and texture.

Though there are receptor cells for touch throughout the body, there are certain areas like the fingertips and face that contain many more, and thus, are more sensitive to touch. This is what enables blind people to read Braille. Next time you come across a sign in Braille, place your shoulder against it. Can you discern between different patterns with your shoulder? Probably not. However, the large concentration of receptors in your fingertips allow you to detect the small bumps easily.

Your skin is constantly adapting to different sensations. For example, when you get dressed in the morning, you might feel the temperature and texture of your shirt very clearly. However, throughout the day, your brain does not continue to process and remind you of this information. Similarly, you do not feel the weight of your watch all day long; only when you first put it on. This is also why the temperature of a hot tub or cold stream might be really pronounced at first until your body has been submerged for several minutes.

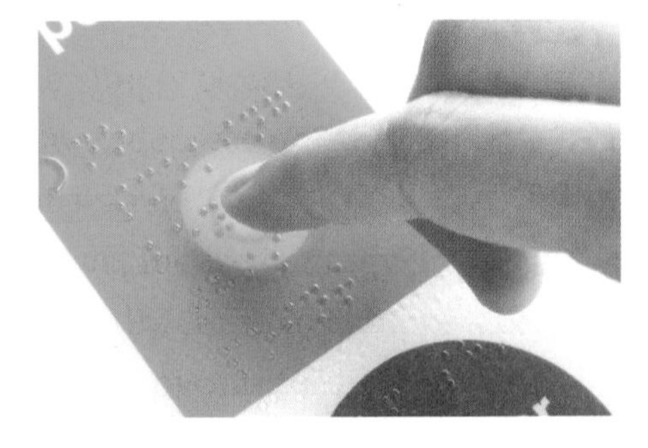

Blind persons are able to read Braille using their fingertips because there are more receptors for touch in this area of the body.

PAIN

Pain is the sensation caused by stimuli that have the potential to damage tissue such as boiling water. This sense is particularly mysterious because physical injury does not always cause pain. Think, for example, to when you were a teenager, climbing trees and playing sports. You might have fallen and scraped your knee, leading to visible injury including blood. However, in the excitement of a backyard basketball game, you probably dismissed it, sensing nothing but a mild sting.

An injury might not feel too bad when it first occurs, but the next day, the pain is much worse.

Whereas the relationship between other sensory receptors and the corresponding sensation is simple and linear, pain perception is not always so straightforward. One proposed reason for this delay in pain sensation is referred to as the **gate control theory** of pain (Melzack & Katz, 1980). According to this theory, neurons in the spinal cord form a proverbial gate which controls the transmission of pain sensation to the brain. When the gate is open, pain is experienced. When the gate is closed, it is not. Even when the gate permits these impulses to reach the brain, the sensation of pain activates the sympathetic nervous system and endocrine system to help the body deal with the perceived crisis. This leads to the secretion of chemicals that are meant to reduce pain.

KINESTHETIC AND VESTIBULAR SENSES

Close your eyes and try to touch the tip of your nose with your index finger. Despite not having any of the other senses to aid in the task, this was probably relatively simple to do. This is all due to the kinesthetic sense. The **kinesthetic sense** is responsible for the sensation of the positions of the body. It transmits information from our muscles and joints to the parietal lobe of the brain, constantly sending signals to the brain about changes in posture, strain on the muscles, and movement.

The kinesthetic sense allows a dancer's brain to interpret the movement of her joints and muscles.

The **vestibular sense** is our sense of balance. Not to be confused with the kinesthetic sense, which tracks the movement of our bodies, the vestibular sense allows us to sense our body's orientation and movement relative the environment around us. This sense is related to the inner ear, where the same cells that detect hearing detect the speed and direction of movement. This relationship explains why one might experience dizziness in relation to ear infections that affect inner ear fluids.

PERCEPTION

All the senses we have discussed provide the brain with information about the external world. But how do perceptions differ when two people are exposed to the same stimuli? For example, someone who likes sushi might have an enjoyable experience and perceive a piece of sushi as fresh and delicious. On the other hand, someone that does not like sushi might experience the same piece of sushi as slimy and disgusting. These are individual differences in **perception**, or the way one's brain interprets and organizes incoming sensory information. Even the same stimulus can lead to a variety of interpretations.

Our perceptual ability allows us to process our sensations as organized and meaningful. This often involves creating a coherent perceptual experience when faced with an abundance of complex and discordant sensory information. Our minds seek organization in a sometimes chaotic world. One important component of our perception is distinguishing figures from the background in which they appear for any sensory system. This is the reason why you are able to pick out a sound and focus on it, drowning out other unimportant background noises; and why you can tell that a vase of flowers is separate from the wall behind it. These might be abilities you take for granted, but imagine not being able to discern these words (the figure) from the page (the background). This process gives meaning to the stimuli we sense.

Two heads or a goblet? The figure pictured can vary depending on which perspective you take.

We also have a tendency to "fill in the blanks" whenever possible to aid in our organization of the world. Even when information is missing, we tend to see whole objects and hear complete sounds, even if they are broken up. If your grandmother calls you and the connection is bad, you might only hear "H-y, -ow a-- -ou?" over the phone and still be able to perceive the intended message: "Hey, how are you?" Using cues from the environment, one is able to accurately piece together information to form a complete and logical picture.

PERCEPTUAL CONSTANCIES

Another useful characteristic of perception involves the stable way we perceive changing sensory information. This is what is referred to as a **perceptual constancy**. Once you are familiar with the size and shape of a car, for instance, you are able to recognize it from any distance or angle. This tendency helps us better organize our sensations. Without this, we might not be able to recognize our own white jacket under different lighting, which makes it look gray. Your stable perception of the jacket as white permits you to see it as such under any condition.

There are several different examples of perceptual constancies, all of which function in the same way. **Size constancy**, for example, is the human tendency to perceive objects as maintaining their known size despite changing sensory information to the contrary. If a person of average height is far away, the image we are sensing of that person may be just inches from the ground, but we know that they are not actually a few inches tall; they only appear that way because of the distance.

Similarly, objects tend to maintain a constant shape in our minds, even when our vantage point affects the image our eyes see. This is called **shape constancy**. For instance, based on relative knowledge, we are aware that most doors have a rectangular shape. If you are looking at a door straight on and it opens slightly, the shape of the door becomes a trapezoid to the eye. Despite that, we understand that the shape of the door is still a rectangle.

Though the shape of a half-opened door appears to be a trapezoid, we never question the reality that the door's actual shape is a rectangle.

Color constancy is another type of perceptual constancy that allows us to perceive familiar objects as maintaining their color despite changing conditions under which they might be viewed. If you have a blonde friend, it is likely that you will perceive her as a blonde even under lighting that makes her hair look brown or red.

A similar concept is that of **brightness constancy**, which explains that the perceived brightness of familiar objects remains intact despite the fact that the amount of light they are seen under might vary from moment to moment. This occurs because we tend to perceive objects in relation to the objects around them. A bright, white smile will always be perceived as brighter than the skin of the face, regardless of how light or dark it is. Your pearly white teeth will reflect more light relative to your skin or hair, allowing perception of your teeth's brightness to remain constant, even under different lighting conditions.

DISTANCE AND DEPTH

Our perception also aids us in determining the distance between ourselves and the objects around us and how much depth the objects have. This is why we are able to drive without hitting other cars. Our brain uses cues from the environment to accurately make these spatial judgments. There are two categories of depth and distance perception cues: monocular cues and binocular cues. **Monocular cues** can be ascertained from the information only one eye provides. In other words, if you were wearing an eye patch over one eye, you would still be able to use monocular cues to determine the distance of objects around you. The other types of cues are **binocular cues**, which require both eyes and cannot be perceived with one eye alone.

MONOCULAR CUES

Monocular cues allow us to determine depth and distance even with one eye covered. One particularly useful monocular cue is known as *interposition,* or *occlusion*. This happens when an object blocks or partially blocks our view of another object, and thus, we perceive it as closer. For example, if you are driving on the street and a large pine tree blocks your view of a large cabin, you will know immediately that the tree must be closer to you than the cabin.

Because the giant pine partially obscures your view of the cabin, you recognize it to be closer.

Another commonly used cue is called *linear perspective*, and this is how artists can create three-dimensional images on a two-dimensional plane. Imagine the last time you drove on a long stretch of highway. The parallel lines of the highway on either side of you appear to come together the farther in the distance you look, even though we know those two lines never meet.

Motion parallax is yet another monocular cue of depth and distance perception. Imagine yourself on that long stretch of highway again, only this time you are looking out the passenger-side window. Though everything outside of the window – the trees, the light poles, the mountains – is stationary, they all appear to be moving very differently. Things that are closer to you are whizzing by very quickly, whereas mountain peaks far off in the distance appear to be stationary. The way you perceive these objects to be moving indicates to your brain how far they are from you.

Linear perspective makes the edges of the road look like they come together far off in the distance.

BINOCULAR CUES

Binocular cues of depth perception, as previously discussed, do require the use of both eyes. This is because, at any given moment, your brain is receiving information from both retinas to create these cues.

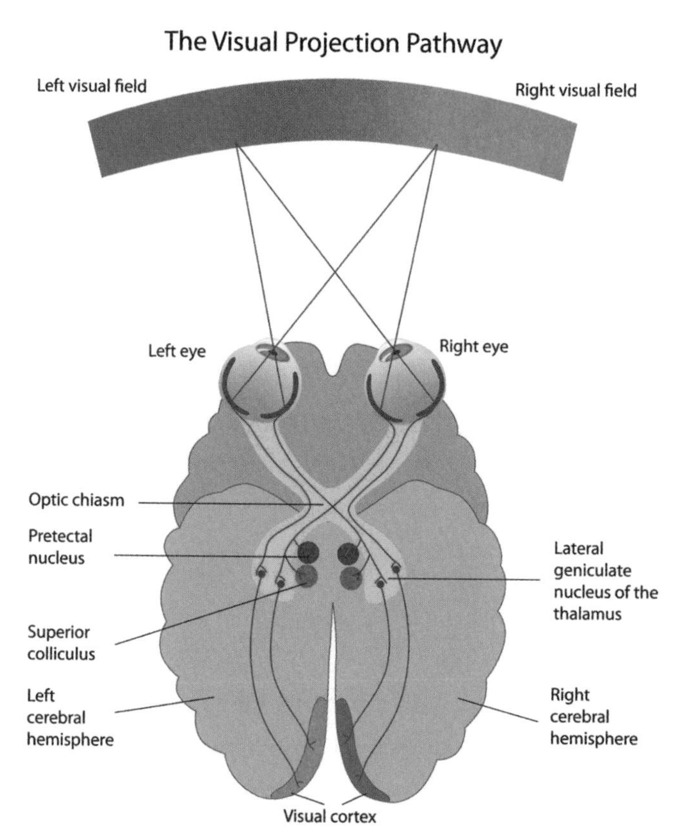

Information from the left visual field is transmitted to the visual cortex in the right hemisphere and information from the right visual field is transmitted to the visual cortex in the left hemisphere.

One such cue is called *retinal disparity*. What we see at any given moment is a complete picture because the two hemispheres from our brain are in constant communication, which allows us to bridge two images seamlessly. However, whether you notice or not, each eye has a slightly different perspective of the world. You can see this by holding up a pencil a few inches from your face and closing one eye. Without moving the pencil, open that eye and close the other one. You will see that the pencil appears to have moved. This is retinal disparity, which is the difference between what each eye sees. When you hold out your pencil at arm's distance and perform the same exercise, you will see that the two images appear more similar. When objects are very close, the disparity will be much greater than when objects are far away, allowing our brain to determine depth.

The muscles of the eyes also provide an important binocular cue: *convergence.* This refers to how much your eyes must rotate inward toward each other to keep an approaching object in focus. The closer an object comes toward you, the more your eyes will converge. This is what happens when someone throws a ball at you. Your eye muscles begin to turn your eyes inward as the ball approaches, signaling to your brain that it is getting closer.

Using these cues from both your eyes as well as the monocular cues discussed in the previous section, we are able to gauge the depth and distance of objects in our ever-changing world.

INDIVIDUAL DIFFERENCES IN PERCEPTION

Even though the information you gather from the external world might be the same or very similar to what someone else senses, the way it is interpreted in your mind can be very different. This interpretation depends highly on the characteristics of the observer.

As the old adage goes, "We see what we want to see," and even in cases of simple object perception, this holds true. Our expectations and motivations significantly influence what we perceive. You might be motivated to see a friendly hello as flirtatious if you are attracted to the person greeting you. If you have just finished watching a scary movie in which the serial killer calls and threatens his victims and your phone rings, you will probably perceive that mundane sound as chilling. That is because the movie created a **perceptual expectancy**, or a predisposition to perceive things a certain way.

These expectations can also cause people to alter what they see in a way that makes more sense. For instance, read the lines below:

PARIS
IN THE
THE SPRING

Many people automatically read "PARIS IN THE SPRING" even though the word "the" appears twice above. We automatically delete that extra word because we do not expect it to be there. This is why we are often advised to have other people edit our work. Mistakes in our own writing can be passed over because our minds read the complete and correct sentence, even if that is not what is on the page. This is also why true/false questions on exams can be the hardest. If you do not carefully read a sentence, you might automatically delete or alter the part that makes it false, and think that it is true.

Our experiences also have a great influence on our perceptions. A chef, who has been trained and has spent years cooking with a variety of ingredients might be able to pick out the different spices in a dish, whereas the average restaurant patron would not. Any kind of training or experience can alter the way one looks at certain objects. This is also true of culture. For example, a Chinese character might be aesthetically pleasing to a Westerner with no knowledge of Chinese. However, the meaning of that character in Chinese culture would certainly affect how it is perceived in China.

Perception can also be a reflection of personality. This is why optimists are seen as perceiving a glass as half-full when a pessimist sees the same glass as half-empty. This idea is behind the use of projective personality tests such as the Rorschach inkblot test, which is a series of ambiguous inkblots that test-takers can interpret in any way they choose. The idea is that certain aspects of one's personality will come to light depending on the interpretation given to these images.

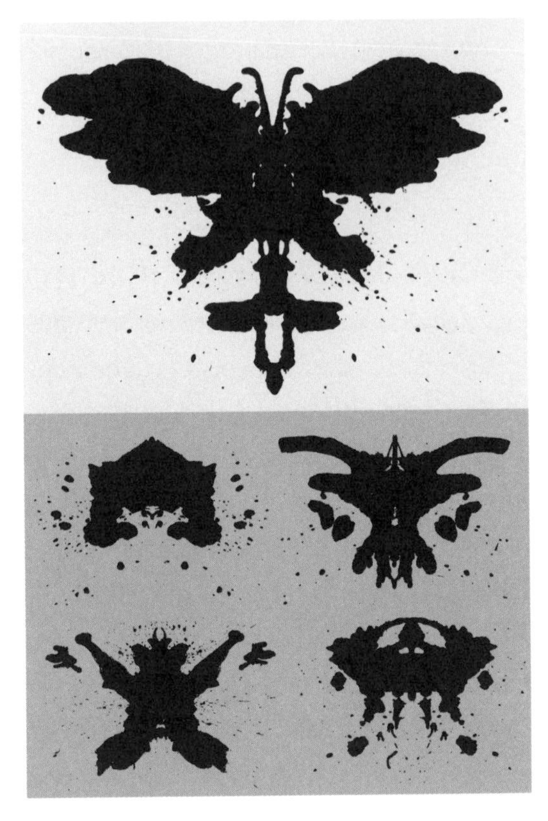

The Rorschach inkblot test allows test takers to interpret the images any way they see fit.

All of these factors are examples of the subjectivity of perception, even though our sensory processes are quite objective.

CHAPTER 3 REVIEW QUESTIONS

1. The receptor cells for vision are called ________________ and ________________.

2. The minimum amount of intensity of a stimulus that will produce a sensation is called:

   a. Difference threshold

   b. Absolute threshold

   c. Just-noticeable difference

   d. Adaptation

3. The frequency of a sound wave determines ________________, while the amplitude of the wave determines ________________.

4. T/F. What we sense is exactly what we perceive.

5. Which of the senses has to do with balance and our body's position in our environment?

   a. Kinesthetic

   b. Vestibular

   c. Tactile

   d. Gustatory

6. Which nerve transmits information from your ears to your brain? ______________________________

7. A sheet of white paper will always be perceived as being brighter than a piece of coal, regardless of the light conditions that they are being viewed in, because of the principle of:

    a. Shape constancy

    b. Brightness constancy

    c. Color constancy

    d. Size constancy

8. Which is the monocular cue of depth perception that uses parallel lines? ___________________________

9. The difference between what each eye sees is called:

    a. Convergence

    b. Linear perspective

    c. Retinal disparity

    d. Perceptual constancy

10. T/F. Our perceptions can be influenced by culture, personality, expectancies and motivation.

CHAPTER 4

CONSCIOUSNESS

THROUGHOUT THE DAY, we experience several different states of consciousness – from sleep, to the effect of a drug like nicotine, to the normal unaltered state of waking. Typically, we spend most of the day in a waking state of consciousness, or **wakefulness**. During this state, we are conscious, awake, and reasonably aware of our external world and coherent enough to process our surroundings.

As was briefly mentioned in Chapter 2, the hypothalamus maintains the activation in the cerebral cortex that must occur for one to be in a wakeful state. During wakefulness, there is more firing of neurons in the brain than during sleep. The brain's waves during wakefulness, as detected by an electroencephalograph (EEG), are *beta waves*. These waves correspond to normal brain activity, encompassing a range from relaxed to excited or panicked.

This waking state allows you to make your way through the world every day, from the moment you get up to shower and brush your teeth, to the moments when you get dressed for work, eat breakfast, and drive to work. Wakefulness allows you to complete all the simple day-to-day tasks of a normal functioning adult including eating, walking, driving, and communicating with coworkers and family members.

Anything other than this state of wakefulness is considered an **altered state of consciousness (ASC).** Normally, an ASC is a temporary change of one's awareness and can be induced by chemical substances. For instance, many of the aforementioned activities would be impossible under the influence of certain sedative or mind-altering substances which may inhibit your ability to communicate or walk. These activities are also generally not possible to do while sleeping.

SLEEP

Aside from wakefulness, we spend a large portion of our time sleeping. In fact, a typical person who sleeps an average of eight hours a night spends about a third of his or her life sleeping. This might seem like a lot, but consider how you feel when you've gone almost 24 hours without sleep. You feel exhausted and badly crave a good night's rest. The fact is, you need sleep to function normally in everyday life. During sleep, consciousness and sensory activity are reduced, and voluntary muscles become inactive, allowing the mind and body to rest.

Several studies have demonstrated that sleep is associated with many essential functions, though they each only partially explain why humans actually need sleep. Some of the research findings suggest that sleep is related to the immune system. Sleep deprivation is correlated with a decrease in white blood cells, which defend our bodies from disease (Zager et al., 2007). Furthermore, lack of sleep has been shown to hinder the healing of burns on rats (Gumustekin et al., 2004). In other words, sleep actually keeps you healthy! Sleep is also important for memory and learning. Research has demonstrated that sleep deprivation affects working memory – the short-term memory used to process information throughout the day (Turner, Drummond, Salamat, & Brown, 2007). Without working memory, higher-level functions are hindered, such as reasoning and decision making, and the ability to commit things to long-term memory. These findings are the reason that students are always advised to sleep well before an exam. Certain stages of sleep are crucial in consolidating learned information into long-term memory.

Sleep follows a rhythm called the **circadian rhythm,** which is a biological cycle lasting 24 hours that is synced to the day-night cycle. This rhythm is partially controlled by a cluster of neurons in the hypothalamus that is sensitive to light. When it gets dark, neurons in the retina transmit directly to this area in the hypothalamus, which controls the body's metabolism and blood pressure, among other important functions. The hypothalamus signals to the nervous system and the endocrine system that it is time to wake up in the mornings and that it is time for bed in the evenings. Obviously, we do not always sleep when it is dark or wake when it is light, because our circadian rhythm adapts and can function without the cues to day and night. However, if you have ever been camping, you have probably noticed how easy and restful it is, in the absence of artificial light, to go to bed early and wake up with the sun.

The circadian rhythm is also affected by travel across different time zones, which is what causes jet lag. If you've traveled from the U.S. to Europe, for instance, you might have had trouble falling asleep at a reasonable hour and waking up early. This occurs because your body is adjusted to a sleep cycle that is in sync with your time zone. When you travel from New York to London where it is 11:00 pm when it is 6:00 pm in New York, you might need some time to adjust, or to synchronize, to that new cycle.

STAGES OF SLEEP

Sleep is complex, and human beings do not simply switch from wakefulness to sleep. Instead, we go through several stages: three non-REM (rapid eye movement) stages and one REM stage (Silber et al., 2007). Before we fall asleep, we experience a stage of increased relaxation when we are slowly losing awareness. In this first stage of sleep, *NREM stage 1*, when we are falling asleep, we experience irregular *alpha waves* as detected by an EEG. During this stage, we are between sleep and wakefulness. Our muscles are relaxed, and pulse slows, as our eyes roll slowly. This stage is very brief, and it is very easy to be woken at this stage. During this stage it is common to be distantly aware of conversations going on around you. Loud sounds or movement on the bed may make you suddenly awake and alert. In fact, you might not even realize you were sleeping at all.

During *NREM stage 2*, a sleeping person becomes progressively harder to wake. The patterns of the brain of a sleeping person during this stage are characterized by *theta waves* and by sleep spindles, which are short bursts of brain activity. In other words, your brain activity has slowed down considerably, which is reflected by slightly wider, longer waves on the EEG than in NREM stage 2. Sleep spindles represent brief moments of increased alertness. Following NREM stage 2, we reach *NREM stage 3*, which was previously broken up into two

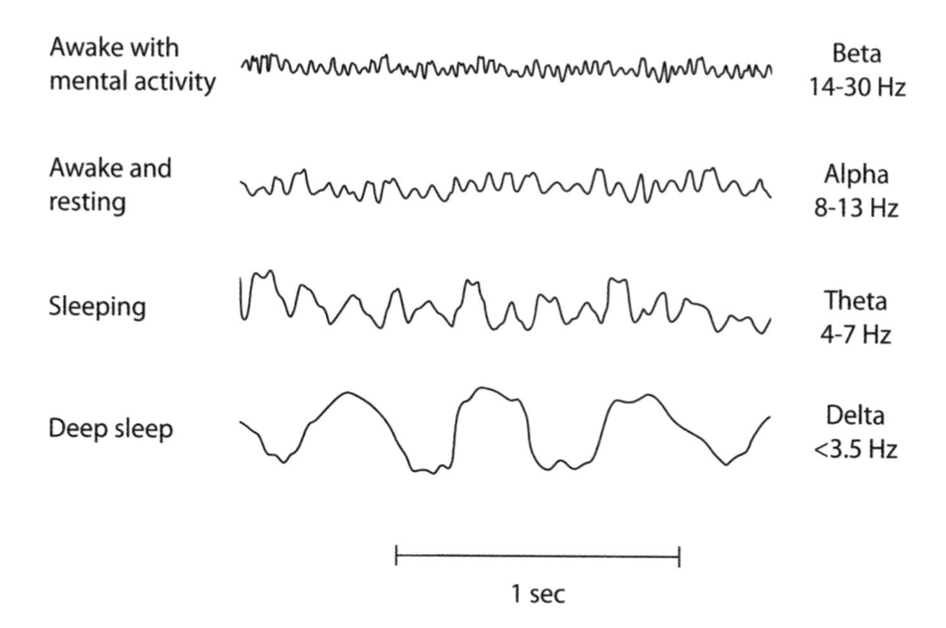

Brain waves tend to get longer and slower as we fall deeper and deeper into sleep. REM sleep, on the contrary, leads to more activity in the brain, and the brain waves of a person in REM sleep would look like those of someone who is awake.

stages. This is when the EEG would show slow-wave sleep. *Delta waves*, which are much slower waves with high peaks predominate this stage. At this point, the sleeping person is unresponsive to the environment, including the presence of lights or noises, and will not easily awaken. Physiologically, heart rate, blood pressure, and temperature drop during NREM stage 3. It is considered the most restful stage and the amount of time spent in stage 3 tends to decrease with age.

After passing through these three stages of non-REM sleep, roughly about an hour after falling asleep, we experience **REM (rapid-eye movement) sleep**. At this stage, our brain waves return to the high-frequency short waves of *NREM stage 1,* and our eyes move rapidly back and forth under our eyelids (hence, the name). Aside from brain activity, blood pressure, heart rate, and other physiological functions are very similar to those that one would detect in a person that is fully awake. Though some dreaming occurs during NREM sleep, most remembered dreams are experienced at this stage.

You might assume that this sleep cycle begins when you fall asleep and ends when you wake up, which might be why early researchers had the misconception that dreams occur right before waking. Further research in sleep has demonstrated that the sleep cycle repeats several times throughout the night. After the first REM stage, a sleeper returns to the stages of NREM sleep and the cycle repeats. Overall, the stages of sleep cycle repeat about four to five times a night. The length of the REM stage tends to increase over the course of the night, and you spend less time in NREM stage 3. These average lengths vary with age. The progression of these stages and average duration also do not account for a variety of different sleep disturbances that afflict up to 50 million Americans at any given time.

SLEEP DISORDERS

The study of sleep has led to the identification of several sleep disorders, which are classified by the American Psychiatric Association (APA) in the Diagnostic and Statistical Manual of Mental Disorders (DSM-5; APA, 2013).

INSOMNIA

Insomnia is one of the most common sleep disorders, affecting as many as 35 million Americans. It is characterized as an inability to fall asleep or to sleep as long as desired. There are different types of insomnia depending on how long one is affected. Transient insomnia lasts less than a week and is usually caused by stressful events. You can probably imagine a time when you had trouble falling asleep the night before a big job interview or a presentation. When stress interferes with sleep, it is because increased activity of the nervous system (particularly the sympathetic nervous system) prevents you from feeling relaxed enough to be able to fall asleep. Insomnia can also be chronic, sometimes lasting for longer than a month. This can be due to a variety of issues, such as hormonal imbalances, long-term interpersonal difficulties, or because of another disorder, like depression.

Secondary symptoms of insomnia demonstrate the effects of sleep deprivation. People who suffer from insomnia often feel drowsy and fatigued throughout the day. They may be irritable and have difficulty concentrating on simple tasks. Many sufferers of insomnia turn to over-the-counter sleep aids to help induce sleep when it does not come naturally. This can lead to dependence on such aids.

SLEEP APNEA

Sleep apnea is a disorder characterized by breathing difficulties or slow breathing during sleep. Typically, a sleeping person breathes in air and exhales carbon dioxide through the nose and mouth. When a person with apnea sleeps, the airway can be partially or completely blocked. He or she will experience a pause in breathing that can last seconds to minutes and recurs throughout the night. The lack of oxygen in the brain disrupts sleep, which allows for the re-opening of the airway. As the person struggles to breathe, he or she may make loud snoring or gasping sounds, but it is important to differentiate the sounds of sleep apnea from normal snoring, because the long-term effects of apnea can be quite serious.

Severe sleep apnea can be a grave health hazard and has been shown to double or triple the risk of stroke (Yaggi et al., 2005). Lack of adequate oxygen is also associated with a higher incidence of cancer (Nieto et al., 2012). As with insomnia, quality of sleep can be reduced and sufferers may experience daytime drowsiness and fatigue. The problem can last for years and is normally recognized by others who witness the difficulty breathing. Sleep apnea can be effectively treated using continuous positive airway pressure (CPAP) face masks, which can help prevent the obstruction of the airway by providing constant air pressure (Smith et al., 1980).

SLEEPTALKING AND SLEEPWALKING

Sleepwalkers are not generally aware that they sleepwalk. They may be shocked to wake up to find they are not in bed.

Sleepwalking and **sleeptalking** are disorders that occur in NREM stage 3, slow-wave sleep, and they involve performing activities normally performed when awake. The activities of a sleepwalker may be harmless, like sitting up in bed or walking to the bathroom; or dangerous, like cooking or driving. Sleepwalkers generally do not have memory of incidents that occur during sleep, though their eyes may be open. Sleepwalkers may also be very hard to awake due to the fact that they are in a very deep stage of sleep, but contrary to popular belief, waking a sleepwalker is not dangerous. Considering the fact that they might leave the house and get behind the wheel of a car, it may be more dangerous to *not* wake them. Both sleepwalking and sleeptalking are more common in children and have a tendency to decrease with age.

NIGHT TERRORS

A **night terror** is another sleep disorder that involves waking in an inconsolable state of panic. Often, sufferers will bolt upright, screaming, crying, and sweating. When they awake, they are likely to be unresponsive to attempts to comfort them. This phenomenon is distinguished from a more common night-time occurrence: nightmares. Most people occasionally experience nightmares, such as dreaming that they are running away from a person with a knife or falling off a precipice. The difference between the two has to do with our sleep stages. Nightmares, like most dreams, occur during REM sleep. Night terrors, on the other hand, occur more frequently during NREM sleep. Unlike nightmares, which can be remembered upon waking, night terrors cannot be recalled the next morning.

NARCOLEPSY

Narcolepsy is a chronic disorder in which the brain is unable to regulate sleep-wake cycles normally, leading sufferers to fall asleep involuntarily. Narcoleptics could be in the middle of any daily activity such as working, reading, or cooking, when they suddenly nod off. These periods usually last about 15 minutes, though they can be longer. These sleep episodes are unique because they lead to REM sleep almost immediately; whereas, during a normal sleep cycle, it takes about an hour or so. This sudden entry into REM sleep can lead to hallucinations while falling asleep, which can be very vivid and often frightening.

Though a single cause for narcolepsy has not been identified, researchers have found that a neurotransmitter called *hypocretin* is correlated with the incidence of narcolepsy (Nishino et al., 2000). People with narcolepsy seem to show shortages of this neurotransmitter in the brain, leading researchers to conclude that it may be part of the problem. This chemical is involved in the regulation of wakefulness and arousal.

DREAMS

When your head hits the pillow and you close your eyes, what do you dream about? Winning the lottery, flying, running away from a madman, falling off a cliff, performing naked in front of an audience, quitting your job? Though the content of your dreams can be very unique, many themes recur in dreams, representing common human fears, concerns, or desires.

Dreams are a series of auditory and visual experiences occurring involuntarily in the mind during sleep. Typically, dreams occur during REM sleep, when brain activity is high. Most dreams last about 5 to 45 minutes and most people dream several times a night, even if they do not remember them (Meier, Ruef, Ziegler, & Hall, 1968). External stimuli can affect the content of dreams. For example, a loud bang outside your bedroom window might be seen in a dream as a fiery explosion.

THE PURPOSE OF DREAMS

Dreams have been the topic of psychological speculation for a very long time, though they are still not fully understood. Different psychologists have come up with very different theories regarding the function and purpose of dreams.

One of the first modern theories of dreaming came from Freud's *Interpretation of Dreams* (1913). Freud believed that dreams are one of the few ways in which our unconscious desires and drives make themselves known. For example, a dream about marrying someone we do not often think about might reflect an unconscious desire to be with them. Dreams can often reflect hidden motives or worries that one is unaware they have. This belief is reflected in psychodynamic therapy, which is often used to interpret the content and symbols of dreams in order to understand individuals and their psyches.

Freud believed that dreams have a *manifest* and a *latent* content. The manifest content is the part of a dream you are able to recall, including what you saw, heard, and thought (Freud, 1911). This information could be useful at face value. As the famed psychologist is allegedly quoted as once saying, "Sometimes a cigar is just a cigar." Dreaming of riding a horse could simply represent a real hobby in your life. However, Freud also believed that some dreams held a hidden meaning, which he called the latent content of the dream. Thus, the symbols and themes in the dream could be interpreted to uncover their true unconscious meaning. So perhaps riding a horse is actually a representation of your desire to escape your current life. If a woman dreamt about riding a horse, a psychoanalytic psychologist may also conclude that the horse represents a phallic symbol and that the dream is a manifestation of penis envy. Obviously, extrapolating meaning from simple images in dreams leaves a lot of room for interpretation – a fact that earned Freud a lot of criticism. Despite this, many dream symbols and themes are quite pervasive, suggesting that dreams do sometimes have primal elements, particularly fear and survival-based elements, that are shared by everyone.

The cognitive perspective provides a very different explanation of dreams. According to this perspective, dreams help us process information gathered during the day and strengthen memory for this information. This is why dreams often have aspects related to something we read or saw during the day. This is true for insignificant imagery, like a commercial, but also for important information to be learned. Research has demonstrated that REM sleep is associated with learning and that after learning difficult material, one spends more time in REM sleep (Smith, Nixon, & Nader, 2004). This research supports the theory that dreams, which occur most frequently during REM sleep, help us consolidate and commit to memory learned information.

Have you ever spent all day performing a repetitive task and then dreamt about doing that task? This can be as simple as assembling a car engine or playing a game of Candy Crush. Sometimes, dreams are simply expressions of our daily lives. Often, people find that they dream about whatever they were doing right before bed. These dreams may not have any other purpose than as an extension of what people think about in their daily lives.

DAYDREAMS

Daydreams, like dreams, are their own curious phenomenon. The main difference between a dream and a daydream is that during a daydream you are not sleeping. Instead, your thoughts shift from the present reality into a state of fantasy, where you might have won the lottery and be vacationing on the beach in Fiji with your favorite movie star. Daydreaming is also a conscious choice. Except in rare cases where you become aware you are dreaming, known as *lucid dreaming*, you cannot control the content of your dreams, but you *can* control your daydreams. They are usually representations of some personal goal or desire.

Though it is often seen as non-productive (and if you are daydreaming in class when you should be listening to your instructor, it probably is), daydreaming can serve useful purposes. Daydreams allow your mind to rest and allow one to de-stress by providing a brief moment during which you are unconcerned with the stressful worries of daily life. This can reduce the increased activity of the nervous system brought on by common stressors. It can also help develop creativity and enhance problem solving and interpersonal skills.

DRUG-ALTERED STATES OF CONSCIOUSNESS

States of consciousness can also be influenced, sometimes immensely, by foreign substances including drugs – both prescribed and illicit. The prevalence of drug use, including mild-altering substances, is nothing new. Since the beginning of time, people all over the world have used substances that affect their mental states. Some take drugs to ease pain, to have a spiritual experience, to achieve a mental state they cannot reach naturally, for a thrill or an escape, or to fit in with their friends. Different substances work differently with the body to produce specific effects.

DEPRESSANTS

Depressants are substances that reduce, or *depress*, the activity of the nervous system. This means arousal levels and excitability are lowered. It is because of impaired reaction time and cognitive function, due to the effect of depressants, that we are cautioned against driving under the influence of alcohol, one of the most commonly used depressants. Barbiturates and opiates are other common examples of depressants. Depressants are often used in the treatment of anxiety since the nervous system is excessively active during bouts of anxiety and substances with a depressant effect help reduce this increased activity. This mechanism explains why some people with social phobia develop alcoholism in an attempt to cope with their problems (Schneier et al., 1989). Since alcohol is always readily available, particularly in social situations, they become dependent on the substance to cope with their anxiety.

- Alcohol

Alcohol is one of the most abused substances in the United States. It can become addictive and have damaging long-term effects on health and well-being. Like other depressants, alcohol helps people relax and enhances their mood, which makes it a drug with high potential for abuse. Alcohol affects several important parts of the brain including the frontal lobe, which is responsible for reasoning, judgment, and impulse control. That is why people under the influence of alcohol tend to be less inhibited and more spontaneous. People might also be more volatile, hostile, or violent because the substance impairs their ability to make reasonable decisions.

People who abuse alcohol sometimes find themselves blacking out completely and losing control of their faculties. For instance, a person heavily intoxicated might be convinced that he is sober enough to drive home, because his logic and reasoning is impaired. It is not uncommon for people who abuse alcohol to wake up not remembering how they got home, or what may have happened while they were under the influence. Many end up regretting the decisions they made while drunk that they would not have made while sober.

The long-term effects of alcohol use, especially heavy use, can be devastating. Chronic use can damage many vital organs in the body, including the kidney and the liver. The liver, for example, which breaks down food to create energy for your body and removes toxins from your blood, can be seriously affected by chronic drinking. In breaking down alcohol, liver cells can become irrevocably damaged. Alcohol has also been implicated in cardiovascular disease and certain cancers (Nelson et al., 2013).

- Barbiturates

Barbiturates are medications, such as Amytal, Nembutal, and Phenobarbital that have sedative properties and have historically been used for the treatment of anxiety, insomnia, and epilepsy. Depending on the type and the dose, they can act as mild sedatives or lead to total anesthesia. In the 1950s, the damaging effects of barbiturates, as well as the potential for physical dependence, were discovered, so the use of barbiturates to treat anxiety has declined in favor of medications with fewer side effects (Galanter & Kleber, 2008). The most common of these medications are benzodiazepines, which include drugs like Valium and Xanax, for the treatment of anxiety disorders, and Ambien, for the treatment of insomnia. In contemporary medicine, barbiturates are still sometimes used to treat epilepsy and as an anesthetic.

- Opiates

An *opiate* is any narcotic substance derived from the opium poppy plant. Morphine, codeine, and thebaine are the major psychoactive opiates. Heroin is a drug that is metabolized into morphine in the body, which produces euphoria and acts as a potent painkiller. Though heroin was originally created as a cure for morphine addiction, it has led to even greater drug problems. Heroin can be administered in a variety of different ways, though injection is one of the most common. Users quickly get addicted to the euphoric rush of the drug and develop a tolerance to it, requiring higher and higher doses to get the same effect. Heroin use is also linked to the transmission of diseases like HIV and hepatitis because of users sharing the same unsterilized needles.

Opiates are derived from the poppy seed.

STIMULANTS

While depressants lower the activity of the nervous system, **stimulants** have the opposite effect. They provide energy and induce temporary improvement in mental and physical capacities, to varying degrees. Some of the most commonly abused stimulants are caffeine, nicotine, amphetamines, and cocaine. Because of the positive feeling and energy that these substances produce, they lend themselves very easily to addiction.

- Caffeine

A lot of people like to drink coffee in the morning to give them the boost they need to start their day. Coffee's *caffeine* content is the reason behind that boost. This mild stimulant can also be found in tea and cocoa, as well as artificially, in many over the counter medications used to treat pain, and cold and allergy symptoms. Though it is one of the safest stimulants, large doses of caffeine can lead to palpitations, headaches, anxiety, insomnia, and diarrhea. Some people even report shaking after consuming caffeine, especially in high quantities, like those found in energy drinks such as Monster and Red Bull.

- Nicotine

Nicotine is the main chemical ingredient in tobacco, which is one of the main reasons behind the formation of tobacco dependency. This is also what makes tobacco addiction one of the hardest to break, despite common knowledge linking tobacco use to lung and oral cancer. Nicotine causes the user to feel relaxed and almost euphoric, though not as intensely as other stimulants. This is because it stimulates reward centers in the nervous system, but with effects peaking very quickly after inhaling, causing the user to smoke more.

Smoking is addictive in part because of the effect of nicotine.

- Amphetamines

Amphetamines are synthetic stimulants that resemble epinephrine (adrenaline), which functions to activate the sympathetic nervous system. One well-known type is methamphetamine, which is produced in homemade "meth labs," often with disastrous results. The drug can be transmitted intravenously or smoked. Users report increased alertness and euphoric well-being. After the drug effects wear off, they also report "crashing," an experience of exhaustion and sadness. Amphetamines have long-term negative effects, affecting many cognitive functions including intelligence and emotion. Users demonstrate higher levels of aggression and are more prone to psychosis than the average person (Berman, Kuczenski, McCracken, & London, 2009).

- Cocaine

Cocaine is a stimulant that is obtained from the leaves of the coca plant. Aside from its stimulant effects, it acts as an appetite suppressant and local anesthetic. In fact, originally, it was used as an anesthetic for surgery. In its white powder form, it is snorted and in its crystallized form, commonly known as "crack," it is smoked. Cocaine blocks the reabsorption of the neurotransmitter dopamine. The increased availability of dopamine in the brain leads to pleasurable feelings, boundless energy, and it blocks the feedback mechanism that makes one feel satisfied, leading the user to crave more of the drug.

HALLUCINOGENS

Hallucinogens are a group of substances that cause changes in perception, thought, emotion, and consciousness. Potent hallucinogens cause people to experience perceptual hallucinations, leading them to feel, hear, and see things that are not really there. In other words, these drugs change how one perceives the world. One of the most well-known hallucinogens is *lysergic acid diethylamide (LSD)*, commonly referred to as acid. This drug causes a user to experience intense sensory experiences and loss of control over their thoughts and feelings. Many LSD users report experiencing "bad trips," which are disturbing, often terrifying experiences. Though the drug does not normally lead to addiction, due to its unpredictable effects, LSD use can be very dangerous.

Marijuana is also considered a mild hallucinogen and has a long history of illicit use as well as medicinal use. It is derived from a mixture of dried, shredded flowers and leaves of the *Cannabis sativa* plant. This is the most frequently used illegal drug in the United States. Marijuana users report feeling relaxed and having an increased enjoyment of everyday activities such as eating and sex. Marijuana can affect memory, coordination, reaction time, and has a host of other unpleasant side effects like "cotton mouth" and paranoia. Outside of recreational use, marijuana has been shown to have effective medicinal uses. For many cancer patients, marijuana can relieve the unpleasant side effects of chemotherapy, like nausea and vomiting, leading to its legalization for medicinal purposes in certain regions in the U.S. (Tramer et al., 2001).

In some jurisdictions, medical marijuana is legal for the alleviation of symptoms due to multiple sclerosis, nausea from cancer chemotherapy, seizure disorders, and Chrohn's disease.

SUBSTANCE USE DISORDER

Though many of these substances are harmful, many of them are used legally in the United States and throughout the world. Many people who use drugs like caffeine, for example, in moderation do not experience permanent damaging effects. However, for many, drugs can destroy lives. The *DSM-5*(2013) has updated the substance use disorder diagnosis to encompass what was previously a distinction between substance *abuse* and substance *dependence*. Many clinicians agree that the distinction is unnecessary as **substance dependence** – what we know as addiction – results from substance abuse, which is an irresponsible use of drugs or alcohol. Addiction is marked by tolerance to a substance and withdrawal symptoms when the use of the substance is discontinued. If you happen to be one of those people that gets headaches or is irritable when you go without your morning coffee, you are exhibiting withdrawal symptoms typical of addiction.

The severity of substance use disorder can vary depending on the number of criteria that apply to a specific case, from a mild to severe substance use classification. Typically, those who suffer from it see marked negative effects in their lives. They might stop performing their job duties or start neglecting their families as a result of their drug use. Some people go into massive financial debt in order to obtain the drug. In many cases, heavy drug and alcohol use can also lead to aggressive behavior including violence. Many users react defensively if confronted about their problem.

CAUSES FOR SUBSTANCE USE

Many drug and alcohol use problems begin in adolescence. Nationwide surveys show that 48.2% of high school seniors have reported using an illicit drug at some point in their lives (Johnston, O'Malley, Bachman, & Schulenberg, 2011). Though the large majority of adolescents phase out drug use, this is where problematic drug use begins for many people. For this reason, early use of drugs like tobacco, alcohol, and marijuana are seen by many as potential red flags for future substance use problems, an idea that is known as the *gateway hypothesis*. Despite this purported link, researchers have found that simply initiating drug use is not a statistically sufficient predictor for the development of an addiction (Vanyukov et al., 2012).

The exact causes of substance use are multi-faceted and

complex, usually involving multiple biological, psychological, and sociocultural factors. Addiction research has indicated that a family history of alcoholism or substance abuse can be triggered by stressful circumstances (Tsuang, Lyons, Meyer, & Doyle, 1998). As a result, many clinicians believe addiction is a medical problem that requires medical treatment. Environmental factors can also predict substance abuse. Children are more likely to abuse substances if their parents, and especially peers, partake in the same behavior (Walden, McGue, Iacono, Burt, & Elkins, 2004). In addition, personality factors such as impulsivity, novelty seeking, and environmental impoverishment play a role in the development of substance abuse problems (Carroll, Anker & Perry, 2009).

OTHER TYPES OF CONSCIOUSNESS

There are many different states of consciousness other than the ones already discussed, some of which will be discussed later in the text, as they are brought on by psychological disorders. This includes states like psychosis and mania.

Meditation is another altered state, in which people purposefully and with a lot of effort alter their own consciousness. Meditation techniques are designed to sustain concentration and direct one's energies toward a state of relaxation. Physiologically, meditation suppresses the activity of the sympathetic nervous system. It can be used in many ways to many ends, to simply clear the mind or to treat health issues like high blood pressure, depression, and anxiety. It is a technique that is commonly incorporated into spiritual rituals, like yoga, with the aim of creating positive, focused energy. People who master the art of meditation can actually come to achieve a certain amount of control over the typically involuntary activity of the sympathetic nervous system.

Another altered state of consciousness is **hypnosis**, a state in which a person is under a trance and is functioning at a level of awareness other than ordinary wakefulness. During this state, people are said to be more suggestible. This suggestibility varies from individual to individual. Some people are much more likely to be hypnotized than others, and once hypnotized, some people are much more suggestible than others. Like meditation, this is a state of consciousness that many people use to treat physical and psychological disorders. Some treatments for substance use disorder rely on hypnotic suggestions. For example, one might listen to audio aids, like CDs, while sleeping that hypnotize the listener into believing that that she does not need or crave cigarettes.

CHAPTER 4 REVIEW QUESTIONS

1. A state of consciousness during which a person is conscious, awake, and reasonably aware and coherent is called:

   ____

2. A circadian cycle spans:

   a. A year

   b. A day

   c. A month

   d. An hour

3. T/F. Most dreaming occurs during NREM Stage 3.

4. Narcolepsy is a sleep disorder in which:

   a. People fall asleep unintentionally.

   b. People wake up in a state of panic.

   c. People have trouble breathing during sleep.

   d. People are unable to fall asleep or stay asleep.

5. T/F. According to Freud, dreams are a reflection of our unconscious state.

6. Which are examples of depressant substances? ____________
____
____
____

7. ______________________ is a class of substances that is derived from poppy seeds.

8. Under which category of substances does marijuana fall?

    a. Stimulant

    b. Depressant

    c. Hallucinogen

    d. Barbiturates

9. T/F. Hypnosis and meditation can be used to treat health problems.

10. ______________________ lead(s) to a rush of euphoria and energy.

    a. Amphetamines

    b. LSD

    c. Alcohol

    d. Marijuana

CHAPTER 5

PSYCHOLOGY OF LEARNING

IF YOU STOP AND THINK about it, even outside formal education, you are constantly learning about the world around you. When you have a new job that involves using special equipment or software, when you attend a funeral for the first time in your life, when you read a book, or when you meet people from another culture, you are learning. The process of **learning** has been studied by many different psychologists from many different perspectives. This process, which involves acquiring new knowledge, skills, and synthesizing information is not a simple, straightforward one. It can be explained in many different ways, all of which represent a different dimension of learning. In some cases, these perspectives represent a completely different way in which we learn. Though psychologists might disagree about the mechanism by which we learn, one thing they can all agree on is that learning is essential for us to adapt and survive.

BEHAVIORAL PERSPECTIVE OF LEARNING

If you recall from Chapter 1, behavioral psychologists are concerned exclusively with observable behavior. True to this perspective, their theories of learning involve the types of learning one can actually see. Though some may argue that not all learning is observable (and in fact, cognitive psychologists do), a behaviorist would say, "What good is learning that cannot be demonstrated?" As such, the aim for many behavioral studies of learning is to do exactly that: demonstrate learning. In behaviorism, there are two main types of learning: classical conditioning and operant conditioning.

CLASSICAL CONDITIONING

Classical conditioning is a behavioral modification technique in which a subject learns to respond a certain way to a conditioned stimulus after that stimulus is paired repeatedly with an unconditioned stimulus that naturally elicits a certain reaction. Sound complicated? This is not a concept that is easy to sum up in one sentence, and the simplest way to understand it is to apply it.

Put yourself in the shoes of hypothetical high school sophomore, Jimmy. Jimmy is not very popular at school. He does not have many friends and, like many of his peers at that age, he looks awkward and lanky, he has acne, and he just got a new pair of glasses. He is bullied by the popular kids at school who often approach him in the halls calling out "Hey, Four Eyes!" right before they blow spitballs at him. Of course, Jimmy's natural response to getting hit by the spitballs is to flinch, as would anybody's. The curious thing is that after several days of the bullies calling out "Four Eyes!" in the hall, Jimmy begins to flinch, even when his assailants are not wielding spitballs. Unbeknownst to them, the bullies have classically conditioned poor Jimmy to react to the nickname "Four Eyes" in the same way he would naturally react to getting pelted by spitballs.

The elements of classical conditioning can also be explained using Pavlov's (1927) famous study with dogs in which he demonstrated that he could teach them basic associational learning. As a physiologist, Pavlov was interested in the dogs' digestion which involved collecting samples of their saliva while being fed. As his study progressed, he noticed that the dogs began salivating before the food was presented and he set out to explain why. What he found was that the animals had learned to expect the food simply by seeing him and the research assistants in the lab. He then set out to teach the dogs to salivate to the sound of a bell, by ringing the bell before the food was presented.

He was successful! Pavlov's dogs came to learn that food was about to arrive based on the sound of the bell. How he taught them this was by continuously pairing the sound of the bell with the presentation of food, in the same way the dogs had learned on their own to expect food when they saw the researchers in the lab. Pavlov knew they had learned to make this association based on the increased amount of salivation when simply hearing the bell. In other words, he could observe their learning.

Dogs do not normally salivate when hearing the sound of a bell, but Pavlov changed all that.

The food, in this experiment, is an example of an **unconditioned stimulus (US)**. This is a stimulus or event that automatically elicits a certain reflexive response, similar to how humans' mouths also water when presented with an appetizing plate of food. The salivation is considered the **unconditioned response (UR).** It is unconditioned because it is not taught nor learned; it is one's natural and automatic response to a certain stimulus.

During the conditioning process, Pavlov turned the sound of the bell into a **conditioned stimulus (CS)**. A conditioned stimulus is originally neutral, like a bell, that when paired enough times with the unconditioned stimulus, the food, it comes to be associated with it. This paired association leads to the development of a **conditioned response (CR).** Pavlov found that even when food was not present, the dogs would salivate simply because of the sound of the bell. This response is a conditioned response and it indicates that learning has taken place (See Figure 5.1).

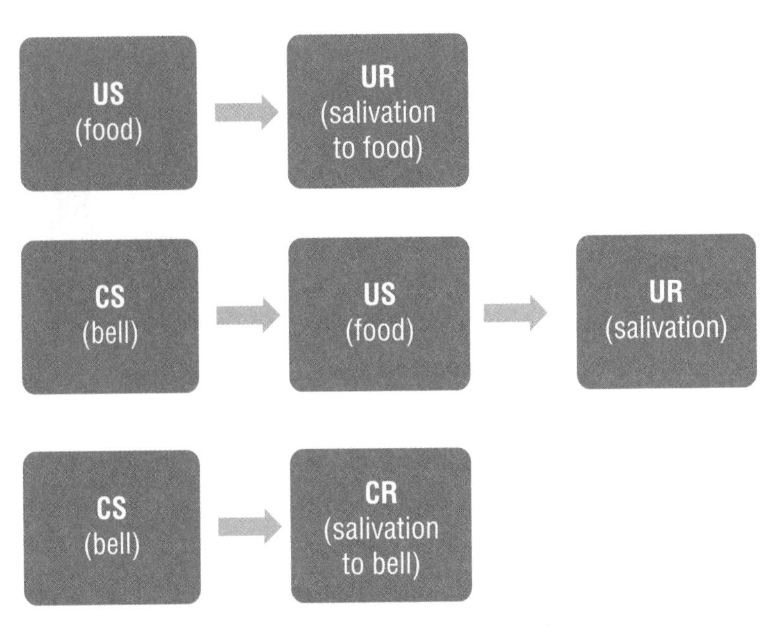

Figure 5.1: Classical conditioning in Pavlov's landmark study.

Using the example of Jimmy and his bullies, the elements of classical conditioning can also be easily identified. A normal reaction to getting hit by something is typically to flinch. The spitballs, in this case, would be the unconditioned stimulus (US), and the flinching reaction would be the unconditioned response (UR). The nickname "Four Eyes" is originally a neutral stimulus, one that, in and of itself, would not cause someone to flinch (maybe grimace or roll their eyes). When the bullies began yelling out "Four Eyes" prior to hitting him with spitballs, the nickname became a conditioned stimulus (CS) and it came to elicit the conditioned response (CR) from Jimmy – flinching even when the spitballs were not present.

Classical conditioning can take place with humans as well as animals, and it does not just occur with sounds. Smells, sights, or feelings can be used to elicit a conditioned response. You might come to associate the feeling of anger toward someone that once insulted you. This is a learned emotional response and perhaps even hearing the person's name or seeing a picture of them can elicit that response. Similarly, the smell of your spouse's cologne might remind you of them and make you feel loving, warm feelings. Like most perfumes, prior to meeting this person, it was probably just another pleasant smell that lingers in elevators or restaurants occasionally. It is after you come to associate that particular cologne with this person that your reaction to smelling it changes. Your response to it has been conditioned over time.

The strength of a classically conditioned response depends on the circumstances under which it was learned. Certain factors create stronger learned responses than others. One factor involves consistency. The likelihood of learning a conditioned response depends on how often the two stimuli are paired. If a dog only hears the sound of the bell once before being fed, and then not again for many weeks, it is probably not very likely to learn to associate that sound with food, at all. That would be like hearing the sound of a police siren outside your apartment one night while you eat dinner and associating the two occurrences. Unless this happened more frequently, that association would not be created. On the other hand if you live near a church that has a bell that rings every day at 6:00 pm, roughly around your dinnertime, you probably *would* come to associate the church bells with dinner. The more frequently it occurs, the more likely it is to be learned.

The timing between pairings is also significant in the rate of learning. Paired occurrences of the CS and US spaced too far apart or too close together in succession would probably have no effect on a subject. If too much time has passed, we are likely to forget the two events ever occurred together. Going back to the example above, if the church bells by your house only ring at 6:00 pm on Sundays, you probably would not learn to associate it with dinnertime because six out of seven nights a week, you have dinner without hearing the bells. The other extreme would also be ineffective. If your playful teenager sat at the breakfast table one morning and pointed a laser pen at your eyes every time you brought a spoonful of cereal to your mouth for about 10 minutes, you would probably find it annoying. But by the following morning, you would not be expecting the laser when you dig into your Cheerios. Learning takes place best when it occurs at a moderate pace.

Intermittent pairing also leads to less consistent learning. If the sound of the bell is played at random and only sometimes around feeding time, a dog is less likely to associate that sound with the food. That is because the bell sound largely remains neutral. It only sometimes alerts the dog that food is coming.

Despite the fact that most classically conditioned responses require repeated pairings, there is one example that you have probably experienced that does not. This is the *conditioned taste aversion*. Have you ever gone to a restaurant or had a certain dish that made you terribly ill? It probably didn't take more than that one incident of food poisoning for you to avoid that food or that particular restaurant for a very long time. This kind of learning comes down to the evolutionary perspective of psychology. We have a biological predisposition to avoid foods that make us sick. It is not something we have to learn twice.

OPERANT CONDITIONING

Operant conditioning is the second type of behavioral learning in which behavior is modified based on its resulting consequences. The basic principle of operant conditioning states that when behavior has positive consequences, we are more likely to repeat it and when it has negative consequences, we are less likely to repeat it. Psychologist Edward Lee Thorndike (1874-1959) referred to this as the **law of effect**. A consequence that makes it more likely that a behavior will be repeated is called a **reinforcement**, because it reinforces that behavior. For example, when you give a puppy a treat for following your command to sit, the treat acts as a reinforcement that makes it more likely that the puppy will oblige the next time he hears the word "sit." A **punishment**, on the other hand, is a consequence that leads to a decrease in behavior. If your child brings home a bad grade on his report card and, as a result, you forbid him from going out with his friends, the punishment makes it less likely that he will let his grades slip again in the future.

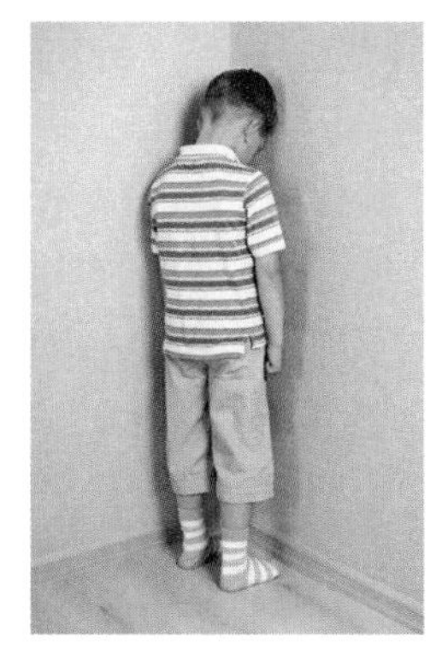

Many parents use punishment to curb their children's bad behavior.

The way in which an operant response is reinforced or punished can be either positive or negative (see Figure 5.2). In this case, positive and negative do not mean good and bad; instead, positive implies the addition of something and negative implies the subtraction of something. What is added or subtracted is either a desirable or undesirable stimulus. A treat for a puppy is a *positive reinforcement*, because the treat is an addition of something positive. A *negative reinforcement* is simply another way to reinforce a behavior only instead of adding a positive stimulus, it reinforces by removing an undesirable one. For example, if your child brings home a straight-A report card, you could reward her with a pizza party – a positive reinforcement.

This is a positive reinforcement because you are giving her something she enjoys: pizza and a party. Another option would be to remove something unpleasant or undesirable, like allowing her to go a week without doing her chores. This is still a reinforcement of the good grades, but it is a negative reinforcement, because of the fact that you are *removing* something unpleasant. Both of these function to the same end, to reinforce the child's efforts in school.

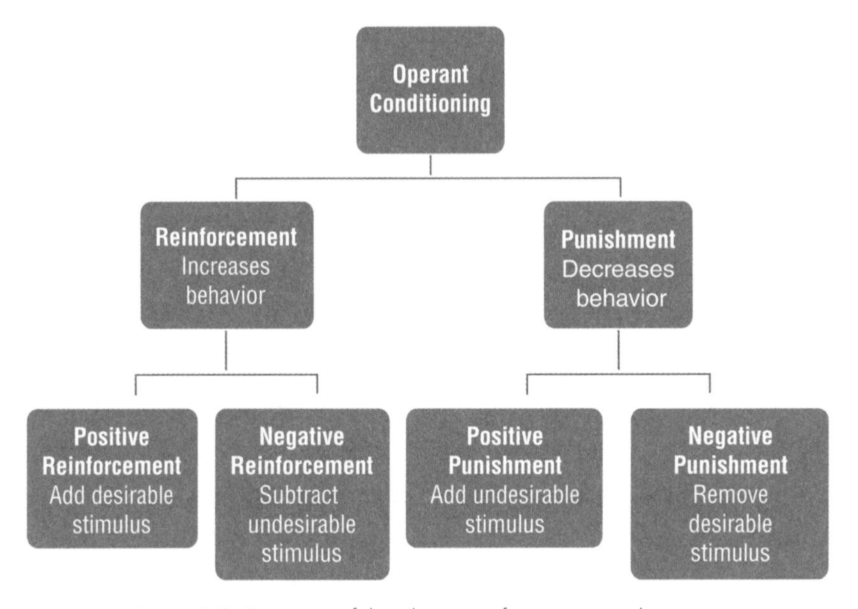

Figure 5.2: Diagram of the elements of operant conditioning.

In the same way, punishment can be positive or negative. *Positive punishment* decreases the probability that a behavior will be repeated by the addition of something undesirable. For example, when speeding to work results in a ticket, one is less likely to speed. In this example, the ticket is a positive punishment, not because it is good, but because you received something you do not want. *Negative punishment* occurs when behavior results in the removal of something desirable or attractive. Parents often punish children for misbehaving by taking away something they enjoy, like their cell phone or video games. The *removal* of something is what makes this *negative* punishment. Both of these would be equally punishing and would result in a decrease in the undesired behavior because the consequences of the behavior were unpleasant.

Operant conditioning has been well established with animals in research. Thorndike (1898) studied learning in cats and was able to demonstrate that they would learn over many trials to escape a box if food was placed visibly just outside. In this case, the animals had an incentive to leave the box – the food. This reward was enough for them to be able to learn to escape the box again and again. In similar studies, B. F. Skinner (1938) placed small animals such as rats and pigeons in what has become known as a *Skinner box.* The box is relatively empty and contains a food cup that gets filled with food when the animals activate a button or lever in the box. This reward reinforces the button-pushing or lever-pressing behavior in the animal, leading to more frequent button-pushing and lever-pressing.

A rat performing in an operant conditioning test in one version of the Skinner box. Typically, the animals learn to perform repetitive tasks, like pushing buttons or levers to get food.

Follow up studies with the Skinner box also demonstrated superstitious behavior in animals as a result of accidental learning (Skinner, 1948). When food was randomly given to pigeons, it would reinforce whatever behavior they had been doing prior to receiving the food – turning counter clockwise or thrusting their heads into the corner of the cage. This would lead animals to repeat such nonsensical behavior in the hopes of receiving more food.

This superstitious behavior is seen in humans, as well. Someone might believe that wearing a special hat had something to do with winning a lot of money gambling, and come to see it as a "lucky" hat and insist on wearing it every time he goes to the casino. Obviously, the hat has no influence on the player's skill or the cards dealt to him, but the association between the two has already been learned. Accidental learning can also inadvertently lead to a decrease in behavior that is erroneously perceived to result in punishment. Have you ever heard your grandparents tell you not to go outside after washing your hair? This and similar old wives' tales are a result of accidental learning. Viruses cause colds, not a chilly breeze over your wet hair. Though this may have happened at some point to countless people (hence the popularity of such a myth), the two are completely unrelated.

Similarly, intended behavior modification strategies can backfire by unintentionally reinforcing the wrong behavior. For instance, if you are trying to teach your teenage son to be more neat and organized, and you do so by giving him an extra $5 on his allowance for every day that he cleans up after himself, you may actually be reinforcing the wrong behavior. That is because the $5 is linked to cleaning up the mess, which requires a mess to begin with. This means that you are accidentally reinforcing your son's messiness, because without it, he has nothing to clean up, so he gets no reward. This is not teaching him to be more neat and organized, which would mean not making any messes to begin with, as intended.

This same mechanism explains why some kids prone to tantrums are not deterred by their parents' angry responses. When a child throws a tantrum, he is merely seeking his parents' attention, and by yelling at the child, the parents are giving it to him. As much as you think that yelling will prevent tantrums in the future, it is actually more likely that they will reoccur because the tantrums are being reinforced.

REINFORCEMENT VERSUS PUNISHMENT

Parents often use principles of operant conditioning to teach their children correct or desirable behaviors. If you are a parent yourself, you are probably wondering which of the two is more effective. Psychologists have put a lot of effort into answering this question. Punishment can have a very powerful effect on behavior. So why doesn't punishment always prevent children from continuing to misbehave?

Several factors come into play to make a punishment effective. For one, punishment should occur swiftly after a behavioral indiscretion. This immediate negative consequence will lead to greater learning. Pet owners are notoriously bad at delivering punishment swiftly. Say your dog, Spot, has been home alone for several hours and to your great ire, he relieved himself on your carpet. You might yell at your dog, pointing angrily at the mess he made, but chances are your dog has no idea why you are upset. On the other hand, if you catch Spot going to the bathroom right in front of you and you begin yelling at him, he will definitely know the behavior that caused you to get upset.

People who tend to be passive aggressive also deliver misguided punishment, because they delay in expressing their anger and often misrepresent the true reason for their irritation. For example, imagine you are out with your partner and you catch him suggestively eyeing an attractive person nearby. If you are someone who tends to be passive aggressive, you would probably suppress your anger in the moment, letting it seethe until later – maybe days later – when, after letting the anger grow for some time, you blow up. This would probably cause your partner, unaware that you were mad at all, a lot of confusion and would not be very effective in teaching him that you are not okay with his wandering eyes. Even worse, you might let your anger out at an inappropriate time in response to an unrelated incident. So if your anger bubbled over when days later your partner left dishes in the sink, he would definitely learn to clean up the dishes, and still have no clue about the reason you were *really* angry.

To be effective, punishment should also be sufficient and commensurate to the misbehavior. A simple scolding might not be enough of a punishment for a child that pushed his little sister. Similarly, taking away access to the television, when a child spends most of their time on the computer, is hardly going to have an effect on behavior. Though still a punishment, these examples are not punishment enough to actually deter future behavior.

Finally, punishment must be consistent; it must follow every instance of the behavior. Compare the following case of two children in middle school: Tommy and Michael. Tommy is always punished for any grade lower than a B on his report card. Michael is also punished for low grades, but depending on her mood, Tommy's mother sometimes accepts a C or two without penalty. What is Tommy learning and what is Michael learning? The lesson is clear for Tommy – a grade lower than a B always has a negative consequence. On the other hand, Michael is learning that sometimes he can get away with a lower grade with no consequence at all. More often than not, when a person knows he can sometimes get away with undesirable behavior, he will take the chance and repeat it. Since he is not always made to feel the consequences of the

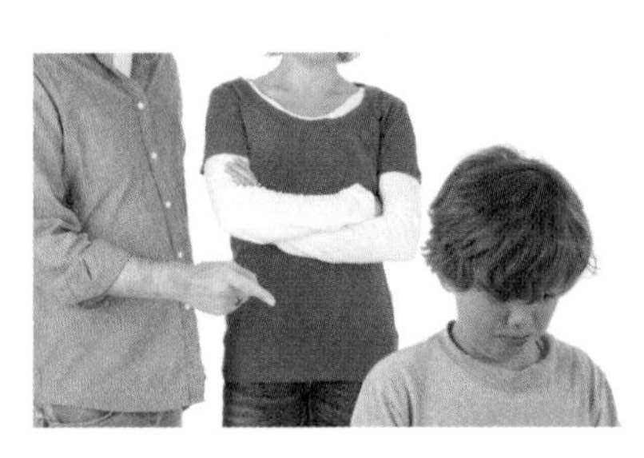

Consistent punishment leads to more effective behavior change.

behavior, the possibility of punishment is not enough to deter it.

Even though, under the right circumstances, punishment can be very effective, it has one very important drawback: alone, punishment only teaches you what not to do, but not what you should be doing instead. Punishment, thus, is most effective when paired with some reinforcement for the correct behavior. Studies have shown that a combination of reward and punishment can be much more effective and lead to faster learning than punishment alone (Brackbill & O'Hara, 1958). Additionally, punishment alone can lead to negative feelings and aggression, especially if there is no occasional praise or reward.

Let's look again at how this could be useful to house train your puppy, Spot. As we noted earlier, yelling at Spot when you catch him going to the bathroom in the house would be an effective punishment, but it does nothing to teach the dog how to correctly go to the bathroom. A smart owner using the principles of operant conditioning would immediately put newspaper down or open the door to the yard and reinforce the dog when he finishes relieving himself outside. This would demonstrate to Spot that urinating on the carpet is unacceptable and results in him getting yelled at, but going outside and doing it on the grass makes his owner happy and he gets a treat.

LEARNED HELPLESSNESS

One unintended result of excessive punishment is a learned response called **learned helplessness**. This is a behavioral response in which humans or animals learn that punishment is unavoidable so they give up, even when faced with opportunities to help themselves. A study by Seligman & Maier (1967) demonstrated the development of learned helplessness in dogs. The dogs were placed in electrified cages where they were shocked at random intervals. Dogs in one group were able to turn off the shock by pushing on a panel in the cage. The dogs in the other group had no control over the shock. When both groups were placed in a different cage where they could both avoid the shock, the dogs in the first group quickly learned to avoid it, as they had been doing in the original cage – pushing on a panel to stop the shock. However, the second group of dogs that previously had no control over the shock, did not attempt to avoid it in any way. Instead, they cowered in the cage and allowed themselves to be shocked.

The dogs in Seligman & Maier's study developed a learned helplessness response.

This passive response is something that occurs with depressed people, who believe that no matter what they do they will never be happy, so they stop trying altogether. Children that were abused also tend to develop learned helplessness, because punishment is unrelated to their behavior and often cannot be avoided. Sometimes ineffective managers who only discipline employees for things they do wrong, without ever providing positive feedback, create this kind of mentality in their employees. "I cannot do anything right so why do anything at all?" As mentioned above, constant punishment with no reinforcement is an ineffective way of obtaining desired behavior. Once developed, learned helplessness can be a very persistent pattern, even across a variety of different situations. Such an attitude learned at work may trickle into a person's home life and her interactions with friends and family.

EXTINCTION AND SPONTANEOUS RECOVERY

In both classical and operant conditioning, a learned response sometimes disappears. This is referred to as **extinction**. In classical conditioning, extinction occurs when the conditioned stimulus stops occurring along with the unconditioned stimulus. For example, if Pavlov continued ringing the bell, but stopped giving the dog food, the response to salivate at the sound of the bell would slowly disappear and the bell would revert back to being a neutral stimulus that elicits no response.

In operant conditioning, if the reward or punishment is discontinued, the behavior may also go extinct. Imagine, for instance, that your instructor provided extra credit every time you raised your hand and answered a question correctly in class. This would probably make you and your classmates more likely to participate in class, because you have been incentivized to do so. What would happen if the instructor suddenly stopped giving extra credit? If you are normally a shy, reserved student, after days of no longer receiving an extra reward for participation, you would probably stop raising your hand. Most people revert back to the responses that come naturally to them. The goal of behavioral conditioning is to make those learned responses natural so that they continue even after the incentives are removed.

Even when a response has become extinct, it does not mean it has been permanently unlearned. In fact, sometimes the previously extinct response re-emerges with no additional training. This is referred to as **spontaneous recovery**. For example, if you feed your pet canned food, they would probably quickly learn to associate the sound of the electric can opener with food. If you switched from cans to dry bagged food, your pet would continue responding to the can opener sound until they realized after enough times that the sound no longer indicated feeding time. This is simple extinction. After a few months of eating only dry food, your pet would not react to the can opener anymore. However, if you went back to the cans one day, the extinct response would re-appear immediately. It would not take as many trials to learn the same response a second time.

GENERALIZATION IN CONDITIONING

In both types of conditioning, one might learn **stimulus generalization** – that is, they might develop a tendency to respond to similar cues, even if they are not identical to the ones present during original learning.

Pavlov's study demonstrated some stimulus generalization. After the dogs had been conditioned to the sound of the bell, they began salivating to other sounds as well, such as the sound of a buzzer.

A study by Watson & Rayner (1920) demonstrated stimulus generalization in a baby boy named Little Albert. Watson wanted to show that using classical conditioning, he could teach the child to fear a neutral stimulus, in this case, a white rat. At the beginning of the study, the boy was allowed to play with the rat, demonstrating that he had no inherent fear of it. Then the researchers began making a loud noise behind Little Albert with a hammer and a steel bar every time the boy touched the rat. He became fearful and after several pairings of the rat and the loud noise, he began to avoid the rat. He would cry and turn away from it, proving that the fear had been successfully conditioned. Little Albert's fear generalized to other furry objects as well. When presented with a rabbit, a furry dog, and with Watson wearing a Santa Claus mask with a furry beard, the child exhibited distress and fearful symptoms. The other stimuli were similar enough to the original white rat to elicit such a response.

Little Albert learned to fear the white rat after repeated pairings of the rat and sudden, loud sounds. Wouldn't you have the same reaction?

Learners can be trained to avoid generalization through a procedure called **stimulus discrimination**. The process involves presenting the learner with similar stimuli, when only one of them is followed by the unconditioned stimulus. This could have worked with Little Albert if he had been allowed to play with the rabbit, the rat and the dog, and each time, the loud clanging sound only startled him while he played with the rat.

In addition to stimulus generalization, operant conditioning can lead to **response generalization**. In response generalization, the conditioned response may appear under conditions other than the one originally learned. For example, an instructor may reward students that come to class on time by giving them an extra credit point on their daily quiz. The response, coming to class on time, is only rewarded in the classroom by that particular instructor. However, it is possible that this response might generalize for a student to doctor's appointments and lunch dates with friends, even though in these other instances, the response is not being directly rewarded.

SIMILARITIES AND DIFFERENCES

Both classical and operant conditioning share many of the same characteristics. They both involve learning by associating different stimuli and responses until we come to know that one depends on another. In other words, we learn to perceive *contingencies,* and become aware that one event depends on another. In classical conditioning, the persistent sound of a dog bowl is a signal that a dog is about to be fed. In other words, eating is contingent upon hearing that sound. In operant conditioning, one comes to learn that a reward is contingent upon good behavior, so that behavior is repeated.

The main difference between the two is that the response learned through classical conditioning is usually involuntary. Once the conditioned response is learned, it is automatic and we are unable to voluntarily prevent it. Bullied Jimmy could not stop flinching at the sound of "Four Eyes" even if he wanted to. By contrast, behavior learned through operant conditioning is voluntary and done to avoid punishment or gain rewards. So even if you have been reprimanded by every professor you have ever had for playing with your phone in class, it would not necessarily stop you from continuing to perform that behavior. Ultimately, the choice to act or not to act is still yours.

COGNITIVE PERSPECTIVE ON LEARNING

Though behaviorists believe that only visible learning matters, cognitive psychologists hold that the unobservable mental processes that occur when we learn should not be overlooked. In other words, they study **cognitive learning**, the mechanism by which our brains actually process information, which they believe can contribute to our understanding of learning as a whole. Cognitive learning may not always be observable, but it can be inferred from observable behavior.

LATENT LEARNING

One example of cognitive learning is called **latent learning**, a term that was coined by Edward Chace Tolman (1886-1959) after studying the behavior of rats in a maze. According to Tolman, this type of learning is not immediately demonstrated. In the study, Tolman & Honzik (1930) placed two groups of rats in the same maze and had them find their way to the end of the maze. One group of rats had pellets of food waiting at the end of the maze as a reward. The other group did not. As you may have guessed, the group that had food at the end of the maze learned to get out faster than the other group, because they had an incentive to do so. This is precisely what one would expect based on principles of operant conditioning.

However, the researchers found that when the group of rats that had not previously been reinforced was placed in the same maze, this time with food at the exit, they ran through the maze just as

Rats tend to learn their spatial environment, allowing them to find the exit when placed in a maze.

well and almost as quickly as the ones that had originally been reinforced with food to exit the maze. Thus, latent learning was demonstrated. Clearly, the rats were learning about the maze while they were in it, even if they weren't demonstrating their knowledge. It was only when they had an incentive to do so, that their performance demonstrated learning.

This kind of learning is known as a **cognitive map**, a type of mental representation of an environment that we use to navigate it. The rats, while unrewarded for exiting the maze, were wandering around creating a cognitive map of the maze. When they needed to use it, they could access the right path to the exit. The same effect happens in human beings. We develop cognitive maps of the environments we frequent – workplaces, neighborhoods, even whole cities. So if your usual route to work is blocked off for construction, you can easily find another route. This illustrates why sleepwalkers can navigate through the rooms of their home while asleep. It is worth noting that technological advancements, like GPS navigation systems, can erode our ability to do this on our own. Research has demonstrated that when we rely on navigation systems, hippocampus functioning is reduced over time (Robbins, 2013). If you recall, the hippocampus is the part of our brain responsible for memory. It is also involved in spatial navigation that we use when looking for and using alternative routes. When we can rely on a machine to give us turn-by-turn directions, we do not put much effort into learning routes on our own, leading to degradation of the hippocampus. Our brains can be just as powerful as a GPS system but we have to develop those skills.

INSIGHT LEARNING

Insight learning was identified by psychologist Wolfgang Kohler (1887-1967) as the kind of learning that takes place all of a sudden by understanding different aspects of a problem to get a solution. In his research with chimpanzees, he found that if a banana was placed outside the animal's cage, the animal figured out a way to reach it by using a long stick (Kohler, 1924). Kohler argued that this behavior reflected sudden insight of the solution.

This type of problem solving sometimes occurs to us, as well. You may be taking a test when you come across a problem that you cannot solve. Perhaps hours later, when you are no longer actively working on solving the problem, the solution will pop into your head. This "a-ha!" moment, one would argue, is one of the ways in which we learn cognitively.

LEARNING SETS

Sometimes when we do not have unexpected insights into the solution of a problem, we develop a **learning set** based on previous learning experiences. This predisposition to acquire new knowledge is founded on the way we have solved problems and learned in the past. This is what occurs when a child sits in a math class. The first time she is given a formula and asked to solve for variable x, it will probably take her a long time to get accustomed to the procedure. However, after solving the same kinds of problems many times, she becomes much faster and more efficient at finding the value of x. This is because she has developed a learning set for that type of problem.

A study involving monkeys demonstrated that learning sets occur in animals, as well. The researcher presented the monkeys with two boxes of different shapes and sizes, and the monkeys were allowed to lift one at a time to find food placed under it (Harlow, 1949). The food was always placed in the same box, even if the location of the box had changed. Pretty soon, the monkeys would learn that the same box was hiding the food, and that is the one they would choose first. The monkeys were behaving the way any of us would. When a solution works, we keep using it.

SOCIAL LEARNING

One method of learning that cannot be understated is the way in which we learn the majority of our behavior. How do we know how to behave at a religious church service for the first time? Or how do we acquire skills at a new job? Simple: we observe others. **Observational learning** is a powerful type of learning that is constantly affecting our behavior. Children, especially, are shaped by what they see. They model the behavior that they observe in others, good or bad. This partially explains why children with siblings and family members who smoke, are more likely to smoke themselves. It is why young children can apply make up to themselves if they get their hands on blush and lipstick without ever being taught, and why teenagers know how to start a car and put it in gear after getting behind the wheel for the first time. Learning has occurred vicariously.

Kids tend to imitate the behavior of adults around them.

This type of learning has been referred to as **social learning**, by psychologists like Albert Bandura (1925-), who strongly believe that people can learn behavior without it ever being reinforced, as long as there is a model displaying that behavior. In one of his greatest contributions to the field, he demonstrated this theory in the classic Bobo doll study (Bandura, Ross, & Ross, 1961). In the study, children were individually placed in a playroom with an adult who acted as a model. The adult was seated in front of an inflatable clown-faced Bobo doll. In one condition, the adult model aggressed toward the Bobo doll – punching it, kicking it, and hitting it with a mallet. When the adult was dismissed and the child was given the opportunity to play with the toys, the researchers observed their behavior. They found that children exposed to the aggressive adult were much more likely to display aggressive behavior toward the Bobo doll, demonstrating that they had learned the behavior simply by watching it.

The children in Bandura's study quickly learned to imitate aggressive behavior.

However, we do not imitate everything that we see others do. We are much more likely to imitate certain behaviors and not others. One reason for this is the different consequences associated with different behaviors. In a follow up study, Bandura (1965) demonstrated the effects of observed consequences on modeled behavior. Children watched a video of a model aggressing toward the inflatable Bobo doll. However, the end of the video was different for each group of children. In one condition, children saw the model rewarded with candies and praise. In another condition, the model was scolded and spanked for the behavior. In a third condition, there were no consequences following the behavior. The findings showed that though all the children learned aggressive actions from the video, the ones who watched the adult get rewarded after the behavior were much more likely to copy it. The ones who watched the adult get punished showed more restraint in their behavior toward the Bobo doll.

This study illustrates *vicarious reinforcement* as well as *vicarious punishment*. Despite the fact that the children were not themselves punished or rewarded for the behavior, observing the consequences that came about for someone else for the same behavior taught them something about it. They learned that they wanted to either copy the behavior or avoid it. Similarly, if you were sitting in class and a classmate's phone went off to the great ire of the professor who proceeded to yell at them, you would probably quickly silence your phone to make sure it does not happen to you. This is an example of vicarious punishment, which would shape your behavior in an effort to avoid punishment. On the other hand, if you find that one of your coworkers got a raise and you did not, you would probably make more of an effort to improve your performance. This raise would have vicariously reinforced good work.

As you can see, this type of learning is pervasive in our daily life and can be applied many different ways. Either intentionally or unintentionally, we are constantly shaped by what we are exposed to. Though this exposure is moderated by our own performance standards and values, many skills are acquired simply by watching.

CHAPTER 5 REVIEW QUESTIONS

1. Every time a toilet flushes in an apartment building, the shower becomes really hot, making the person in it jump back to avoid getting burned. Over time, one tenant begins jumping back automatically when he hears the flush, before the water gets hot. Identify the elements of classical conditioning:

a.	Unconditioned Stimulus	______ Toilet flushing
b.	Unconditioned Response	______ Jumping back at the change in temperature
c.	Conditioned Stimulus	______ Hot water temperature
d.	Conditioned Response	______ Jumping back at the sound of the flush

2. Normally, a classically conditioned response requires repeated pairings, with the exception of:

   a. Auditory conditioning

   b. Conditioned taste aversions

   c. Emotional conditioning

   d. Operant conditioning

3. In operant conditioning, ______________________________ increase(s) the likelihood that a behavior will be repeated, while ______________________________ decrease(s) the likelihood that a behavior will be repeated.

4. The students in Dr. Haaga's class do not have to take the final exam if they have a grade average above 95% by the time of

the final. This is an example of:

a. Positive reinforcement

b. Negative reinforcement

c. Positive punishment

d. Negative punishment

5. Learned helplessness was demonstrated in a study involving:

a. Pigeons pecking at buttons

b. Dogs being shocked

c. Monkeys guessing which container held food

d. Monkeys reaching for bananas

6. ______________________________ is when a learned classical or operant response disappears.

7. In one study, Tolman & Honzik demonstrated rats' abilities to form ______________________________ of a spatial environment.

8. T/F. Children do not learn behavior by observing it.

9. Your coworker was reprimanded for leaving work early. Since

then, you make more of an effort to leave work when you are supposed to. This is an example of ______________________

____

10. Which social learning theorist studied learned aggression in children?

    a. John B. Watson

    b. Albert Bandura

    c. B. F. Skinner

    d. Ivan Pavlov

CHAPTER 6

MEMORY

WHAT DID YOU HAVE for breakfast this morning? Where were you when the 9/11 terrorist attacks occurred? How do you play the guitar? What is the capital of Italy? How do you feel about communism?

Most people have a vivid memory of where they were on 9/11. Later in the chapter, we will find out why.

The answers to all these questions, different as they may sound, lie in memory. **Memory** is a process in which information is encoded when learned, stored, and retrieved when needed. It is widely accepted that memory has multiple stores, a concept that was first recognized by Atkinson and Shiffrin (1968), who divided up memory stores into three parts: a sensory register, a short-term store, and a long-term store. Though the theory has evolved over time, the fundamental concepts make up the **information processing theory**; it outlines the same three major components (Figure 6.1).

The multi-store model of memory
(Atkinson & Shiffrin, 1968)

Rehearsal
Sensory Store
Attention
Short Term Store (STM)
Transfer
Retrieval
Long Term Store (LTM)
Information lost (forgetting)

Figure 6.1: The information processing model of memory theorizes that memory passes through sensory registers and short-term memory before it is conserved in long-term memory.

SENSORY MEMORY

At any given moment, your senses are being bombarded with information from your external environment. You might be taking a drive and seeing the cityscape pass you by – buildings, trees, and people. You see other cars moving about you. You feel the temperature inside the car and the texture of the steering wheel, while the sounds of your radio and the engines around you greet your ears. Each sense has its own **sensory register**, as we know from Chapter 3, which receives and holds incoming stimuli from the environment, but only for a very short time. These registers have an almost unlimited capacity, but information is stored just long enough to be attended to and transferred to short-term memory, or to disappear from memory, altogether.

Think about it: of all the things you drive by, what kind of detail do you remember? Do you remember all the bumper stickers and car models driving around you? Do you remember what the person crossing the intersection is wearing? Probably not. The reason for that is that even though this information was registered by your senses, you were probably not paying attention to every detail of your surroundings. **Attention** determines what you pass from your sensory inputs into your short-term memory. It involves selectively concentrating on one aspect of your surroundings, while other aspects fade into the background. If you are sitting in lecture, you are likely paying attention to the speaker's words, since that is what you probably deem most important (one would hope). If someone is having an audible conversation in the hall just outside your classroom, but you are intently paying attention to the lecture, you probably would not be able to remember the details of the conversation outside. That is, unless you shifted your attention to it.

Our attention can shift very quickly, depending on our interest and the strength of the stimulus. Bright lights or loud sounds would probably immediately take your attention. On the other hand, subtle movement like someone taking notes in class in your peripheral vision probably would not make you take notice. Meaningful information, such as your name, would also grab your attention. This accounts for the *cocktail party phenomenon* (Treisman, 1960), which is our ability to focus our attention on a particular stimuli while filtering out all other stimuli, the way one would at a party. So if you are

Even in a loud environment, hearing your name will usually call your attention easily.

having drinks and chatting with your coworkers at Happy Hour and you overhear your name, your attention would probably shift to that other conversation.

SHORT-TERM MEMORY

All the information you are currently attending to is held in **short-term memory (STM),** or working memory. Short-term memory serves to hold information briefly and allow you to work on it – that is, to think about it. The capacity of this memory store is very limited. According to one psychologist, human short-term memory has a span of approximately seven items plus or minus two (Miller, 1956). He called it the "magical number seven." According to this theory, it would be simple for you to work with a series of seven numbers but if you had to repeat back a list of ten numbers, you would probably do so with some error. This is why it was easier to remember phone numbers before it became necessary to use the area code. While this theory holds true for series of digits, the capacity of short-term memory varies depending on the material to be recalled. Some psychologists believe that spontaneous decay is responsible for the capacity of short-term memory – that is, that information in STM quickly disappears unless it is rehearsed. However, others believe it is due to interference, as new content gradually replaces old content.

One widely accepted model of short-term memory was later proposed by psychologists Baddeley & Hitch (1974). According to this model, the short-term memory store is itself divided into three components: the phonological loop, the central executive, and the visuo-spatial sketchpad, each having its own important role in STM. The **central executive** acts as a supervisory body, coordinating the other two parts of the system and deciding what to attend to. Using the cocktail party phenomenon as an example, the central executive would be the part of short-term memory that directs your phonological loop to listen to the conversation when your name is said. The **phonological loop** would be responsible for temporarily storing auditory information. It has dual functions: to store verbal information and to rehearse it so it does not decay.

This rehearsal, called rote rehearsal, is one way to prevent loss of information from short-term memory. **Rote rehearsal** is the process of keeping information in short-term memory by simply repeating it, out loud or in your head. For instance, if someone shouted a phone number at you and told you to dial it, you might employ this method to keep the number in mind until you are able to find your phone in your purse or take it out of your pocket and begin to dial. If something prevented you from rehearsing the number in your head, like having to carry a conversation with someone, you would be unable to remember the number.

The third component of Baddeley and Hitch's model of memory is the **visuospatial sketchpad**, which temporarily holds visual information, such as the shape or color of a chair. This part would also be involved in tasks pertaining to spatial movement, which is useful when you are, say, walking through a large museum.

Many years after the original model was proposed, Baddeley added a fourth component to the original three, called the *episodic buffer*. This component links information from the different parts of short-term memory, incorporating visual and auditory information to create a complete unit (Baddeley, 2000). This component of the theory accounts for the fact that we are able to process and recall complete, complex scenes.

Research such as this has led to a greater understanding of how short-term memory works and how to best maintain information in it. Aside from rote rehearsal, a technique called chunking can help accomplish this task. **Chunking** helps reduce the pieces of information one has to remember by grouping them. For instance, it might be difficult for you to remember the following string of letters:

YFACOIBNMCLD

This is probably challenging, in part, because the amount of letters is slightly larger than your STM capacity. In addition, none of these letters have any meaning; it is a string of meaningless information. However, if you group the letters into more meaningful chunks, they are much easier to recall:

NYC FBI DC LMAO

Not only do these acronyms shorten the pieces of information you have to remember to four instead of twelve, it also makes them meaningful to you. Otherwise, verbal information tends to have little meaning in short-term memory because it is encoded phonologically, or by how it sounds. Even when information is read rather than heard, it is encoded by sound. Evidence of this comes from the errors people make in short-term memory recall. When presented with five-word sequences, words that sounded similar – such as *mad*, *mat*, *map*, *tap*, and *cap* – had a large adverse effect on short-term memory (Baddeley, 1966). This supports the existence of the phonological loop, as described above. If information was not encoded phonologically, these words would not be so easily confused given the fact that they all have very different meanings.

LONG-TERM MEMORY

When information from one's short-term memory has been attended to and rehearsed sufficiently, it moves into **long-term memory (LTM)**. This is where information becomes relatively permanent in our memory, allowing us to retrieve it to work with it in STM when we need to. Anything you've ever learned – whether it is a skill like riding a bike, the meaning of words, the details of news events, or principles of psychology – is stored in your long-term memory. The capacity of

LTM is much greater than STM. We are able to remember a massive amount of learned information, including the lyrics to songs we have not heard in decades.

Most information in LTM is encoded in terms of meaning. Generally, we do not store information word for word; we remember the general meaning, like one might remember the general plot of a movie without necessarily being able to provide specific dialogue from the movie.

There are two methods of processing that can help us maintain information in long-term memory: rote rehearsal and elaborative rehearsal.

Rote rehearsal is how actors learn their lines.

Rote rehearsal, as discussed in the previous section on STM, is a way of holding information in memory by repeating it. This is the way that actors learn lines and the way we learn the alphabet. This tool, while useful, is not nearly as effective as the second method, which helps you learn the meaning of new content. **Elaborative rehearsal** is a way to commit information into long-term memory by relating new material to information already stored there. It is a deeper form of processing because it focuses on the meaning of new information and on creating associations in the brain with already-known information. For example, if you are a teacher or a parent and you can relate the concepts of behavioral conditioning we learned about in Chapter 5 to activities you already do with your children or students, you probably had an easier time remembering those new concepts than someone who did not make this association.

Elaborative rehearsal works, in part, because of the way our nervous system transmits information. As you know, our neurons are organized in an immense network in our brain and the rest of our nervous system. When you think about a particular topic, you set off a chain of neural activity in the brain, surrounding not only that topic, but also related concepts. To demonstrate, stop reading for a second and think about French fries.

Did any other thoughts or images occur to you while you thinking about French fries aside from how they look and taste? Did you perhaps think about ketchup? Or about your favorite French fries from McDonald's? Or maybe you thought about your high cholesterol. Or perhaps the thought triggered a memory of when you last had French fries. All of these separate, but related, concepts easily come to mind when you think about any topic. Cognitive psychologists refer to this as the *spreading activation theory* of memory (Anderson, 1983). This activation occurs because these particular concepts, ideas, or experiences are often associated in your mind with French fries. In the same way, elaborative rehearsal takes advantage of that existing network to create associations between new information and existing knowledge. Think about it, if you were going to build a house, wouldn't it be easier to put up the walls when the foundation has already been laid rather than start from scratch? Your mind already contains a lot of valuable information and just about anything new you can possibly learn is probably already linked to something you already know. If you let that existing knowledge serve as a foundation, you will have an easier time understanding the new information.

Mnemonics are another technique that we can, and often, employ to remember new information. These can be jingles or acronyms that transform to-be-remembered information into something that is easier to remember. For instance, you may have learned PEMDAS as a quick way to remember the order of operations in mathematics (parenthesis, exponents, multiplication, etc.) or ROY G. BIV as a way to remember the colors of the spectrum (red, orange, yellow, etc.). These techniques have been shown to work compared to the application of other learning styles to remember novel vocabulary (Levin & Nordwall, 1992).

Despite all of these useful techniques, information stored in LTM is not impervious from being forgotten. Either because of failure to recall, or interference – similar to that which affects maintenance in STM – information can be forgotten, even if it was once learned. One failure to retrieve a word from LTM is called the **tip-of-the-tongue (TOT) phenomenon**. This has probably happened to you at some point when you were trying to remember the name of the actor in "Die Hard" or the name of that medical condition that an old friend had. TOTs can be frustrating because you know that you know the information, you just cannot access it. "It is on the tip of my tongue!"

Sometimes even if we cannot remember that the actor's name is Bruce Willis, we are able to picture his face.

SERIAL POSITION EFFECT

Hermann Ebbinghaus (1913) found in an early study of memory that recall of an item varies depending on the position of the item in a list. He called this effect the **serial position effect**. More specifically, we are more likely to remember the items that come first on a list, which is known as the *primacy effect*, and the items that come at the end of a list, known as the *recency effect*. One proposed explanation of the primacy effect suggests that items that come first on a list have been more effectively stored in long-term memory because greater processing has been devoted to them. The recency effect has been suggested to occur because items most recently heard are still present in working memory when recall is solicited. The items in the middle of a list suffer due to their position, presented too long ago to still be in short-term memory and with less time than the first items to be adequately rehearsed.

The role of the serial position effect is not limited to items on a list. In fact, as we will discuss later in the text, first impressions with people tend to be more memorable, as well. A recent study also identified the primacy effect in operant conditioning (Shteingart, Neiman, & Loewenstein, 2013). In the study, participants were given repeated-choice tasks, which earned them large or small amounts of money depending on whether they pressed a high-risk button or a low-risk button. Researchers found that the outcome of the first choice had a disproportionately large effect on participants' subsequent choices. So, for example, if a participant earned a large amount of money by pressing the high-risk button on the first trial, he would be more likely to continue pressing the high-risk button even if many subsequent trials were unsuccessful.

What can this add to our existing knowledge of operant learning? For one, if you are punished harshly the first time you do something bad or inappropriate, you will probably be more likely to remember that punishment in the long run, even if there are subsequent instances of the behavior that were not punished. Our memory tends to anchor to the first experience.

TYPES OF LONG-TERM MEMORY

Long-term memory is not simply a large empty storage; it is divided into two categories of memory, based on their characteristics. Each of these is stored in a uniquely different way in memory. **Explicit memories** make up one of these categories; they are memories that are consciously available to us. These are events or information that we are aware of and that we are able to describe, which is why they are also known as *declarative memories*.

Do you remember your first kiss? That is an explicit memory. Do you know who the Prime Minister of the United Kingdom is? That is an explicit memory – a memory that you have and can consciously access.

These two examples illustrate two different types of explicit memories: episodic memories and semantic memories.

Episodic memories are memories for events in time. These can be as meaningful as your first kiss or as ordinary as the last time you went grocery shopping. These are the specific events that we have experienced and can place in a specific location at a specific time. **Semantic memories**, on the other hand, represent our knowledge of factual information. These do not have any link to a specific event; they are merely general knowledge. The distinction can be tricky. For instance, your brother's birth date is a simple fact. It is something you learned and you know, which makes it a semantic memory. However, your memory of what you did last year with your family on your brother's birthday is an episodic memory. The difference is that the latter is a memory that represents a specific event in a specific time and place, while the former is just a fact. Other examples of semantic memories include the meaning of words, capital cities around the world, and facts about dolphins. Research has shown that young adults tend to have better episodic memories compared to older adults, because of episodic memory's reliance on the context in which it was encoded. Older adults may have more trouble placing an event that happened many years ago. However, episodic memory, which does not depend on context, does not vary much by age (Spaniol, Madden, & Voss, 2006).

Memories of when you or your child graduated from college would be considered episodic memories. These are linked to a specific time and place.

The other major category of long-term memories is **implicit memories**. These are non-declarative memories that we may not be aware that we have and that are more difficult to put into words than explicit memories. One example of such a memory is what is referred

Skills like playing an instrument or riding a bike are examples of procedural memories.

to as a **procedural memory**, or a learned skill. These are memories that you must develop by doing. If someone asked you, "How do you play the piano?" it would be difficult to put into words without physically teaching them how to play. That is because this is a learned skill, one that often improves with practice and that can be remembered after many years out of practice, hence the saying "You never forget how to ride a bicycle." Another type of implicit memory is called an **emotional memory**, which is a specific, learned emotion. The feeling of disgust when you see a cockroach, or love when you think about your spouse would be examples of emotional memories.

DIFFERENCES BETWEEN EXPLICIT AND IMPLICIT MEMORIES

Evidence for the separation of explicit and implicit memory has been found in the study of amnesic patients. Researchers found that amnesic patients that had impaired abilities in long-term verbal memory showed no impairment in the ability to solve a motor task, showing improvement each time they performed the task even though they could not remember being exposed to it previously (Brooks & Baddeley, 1976). These findings indicate separate mechanisms for declarative memories and implicit memories – in this case, procedural memories.

The effect of **priming** has also demonstrated the difference between explicit and implicit memories. Priming is a process in which prior exposure to a stimulus affects one's response to a later stimulus. For example, the experience of sitting in a dark theater watching a scary movie would probably make you more jumpy and susceptible to fearful responses when you walk to the parking garage after the movie. While this is an obvious connection, the effect of priming, though influential, often goes undetected. For example, one study showed that exposure to hot temperatures increased aggressive thoughts (DeWall & Bushman, 2009). Participants exposed to words related to hot temperatures were more likely to have more aggressive responses to an ambiguous word-completion task. So if a participant had to complete the word: K I _ _, they would be more likely to do so as KILL or KICK, rather than non-aggressive words like KISS or KIND. If asked, the participants would probably not be able to cite the priming effect of hot temperature as a reason why they completed the words the way they did.

Research on the biology of memory has also provided support for the separation of these two types of memory. As discussed in chapter 2, the hippocampus plays an important role in the development of long-term memories. More specifically, the structure is crucial for semantic and episodic memories (Eichenbaum & Fortin, 2003; Manns, Hopkins & Squire, 2003). Implicit memories, on the other hand, do not rely heavily on the function of the hippocampus. Instead, some implicit memories, such as procedural memories appear to require the use of the cerebellum and motor cortex (Gabrieli, 1998; Hermann et al., 2004). Emotional memories are associated with the function of the amygdala, which if you recall, is involved in processing emotional reactions (Cahill & McGaugh, 1998). These findings are supported by the extraordinary case of Clive Wearing, a British musician whose hippocampus was badly damaged as a result of illness (Wilson & Wearing, 1995). Since then, Wearing has been unable to form long-lasting memories and his consciousness appears to reset every 20 or 30 seconds, the

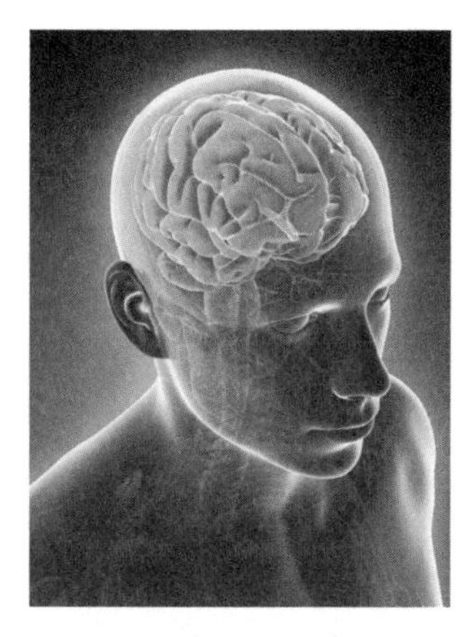

The hippocampus, highlighted here, is involved in the development and maintenance of long-term memories, particularly explicit memories.

span of his short-term memory. However, extraordinarily enough, his ability to play the piano – a procedural memory – has not been affected. Neither has his love for his wife – a strong emotional memory.

FORGETTING

One of the most pervasive theories of forgetting is called **decay theory**, which explains that memories deteriorate because of time passed (Thorndike, 1914). As time goes by without rehearsing information, the memory for that information slowly fades. You have probably noticed examples of decay theory in your own life. If you just returned from a trip to California two days ago, the memories of the vacation are probably still fresh and detailed in your mind. After a few months, the unimportant details – such as the name of your waiter or the location of your hotel – will probably begin to fade unless you spend time regularly going over the details of the trip. After many years, the vacation might not be distinguishable from other visits to the state and you may not even remember with whom you went. This is because that information has decayed over time.

Preventing decay requires rehearsal. Information learned in school will be largely forgotten unless it is periodically rehearsed. The plot of a movie you only saw once will likely be forgotten on a long enough timeline unless you occasionally discuss the plot or watch it again. When you think about information again and again, you signal to your brain that this information is important and your neurons go to work to help you maintain that information in LTM. The memory traces created by a specific concept are strengthened every time you access that memory, and they are weakened over time if you do not.

In addition to simple decay, many biological factors play a role in forgetting, as well. Accidents, surgeries, disease, or head injury can all impact parts of the brain associated with memory and can cause memory loss. Alzheimer's disease is commonly cited as a factor in memory loss in people over 65 years old. Head injuries and disease can also lead to **retrograde amnesia**, a condition in which patients are unable to remember information learned before an accident or disease. Inversely, they can lead to **anterograde amnesia**, which is the inability to create new memories. With certain cases of anterograde amnesia, long-term memories from before the onset of amnesia remain intact. In the case of Clive Wearing, he suffers from both retrograde amnesia – unable to remember his previous long-term memories – and anterograde amnesia – unable to create new memories.

INTERFERENCE AND ERRORS OF RECONSTRUCTION

The examples of forgetting described above are all related to failure in recalling long-term memories, but that is just one of the explanations of forgetting. Problems in encoding during learning also underlie forgotten information. Inadequate learning, like not enough rehearsal, will result in forgetting. Interference of learning can also lead to forgetting. There are two kinds of interference: **retroactive interference**, in which new material to be learned interferes with material already stored in long-term memory, and **proactive interference**, in which old material interferes with new material you are trying to learn.

Retroactive interference would occur when new material – for example, material learned in the psychology class you are currently taking – affects your ability to recall previously learned information, such as what you learned in last term's English class. Proactive interference might take place if you try to learn a new language. Your knowledge of your first language might interfere with your ability to learn the grammar rules of the new language.

Errors in reconstruction can also lead to forgetting. Frederic C. Bartlett (1932) studied memory by asking people to reproduce a story they had read. He found that people tended to change details of the story they read over time, changing unfamiliar elements to match their own experiences and their cultural expectations. According to Bartlett, different parts of the story were changed upon retelling because of the reconstruction process taking place. So instead of thinking of memory as an object that you can put in your attic and retrieve exactly as you left it whenever you want, think of it as a piece of furniture you have to take apart and reassemble each time you want to use it. You may lose or replace some pieces of it over time, so in the end it will not be exactly the same as when you first got it.

- Eyewitness Memory

Eyewitnesses may be asked to identify the perpetrator of a crime out of a line up. The accuracy of this judgment is crucial in our legal system.

Errors such as interference and errors in reconstruction are extremely important in eyewitness memory, where the testimony of a witness can have life or death implications for the person on trial. Research on eyewitness memory has demonstrated time and time again that it can be very flawed. In one study, Loftus and Palmer (1974) had participants watch a video of a car accident. The participants were then asked various questions about the video. In one condition, the participants were asked questions such as, "About how fast were the cars going when they hit each other?" In another condition, participants were asked the same question worded slightly differently. Instead of "hit" or "bumped," they were asked how fast the cars were going when they "smashed into" each other. They found that with this wording – which brings to mind a more serious accident – participants tended to overestimate the speed of the car, compared to the wording that implied a less severe accident. Despite having seen the same video, their memory of the events was changed.

Hearing details or being asked misleading questions about an event, like a robbery, can actually change your memory of what you saw.

Another study of eyewitness memory studied the suggestibility of eyewitnesses. Researchers Zaragoza & Mitchell (1996) had participants watch a video of a burglary. Then they asked the participants misleading questions about the video which provided details, action, and dialogue that supplemented the scene, but that were ultimately not part of the original video. They found that repeated exposure to the misleading information increased the likelihood of source attribution error. In other words, people became unable to discern between the facts presented in the video they watched (the original source) and the false facts in the questions they were asked. These findings illustrate how easily a memory can be altered. Considering the stressful circumstances under which eyewitnesses are in a crime scene, it might be prudent to take more solid evidence into consideration.

Errors in source attribution have probably happened to you at some point, as well. For instance, you may have read a fake statistic from a parody news source like *The Onion*, and later recalled that information as a real fact that you saw on CNN. In most cases, unless you verify, there is no way to know for sure that what you recall is accurate.

SPECIAL TYPES OF MEMORY

FLASHBULB MEMORIES

Where were you when terrorists attacked the World Trade Center on 9/11? Or when Kennedy was shot? Or when Michael Jackson died? If you lived through any of these events, it is likely that you have a *flashbulb memory* of the experience. A **flashbulb memory** is a very clear and detailed memory of an event that is often surprising and emotionally impactful. Normally, the events surrounding a flashbulb memory are maintained for many years to come, unlike regular memories that decay over time.

Shocking and emotional events like a presidential assassination tend to create long-lasting, clear memories.

For instance, you probably remember not only where you were when you heard about the 9/11 attacks, but who you were with and what happened in the days that ensued. However, detailed as they may be, studies have found that these memories are not as accurate as people believe them to be. In one such study, students recorded their memories of 9/11 on September 12, 2001. They were tested again one, six, and 32 weeks later, and though they remained confident in the accuracy of their memories, the actual accuracy compared to the initial recording had declined, similar to the decay one would expect from the memory of an everyday event (Talarico & Rubin, 2003). Many factors affect the accuracy of flashbulb memories, including the importance of the event, the consequences of the event, how distinct it is from other happenings, and personal involvement and proximity, which all increase the accuracy of flashbulb memories (Sharot, Delgado, & Phelps, 2004). This suggests that people who were living in New York at the time of the attacks probably have a much more accurate memory of the event than those who were not.

EXCEPTIONAL MEMORIES

Though for most of us, memory is fairly flawed, some extraordinary individuals have total recall of images, sounds, and objects with extreme precision. This is what is known as a **photographic memory** or an **eidetic memory**. Though many people have claimed to have an eidetic memory, most of them rely on mnemonic strategies to develop their exceptional abilities. Many memory researchers have attempted to identify people with eidetic memory and failed. In one such experiment, Wilding and Valentine (1997) searched for people claiming to have a photographic memory and of a total of 31 people, none had a truly photographic memory, even though some did have superior memory ability.

Another form of exceptional memory is referred to as **hyperthymesia**, which is a superior form of autobiographical memory, or a person's life stories. People with this type of memory tend to spend a lot of time thinking about their past, and they have an amazing ability to recall specific events as well as trivia from the past. The first instance of this memory phenomenon was described in 2006 by researchers Parker, Cahill, & McGaugh with the case of AJ, a woman who could remember anything dating back to when she was just 14 years old. Preliminary research on AJ on other similar cases found that areas in the brain tied to autobiographical memory, like the temporal and parietal lobes, tended to be larger in their brains than in normal brains. Other parts of the brain closely linked to obsessive-compulsive disorder (OCD) were also larger, leading researchers to believe that people with hyperthymesia might have an obsessive tendency to hoard memories (Leport et al., 2011).

RECOVERED MEMORIES

Recovered memories are memories of an experienced wherein all memory had been lost until the event was later suddenly recalled. Memories like this tend to surround some traumatic experience in childhood, like physical or sexual abuse that later emerges in therapy or hypnosis. Like eyewitness memory, research on recovered memories has shown that these recovered memories can also be false and a result of suggestion (Loftus & Pickrell, 1995). In one study on the subject, researchers were able to successfully plant a memory of getting lost in a shopping mall, demonstrating that each time the participants were asked about the false event, they seemed to remember it more. One participant, even after being debriefed about the purpose of the study, had trouble shaking the false

Could simple suggestion make you think you once got lost in a mall even if that never happened?

memory, claiming to clearly remember walking around the dressing rooms looking for her mother.

Despite results such as these, many true recovered memories of rape, assault, or war, have been documented as accurate. After a horrific experience, people's minds are able to repress their memories, only to recover them upon seeing some object or place that brings the memories flooding back (Arrigo & Pezdek, 1997). Since it is impossible to tell whether memories are real or false, recovered memories are often legitimized by corroborating evidence, such as physical evidence or secondary witnesses.

CHAPTER 6 REVIEW QUESTIONS

1. T/F. The capacity of short-term memory is greater than the capacity of long-term memory.

2. The kind of rehearsal that best maintains information in long-term memory is called:

    a. Rote rehearsal

    b. Elaborative rehearsal

    c. Mnemonics

    d. Priming

3. A researcher has demonstrated that when people have been walking around in a cemetery, they are more likely to show morbid thoughts in a word completion task. This is an example of:

    a. Serial position effect

    b. Priming

    c. Elaborative rehearsal

    d. Tip-of-the-tongue phenomenon

4. The information we receive from the environment is stored in the ______________________________ before being directed into short-term memory.

5. Match the type of memory to the correct example:

a. Semantic memory ____ How to swim

b. Episodic memory ____ The meaning of the word 'obfuscate'

c. Procedural memory ____ Memory of president JFK's assassination

d. Flashbulb memory ____ Memory of the marathon you ran last month

6. The ______________________________ is crucial to the formation of new episodic and semantic memories, while the ______________________________ is important to forming new emotional memories.

7. James is having trouble memorizing the names of European countries because all he can think about are the name of the US states he learned last week. What is this called?

   a. Retroactive interference
   b. Proactive interference
   c. Retrograde amnesia
   d. Anterograde amnesia

8. T/F. People do not normally make mistakes when reconstructing memories that were accurately encoded.

9. People that can accurately remember detailed autobiographical memories are said to have:

    a. Eidetic memory

    b. Hyperthymesia

    c. Flashbulb memory

    d. Amnesia

10. Who is the researcher that has demonstrated the inaccuracy and suggestibility of eyewitness memory and recovered memories? ______________________________

CHAPTER 7

INTELLIGENCE AND COGNITIVE ABILITIES

PSYCHOLOGISTS, PARTICULARLY cognitive psychologists, have devoted a lot of effort to studying human *intelligence* and the abilities that would make one intelligent, or "smart." Despite this, it has been very difficult to truly define and understand the concept. Since intelligence cannot be directly observed, it must be studied indirectly, using measures that allow psychologists to infer intelligence based on behavior. This begs the question: what behaviors indicate intelligence? Do good scores on test grades make one intelligent? Does creativity make one intelligent?

Most people, outside of the field of psychology, consider intelligence a mix of several different abilities, including problem solving ability, verbal ability, and social competence (Sternberg, 1982). Psychologists agree with laypeople that intelligence includes verbal abilities and problem solving abilities, but not social competencies. The debate about what actually constitutes intelligence has gone on for more than a century. Similar to the findings above, people tend to disagree on what they consider to be intelligence. The one general consensus among many researchers is that it is not simply one general concept, but that it is composed of many separate abilities. As to what those abilities are, the theories differ.

CONTEMPORARY THEORIES OF INTELLIGENCE

Psychologist Robert Sternberg (2003) has proposed the **triarchic theory of intelligence**, which supposes that the concept of intelligence, as we know it, is composed of three broad skills: analytical skills, creative skills, and practical skills. According to Sternberg, *analytical intelligence* is the ability to learn and solve problems. This is the kind of intelligence that one would see with a person that easily learns new information and effectively carries out tasks. Sternberg suggests that the ability to solve new problems in novel ways is a separate skill that he calls *creative intelligence*. Finally, he suggests a third component of intelligence: *practical intelligence*, the ability to effectively solve everyday personal problems.

Another prominent intelligence theorist is Howard Gardner, who proposed the **theory of multiple intelligences**, along with his associates (Chen & Gardner, 2005). This theory suggests that intelligence is made up of at least eight distinct abilities that are independent of each other including: logical-mathematical, linguistic, spatial, musical, bodily-kinesthetic, interpersonal, intrapersonal, and naturalistic. A ballet dancer or a football player, for example, might show exceptional spatial and bodily-kinesthetic ability even if their musical or logical-mathematical ability is not extraordinary. Similarly,

As we will see later in the chapter, musical intelligence might not necessarily be captured by a standard intelligence test.

someone with high interpersonal intelligence might be great at communicating and relating to others, independent of their other abilities. Intrapersonal intelligence refers to the ability to accurately understand oneself and one's motives. Naturalistic intelligence would be the ability to interact with nature – an intelligence that would probably be present in an outdoorsman or a gardener.

INTELLIGENCE TESTING

Intelligence tests are designed to measure intellectual abilities in order to provide a global ranking of intelligence. This ranking is what you probably know as an **IQ**, or **intelligence quotient**. The distribution of IQ scores ranges from 0 to more than 200, with the average being 100. An IQ can be derived from several standardized tests designed to measure one's intelligence. The first such test is the *Stanford-Binet Intelligence Scale* (Terman et al., 1915). The test was updated repeatedly and currently measures four distinct abilities related to intelligence: verbal reasoning, visual reasoning, quantitative reasoning, and short-term memory.

Currently, the most commonly used intelligence test is the *Weschler Intelligence Scale-Fourth Edition (WAIS-IV)* for adults (Weschler, 1955). As opposed to the Stanford-Binet, this test has two major parts – one focusing on verbal skills and another focusing on performance skills. The latter asks test-takers to perform simple tasks such as copying patterns and arranging figures. This test has also been modified for children.

RANGES OF IQ

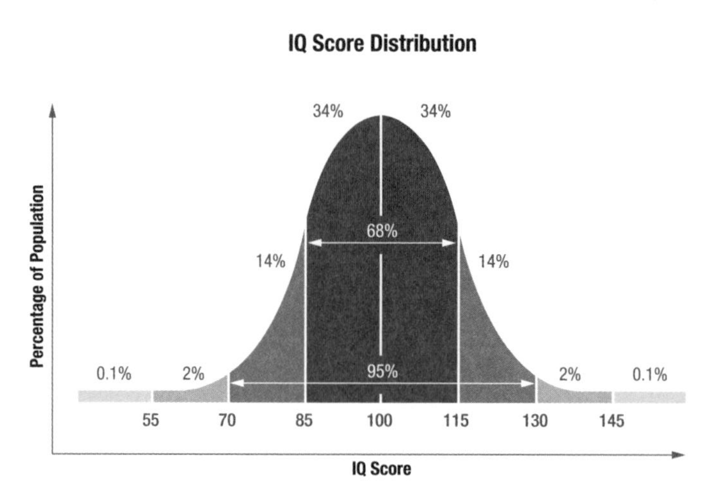

The average IQ is about 100 with the majority of people hovering around that number, as illustrated by the bell curve.

The average IQ score is 100 on a standard bell curve, with nearly 70% of people scoring between 70 and 130. People with scores below 70 on a standard IQ test are considered to have some type of *intellectual disability*, previously referred to as *mental retardation*. Between 50s and low 70s, one would be considered to have a mild degree of intellectual disability, which would indicate adequate functioning in life and the ability to learn skills comparable to a sixth grader. An IQ from the mid-30s to low 50s would indicate moderate disability. At this level, people function at a second grade level. IQ scores between the low 20s and mid-30s indicate severe intellectual disability, which can affect basic daily functions. People with severe intellectual disability cannot learn vocational skills, though they can usually perform simple tasks under supervision. IQ scores below 20 or 25 indicate profound disability and the requirement of constant care.

These scores are generally only used as a benchmark, and a low IQ alone cannot be used to diagnose intellectual disability. A person must also demonstrate an inability to function independently in daily life. In addition, people with intellectual disability sometimes display exceptional abilities in other areas, such as mathematics, memory, music, or art.

In many cases, the cause of intellectual disability is unknown but about 25% of cases – particularly severe disability – stem from genetic or biological disorders, like Down syndrome, which is the result of an extra 21st chromosome (Plomin, 1997). Intellectual disability, including cases caused by biological factors, can be moderated with education and training. Many children with mental disabilities are currently educated alongside non-disabled students, in a practice called **inclusion**.

Typically, cases of severe intellectual disability are due to genetic or biological disorders like Down syndrome.

At the upper end of the intelligence scale are people with exceptionally high IQs. They have above-average mental abilities and are considered *gifted*. Giftedness is believed to be innate, unlike learned or acquired skills. It can be general or specific to one particular mental ability, like mathematical knowledge or verbal skills. According to Joseph Renzulli (1978), giftedness consists of behaviors that reflect an interaction between above average ability, high levels of task commitment, and high levels of creativity.

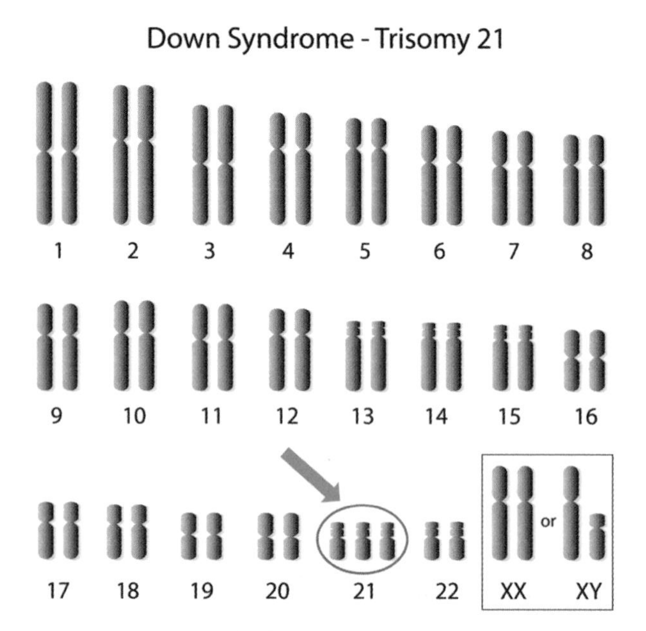

Down syndrome results from an extra 21st chromosome that is present in each cell of the body.

CRITICISMS OF IQ TESTING

Though several intelligence tests, as described above, are accepted and widely used, they are not without their controversy. Intelligence testing is often criticized for having a scope that is much too narrow. As many psychologists agree, intelligence is composed of many different abilities, and most tests focus on a small fraction of them. A child that has exceptionally gifted musical ability might score very low on a test that has only verbal and mathematical components. Some psychologists also argue that it is unfair to sum up the whole of someone's mental abilities with a simple number (Maloney and Ward, 1976).

In addition, the reliability and validity of many IQ tests have been called into question. For a test to be good, it must be reliable and it must be valid. Let's take a look at these two concepts more closely. **Reliability** refers to a test's dependability and ability to produce consistent results. For example, if you weigh yourself on a scale every 20 minutes and the scale reads 150 pounds the first time, 159 pounds the second time, and 143 pounds the third time, it would not be a reliable scale. It does not consistently measure weight. In intelligence testing, one would suppose that different versions of the same test would arrive at the same score for an individual, because IQ tends to remain relatively stable for individuals. This would mean that an IQ test is reliable. However, this alone does not mean the test is good.

For a test to be good, it must also be valid. **Validity** refers to a test's ability to measure what it actually proposes it measures. A test can be very consistent, or reliable, in measuring something and still be measuring the wrong thing. For example, imagine that for your psychology midterm, you were given an exam full of math questions. This test might be very reliable, but it is not valid in measuring your learned psychology knowledge. Intelligence testing can stretch the boundaries of validity because, as we have seen, if intelligence is comprised of many different skills – including visuospatial and musical skill – and an intelligence test only measures mathematical and verbal skill, then it does not validly measure the construct as a whole.

One way to measure the validity of intelligence tests is to compare an individual's scores on two different IQ tests. The idea is that if both are designed to measure the same thing, both should give the same results. However, even if both tests correlate, it does not mean that they are both measuring intelligence correctly. Another way is to compare IQ testing to school achievement, variables that are often correlated (Aiken & Groth-Marnat, 2005).

In addition, the reliability and validity of IQ tests have been criticized with populations of different cultures, because most IQ tests require that the taker be fluent in the language of the test. If you just immigrated to the US from a Spanish-speaking country and you are given an English intelligence test, it probably would not be a very good measure of your intelligence. Tests have been designed for cases such as these, including *performance tests*, which consist of some activity

– like puzzle-solving or navigating a maze – and *culture-fair tests* that eliminate the need for words by using other measures, such as drawings. The obvious criticism of these types of tests is that they measure only specific skills in intelligence and not others that traditional tests tend to measure. Thus, these types of tests tend to be somewhat less reliable.

HEREDITY AND ENVIRONMENT

The concept of intelligence has been at the heart of the nature versus nurture debate. Psychologists and laypeople want to know: is intelligence inherited or the result of our environment?

To study this question, psychologists have used twin studies (Erienmeyer-Kimling & Jarvik, 1963). First researchers compare the IQs of twins raised together, whom in addition to genetic similarities, also share environments. As a result, their IQs tend to be very closely correlated. They also tested identical twins separated before 6 months of age and raised in different families. Researchers found that even when raised in different environments, identical twins tended to have very similar IQs, even more similar than non-twin siblings raised in the same family. Adoption studies corroborate these findings. Adopted children tend to have more similar IQs to their biological mother than to their adoptive mother (Loehlin, Horn & Willerman, 1997).

Twins are unique in that they share exact genetic material. Differences in personality, preferences, or talents would be influenced by their environment.

These findings strongly suggest that intelligence is closely linked to genetic forces. However, most psychologists agree that heredity is only one part of the story and that the environment determines how much we are able to achieve past that starting point. Everything from access to education to nutrition can have an effect on intelligence. Nutrition, particularly during pregnancy, has shown to have a positive effect on children's IQ scores (Harrell, Woodyard, & Gates, 1955).

Another study has demonstrated the importance of stimulation in the environment (Skeels, 1942). Researchers studied children in orphanages, where they had no adults to play with, talk to, or to read them stories. Some of the children were placed in adult wards and tested over an 18 month period, and during this period, their IQs rose an average of 28 points. Conversely, the children left in the orphanage with little stimulation showed an average decrease in IQ of 25 points.

As with many debates in psychology, the true underlying cause of intelligence probably cannot be attributed to heredity or environment alone. The two interact within individuals to contribute to differences in intelligence and mental abilities.

COGNITION

Cognition is a representation of all types of thinking including the processes of attention, memory, communication, reasoning, problem solving, and decision making. You are constantly using several of these processes in your daily life. Cognition allows you to process information, apply knowledge, and make sense of the world around you.

Any given thought can be made up of different elements. For example, if you think about your favorite food, a simple sentence might pop into your head like "I could go for some sushi right now." You might also imagine the taste and texture of sushi in your mouth. You may also think of related concepts, like the fact that you eat sushi with chopsticks. All of these are examples of different types of thought. These are the basic elements of all thoughts: language, images, and concepts.

LANGUAGE

Language is a complex system humans use to communicate. Three basic properties differentiate language – the way humans communicate – from the way animals communicate. First, our language has meaning that is unlike its sound. Though animals communicate information through squeaks and growls, they do not have the meaningful units that make up human language. Secondly, our language is generative, meaning that our words and grammar allow us to combine elements to create an endless variety of things to say. This is why language evolves over time, introducing verbs like texting and tweeting into our lexicon. Finally, human language allows us to communicate about objects, people, places, and ideas that are abstract, imaginary, or simply not present.

Language can be broken up into specific to more general parts, starting with *phonemes*, which are units of sounds like, the sound of *a*, *th*, and *k*. Phonemes are combined into *morphemes*, which are the smallest meaningful units in language: words, prefixes, and suffixes. Morphemes are distinguished by the fact that they have some meaning. For example, *cat* is a morpheme because it has a meaning. However, *dut*, another combination of phonemes would not be considered a morpheme because it has no meaning. One or more morphemes are combined to create words. Words are further combined to create *sentences*, which are phrases that communicate a complete thought.

If you have ever taken an English class, you are probably at least somewhat familiar with the way words are organized within a language: grammar. One important component of **grammar** is *syntax*, the rules that determine how words and phrases can be combined; the other is *semantics*, the meaning that we assign to individual components of language. For example, the word *create* can have many different meanings. An artist does not create in the same way a carpenter creates or the way a musician creates. In each of these examples, creation can have various meanings: paint, build, and compose.

Following this example, the language people speak can affect the way in which they conceptualize the world. This is a theory first proposed by Benjamin Whorf (1956), which he called the **linguistic relativity hypothesis**. If you speak two different languages and you have ever tried to translate a phrase common to one language that does not exist in the other language, then you probably have a good practical understanding of this hypothesis. For example, the Spanish phrase "¡Buen provecho!" or "Bon appétit" in French, which is used to tell someone to enjoy their meal does not have a direct English translation. In fact, the literal translation of the Spanish phrase would be "Good advantage," which has nothing to do with a meal, at all. According to the linguistic relativity hypothesis, this is a sentiment that probably does not occur to English-speaking persons to use very often.

This theory is not without its critics, however. Many psychologists believe that experience and culture have just as much effect on language as language does on one's view of the world. Evidence of this is that language is constantly evolving according to societal need. Words are created to express new ideas, as is the case with many technological tasks – Googling, Instagramming, texting, sexting, etc. – that did not exist a few short years ago. The meaning of existing words also evolves over time, like for example, the meaning of the word *wicked*, which is defined as evil, has been given a positive connotation to mean that something is great or brilliant. In this case, it is not the language that has changed our conceptualization of the world, but vice versa.

LANGUAGE DEVELOPMENT

Language learning begins very early on in life and children are able to easily absorb language. Babies usually begin by crying and cooing to communicate. By about four months of age, they begin *babbling*, or making vocalizations that sound like human speech. Babies tend to produce their first words around one year of life. This is followed

by the use of **holophrases**, one-word utterances that have meaning. For example, a baby could cry out "Bottle!" while reaching out their hands to indicate that they are hungry.

From 13 to 18 months, word knowledge increases very quickly, and children can learn words from a single exposure to them (Woodward, Markman, & Fitzsimmons, 1994). Around two years of age, toddlers begin combining these words into phrases. This gives way to longer and more complex sentences and the correct application of the rules of grammar in their language development. It is very common for children to *overregularize* these rules, like for example, adding *-ed* to a word that does not require it (like *drinked*) after learning that the past tense of many words is constructed by adding *–ed*. Eventually these irregular tenses are learned as well and children begin to use proper verbs and articles in their speech.

This rapid growth of language development led linguist and psychologist, Noam Chomsky (1972) to suggest that language acquisition is a process that is built into us, what he called the **language acquisition device (LAD).** According to this theory, humans are hardwired in a way that facilitates language learning and explains why children of all cultures learn to speak their language without much effort or instruction.

Behavioral psychologist, B. F. Skinner (1957) has his own theory of language learning, which suggests that children learn by being reinforced for grammatically correct speech. This process of reinforcement, according to Skinner, begins very early on, when mothers reinforce words that sound like "mama" with positive attention. Following the basic principles of learning, including reinforcement and imitation, the rules of language are acquired. Many psychologists suggest that this learning alone cannot account for how quickly and accurately children can learn language, supporting Chomsky's idea that there is an underlying innate capacity for language.

IMAGES AND CONCEPTS

The other two components of thought are images and concepts. Since not all thoughts are verbalized, we also think in images. **Images** are mental representations of sensations. A large part of our thoughts are image-based, which is why you can imagine the taste, texture, and smell of a juicy burger. We are constantly visualizing memories and future possibilities, sometimes in a way that is difficult to put into words. If I ask you to imagine the smell of winter or the look of light coming through dense trees, you can probably easily imagine it, without necessarily creating verbal descriptions of this imagery.

Concepts, the third element of cognition, are categories used to classify new information. For example, if you think of potato chips, you might also think about other categories that you classify this snack under, like "junk food," "foods that are bad for you," or "snacks for watching the Super Bowl." Concepts are not necessarily clear cut and may sometimes overlap. Nonetheless, these concepts help us organize and make sense of the world. So if you see an animal you have never seen before that walks on four legs, has fur, and barks, you would be easily able to classify it as a dog even if you've never seen that particular breed before.

PROBLEM SOLVING

Problem solving is a large part of cognition. Any time you are in an undesired state and you would like to get to a goal state, you are thinking about solving a problem. For example, how can I live off $150 worth of groceries for one week? Or, how can I get to work on time with all this traffic? Problems such as these may have affected you from time to time. In both of these cases, you are trying to figure out a way to achieve a goal – the desired state – in a way that may not be obvious.

Once you have correctly defined the problem, it is time to employ methods that will help you arrive at a solution. One common problem solving method is the **trial and error strategy**. This method involves producing solutions and testing them to see if they work. If you've forgotten your password to your email, you would probably use this strategy by testing old passwords at random to see if any of them work. This strategy is effective when solution choices are limited. When they are not, it can be very ineffective and time consuming. For example, if you are trying to guess someone else's email password, you would probably have no idea where to even begin. Trying random strings of letters and numbers is unlikely to get you access to that email account.

Another option for problem solving is what is known as an **algorithm**, a step-by-step process that guarantees the correct response. A mathematical formula is an example of an algorithm. If followed properly, the steps of a formula will lead to the correct solution. Let's say that your problem is that you want to unlock an old briefcase. An algorithm could be used in this example to open the briefcase by trying every possible number combination starting from 0000 and going up to 9999. One of those is guaranteed to be the correct combination. The obvious downside is that this method would take an extremely long time.

It is because of this and because some problems have no known algorithms that many of us use **heuristics** instead. These are mental shortcuts that can save time, though they do not guarantee a solution. When you are making choices in the grocery aisle, you probably use

Mathematical formulas are examples of algorithms.

heuristics. For example, a jar of spaghetti sauce might be available in 3 sizes at 3 different prices. Many of us would choose the larger size, assuming that you are getting more sauce for only a few cents more – more bang for your buck. Though it may not necessarily be the case, it saved you the time you would have spent trying to do the math.

PROBLEM SOLVING BARRIERS

Many factors can become obstacles when solving problems. One such barrier comes from our natural biases, or preexisting expectations, that color the way we see things. This can lead us to focus excessively on *irrelevant information* in a problem that will not help us arrive at a solution. It can also lead to forming *unnecessary constraints*. This occurs when we assume there is a requirement for a solution that is not really needed.

For example, using only four straight lines and without lifting your pencil off the paper, connect all the dots in this diagram (Burnham & Davis, 1969):

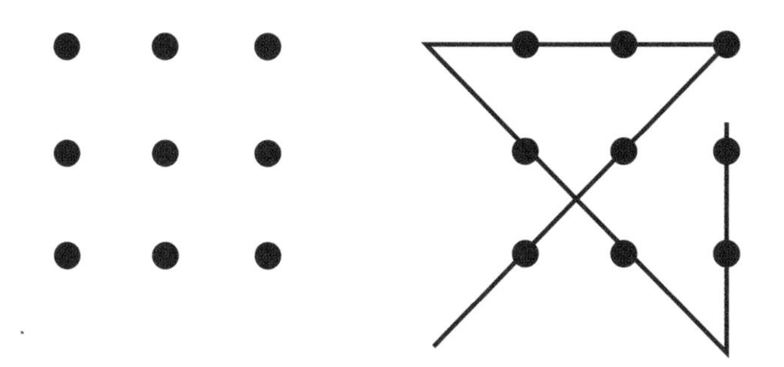

This problem (left) might be difficult because we assume that the lines must fit within the "box" of dots, when the solution (right) requires us to draw outside the box. In this example, one is placing unnecessary constraints on the problem.

Other barriers involve becoming fixated on a certain approach. This is known as a **mental set** and it is a tendency to approach problems in a familiar way, preventing the use of novel approaches.

Mental sets develop as a byproduct of learning and they allow us to become more effective at solving similar problems. However, these become a hindrance when a better solution exists that requires a novel method. An example of a mental set is known as *functional fixedness*, and it is our tendency to only see the intended use of objects. Duncker (1945) created a paradigm in which people were asked to mount a lit candle on a wall using a box of tacks, and a book of matches. In this situation, many people find it hard to arrive at the solution because they become fixed on the box's function – to hold the tacks – which prevents them from seeing it as a potential candle holder that can be tacked onto the wall.

Getting through these barriers requires one to be open to new ways of representing and solving a problem. Brainstorming can be an effective way to arrive at new solutions. This involves generating many ideas, even if they aren't instinctively great ideas and then narrowing them down. This process can help lead to a better solution than simply going with the first acceptable solution that comes to mind. Similarly, providing an *incubation* period, in which we take a break from the problem and come back to it with a fresh perspective, can lead to novel solutions.

DECISION MAKING

In addition to problem solving, our cognitive abilities are used for another major task of everyday life: making decisions. When we make a decision, we must choose the best alternative among many. Decisions can be as simple as what shirt to put on or where to go for lunch or as important and complex as which job to take or what kind of car to buy.

Often, making a decision involves rationally analyzing the pros and cons of each alternative to arrive at a *compensatory decision*. Compensatory decision making is a process that involves identifying the set of attributes or features that are relevant to the decision and assigning a relative importance or weight to each attribute. For example, with something as important as accepting a new job, you might consider a variety of different factors such as salary, hours, benefits, and distance from home. Each of these factors probably has varying importance to anyone making the decision. Perhaps salary is the most important factor to you, so it is weighted more heavily than the others. When it comes to this decision, a great salary might offset, or compensate for, undesirable hours or a long commute. This type of decision making involves closely analyzing all the different options and making the most rational decision.

However, like in problem solving, we do not often take the most accurate, laborious route to picking an alternative. Instead, we use heuristics, or shortcuts, to simplify our decisions.

DECISION MAKING HEURISTICS

There are several different types of heuristics we use to make decisions. For example, imagine seeing a young man with spiky hair, facial piercings, and tattoos, wearing leather pants and a T-shirt with the sleeves torn off, walking down the street. If asked whether you think the young man is a famous rock musician or an investment banker, which would you choose? Most people would "judge a book by its cover," so to speak, and assume him to be a famous rock musician, simply because he fits the stereotypical profile of one. This is what is known as the **representativeness heuristic**. It is a tendency to make decisions about something based on how much it looks like a prototypical case, and this tendency can lead us to make flawed judgments or decisions. Statistically

Making assumptions about people based on their appearance might lead to errors.

speaking, it is much more likely that you would see an investment banker on the street than a famous musician. However, because he looks more like what you would expect a famous rock musician to look like, you would probably easily make that mistake.

Another common heuristic that can affect your decisions is the **availability heuristic**. This is our tendency to estimate the likelihood of an event based on how easily it can be recalled. This occurs because the less effort it takes to come up with an example of an event, the more likely we think that event is. To this effect, events that receive a lot of press coverage tend to be overestimated. For example, many people are afraid of being attacked by sharks. This fear is unjustly biased by the availability heuristic. When shark attacks do occur, you hear a lot about them. Movies like *Jaws* make sharks appear extremely dangerous. However, in reality the total number of fatal, unprovoked shark attacks worldwide was only 10 in 2013 (ISAF, 2014). One is many times more likely to die in the car on the way to the beach than to be attacked by a shark in the water, but because of the availability heuristic, our perception of the danger is skewed.

People also have a tendency to favor their own beliefs in their thinking. This is what is known as the **confirmation bias**. If you are one of those people that believe that every time you wash your car, it rains, you are probably biased by this heuristic. We tend to seek out and notice information that confirms our existing beliefs and to ignore information that contradicts them. Even though there are probably many instances where you washed your car and it remained sunny and clear for several days, we tend to forget these days. The days when it started sprinkling a few hours after you pulled away from the car wash – those are memorable. And those instances are in line with our preexisting beliefs. Research has demonstrated this effect, finding that people have a tendency to test hypotheses by searching for evidence consistent with their ideas (Nickerson, 1998).

Decisions can also be biased by the way information is presented, known as the **framing effect.** Researchers demonstrated this effect by showing a reversal of decision preference when the same problem was presented in a different way (Tversky and Kahneman, 1981). In the study, participants were asked to choose between treatment alternatives for an unusual disease that is expected to kill 600 people. One group of participants were given the following two options:

- Option A: "200 people will be saved"
- Option B: "there is a one-third probability that 600 people will be saved, and a two-thirds probability that no people will be saved"

Presented with these choices, framed by the number of lives saved, most people chose option A, the safe choice that would guarantee 200 people would be saved.

The other participants were given the following choices:

- Option C: "400 people will die"
- Option D: "there is a one-third probability that nobody will die, and a two-third probability that 600 people will die"

These participants preferred option D, even though it is identical to option B, which the majority of people did not choose when the options were A and B. Why the change of opinion? This study simply manipulated the wording of the question. Even though options A and C are identical, it is a lot harder for one to make a decision that will result in the deaths of 400 people (even when it is, in fact, saving 200). So when the problem is presented in this way, in terms of losses or deaths, most people choose the riskier option.

Certain biases can also affect already-made decisions, not just future ones. One such bias is called **hindsight bias**, or the knew-it-all-along effect, which is a tendency to see events that already occurred as being more predictable than they were before they happened. This explains

The Denver Broncos, who have won two Super Bowls, were the clear favorite to win Super Bowl XLVIII to underdogs Seattle Seahawks.

why the majority of the U.S. believed that the Seattle Seahawks would lose the 2014 Super Bowl to the Denver Broncos, before their big win. If those football fans were asked, after the fact, about who they *thought* would win, the numbers would be a little different. It is also why many people living in coastal areas complain that they *knew* that an incoming hurricane would not hit, only after it weakens or changes course, when they have already put up their shutters. It is easy to make that judgment when you know the outcome. However, when you were waiting for the weather forecast and deciding whether or not to prepare, you were probably not so sure.

All of these heuristics and biases can strongly affect our decisions. Though they can be very useful in providing shortcuts to decision making, they can also lead to errors; it is helpful to be aware of this when faced with an important decision.

CHAPTER 7 REVIEW QUESTIONS

1. Which of these is not one of Gardner's proposed multiple intelligences?

    a. Interpersonal

    b. Creative

    c. Linguistic

    d. Spatial

2. Robert Sternberg proposed that intelligence is made up of three different components: analytical intelligence, practical intelligence, and creative intelligence. This is known as ____
    ____

3. If an intelligence test demonstrates consistent results but does not correlate with other measures of intelligence, it likely has problems with:

    a. Reliability

    b. Validity

    c. Culture-fairness

    d. None of the above

4. T/F. Research has been unable to link intelligence to genetic factors.

5. IQ scores between the mid-30s to low 50s correspond to what level of intellectual disability?

    a. Mild

    b. Moderate

    c. Severe

    d. Profound

6. The theory that humans are hard wired with mechanisms to facilitate language learning is called ____________________

    ____

7. The formula to convert temperatures from Fahrenheit to Celsius is an example of:

    a. A heuristic

    b. Brainstorming

    c. An unnecessary constraint

    d. An algorithm

8. Jonas hates weathermen because he believes they are always wrong. Which of these is true?

    a. Jonas is being influenced by the confirmation bias, because he only remembers examples of when the forecast is wrong.

b. Jonas is being influenced by the confirmation bias, because he only remembers examples of when the forecast is right.

c. Jonas is being influenced by the representative bias, because weathermen do not look very intelligent.

d. Jonas is being influenced by the representative bias, because the weather does not look like the weatherman said it would.

9. The availability heuristic is: ______________________________
____
____
____

10. T/F. The way the options are worded in decision making affect how people decide.

CHAPTER 8

MOTIVATION AND EMOTION

THE CONCEPTS OF MOTIVATION and emotion are closely linked in psychology. **Motivation** is a process that moves people to behave in a way directed at meeting some need or desire. For example, being too hot might motivate you to turn on the air conditioner. Being hungry would probably motivate you to cook or order food. **Emotion** is a conscious experience of a feeling that is characterized by physical arousal, behaviors that reveal feeling to the outside world, and an inner awareness of the feeling. Emotions, like joy, anger, or fear, can all be motivating drives. For example, being annoyed with a coworker might motivate you to avoid that person for the rest of the day.

UNDERSTANDING MOTIVATION

Several different approaches to motivation attempt to explain how and why we are stirred to move toward specific goals.

INSTINCT THEORY

Early research on motivation focused on the role of instincts, which exist both in people and animals. **Instincts** are innate behaviors which can be triggered by external or internal cues. William McDougall (1908) listed about 18 different human instincts including curiosity, acquisition – i.e. gathering possessions – and flight – i.e. running away. Over the years, this list grew to have thousands of proposed instincts. However, the theory grew unpopular over time due to the fact that many human behaviors, like deciding to get a higher education, cannot be considered instinctual. In addition, the theory merely describes behaviors, but does not explain why these behaviors occur.

DRIVE REDUCTION THEORY

According to one theory of motivation, a need – such as hunger or thirst, called a *drive* – creates a tension that we are subsequently motivated to decrease (Hull, 1943). This theory is called **drive reduction theory**, an approach that suggests that behavior is a result of these needs, or drives. This theory proposes two kinds of drives: *primary drives*, which include the needs that maintain survival, like hunger, thirst, and the sex drive; and *secondary drives*, which are learned from experience or conditioning. Primary drives can be differentiated from secondary drives because primary drives are common to animals as well as humans; but secondary drives are not. An animal would have a drive to obtain food in the same way as a human, but not the drive to acquire money or learn a skill – secondary drives.

Drive reduction theory further explains that the body attempts to maintain **homeostasis**, a level of internal stability and balance. When there is a drive, like hunger, the body is in a state of imbalance. This state, in turn, will stimulate behavior that will bring the body back into balance.

Though drive reduction theory explains why people are driven to certain behaviors to reduce tension, it fails to explain certain human motivations, like thrill seeking behavior, which aim to increase inner tension. People who enjoy roller coasters and skydiving are not seeking to reduce an inner tension; they are motivated by other incentives.

INCENTIVE THEORY

Another view of motivation focuses on the rewards of behaviors, or the **incentives**. As many behaviorists would tell you, we are motivated by the rewards and punishment of our actions. We might be motivated to work overtime because of the reward of extra pay. We avoid getting to a movie late so that we do not get a bad seat. There are two types of incentives, or motivations: extrinsic and intrinsic.

A person might enter competitive running because he is motivated by the idea of earning a medal.

Extrinsic motivation is external. For example, a salary is an external motivation, or incentive, to work. When an athlete plays well to earn a championship ring or a child does her chores to earn her allowance, they are extrinsically motivated. *Intrinsic motivations*, on the other hand, are internal and they are driven by enjoyment of a task. Some children may like playing "house" with the broom and the vacuum so they do their chores, not for the extrinsic reward, but for the natural enjoyment of the activity in the same way an athlete may play a sport for the love of the game.

Research has demonstrated that providing extrinsic incentive for activities that already offer intrinsic motivation can actually decrease the intrinsic motivation (Deci, 1971). This is what is known as the

overjustification effect. Researchers had participants work on a puzzle on three different occasions. One group, the control group, solved puzzles on their own time with no added incentives. The incentive group solved puzzles in the same way on the first occasion. However, for the second session, they were paid to complete each puzzle. For the third session, they were not paid to complete the puzzle. They found that the control group maintained a steady rate of puzzle completion, doing so out of enjoyment. The incentive group showed an increase in puzzle completion when they were paid, and a subsequent decrease in completion during the third session when the external reward was taken away. The results illustrate the overjustification effect: when paid to do a task that people already enjoy, they lose interest in doing it for free. This is why sometimes trying to make money off a hobby, like writing or painting, can lead people to stop enjoying their hobbies for their own sake.

MASLOW'S HIERARCHICHAL THEORY

One of the most famous humanistic psychologists, Abraham Maslow, conceptualized motivation in a different way. His theory, which became known as the **hierarchy of needs** organizes motives from the most basic to the most complex (Maslow, 1943; See Figure 8.1). According to Maslow, our basic motives reflect the needs of the body such as satisfying hunger, thirst, and getting sleep. There are also basic safety needs which we strive to meet, like having good health, stable employment, and stability in the home and community.

Further up in the hierarchy, we have the need to be loved and belong. According to the theory, one would focus on this need once the two below it, physiological needs and safety needs, are met or largely met; a theorem for which the hierarchy model has been criticized. Skeptics cite people in developing countries who do not always have physiological needs met or stability in their environments who still form close relationships with friends, family, and lovers. In

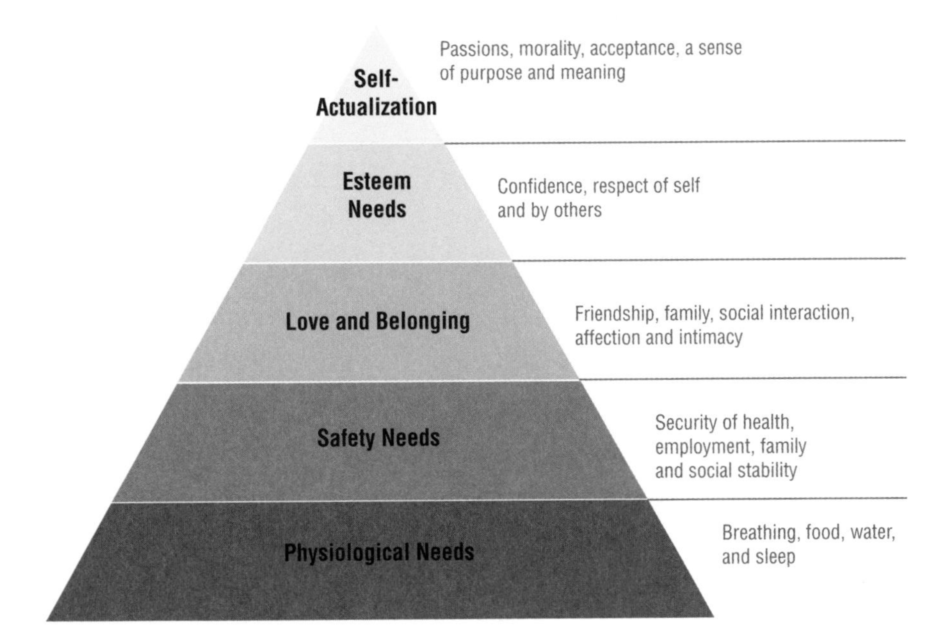

Figure 8.1: Maslow's hierarchy of needs.

fact, sometimes those situations of strife can serve to bring people closer together.

Above love and belonging, the hierarchy cites esteem needs as the next important need, involving confidence and respect of self as well as respect from others. Finally, Maslow states that we seek **self-actualization**, a point at which we have sufficiently satisfied lower needs and achieved fulfillment and satisfaction in life as a result of achieving our full potential.

MOTIVATION OF HUNGER

Several hours after you get to work, your stomach starts to rumble, indicating hunger. This would motivate you to take a break for lunch. This is a relatively simple concept. You get hungry; you eat.

However the underlying mechanisms of hunger are much more complex than this sequence would have you believe. In fact, sometimes when you are really busy, stressed, or distracted, even though your body has an increasing need for food, you do not experience hunger. This is because hunger is regulated by several biological and environmental processes that must all work in sync to create the experience of hunger.

BIOLOGICAL FACTORS

The stomach is one of the biggest influences in the motivation of hunger. An early study tested this by having participants swallow an air filled balloon that filled the stomach (Cannon & Washburn, 1912). The contractions of the stomach were recorded and participants were instructed to push a button whenever they felt hungry. The study found that the feeling of hunger was directly related to the contractions of the stomach.

Other studies examined the brain's role in hunger. If you recall, the *hypothalamus* is the part of the brain that regulates many important bodily functions, including hunger, thirst, sleep, and stress. Two areas of the hypothalamus have been implicated in the activation of hunger and subsequent cessation of hunger. The *lateral hypothalamus* has been shown to start the feeling of hunger, and when the area is artificially stimulated in rats, the rats eat even when they are full (Teitelbaum & Epstein, 1962). Another area of the hypothalamus called the *ventromedial hypothalamus* has the opposite effect on hunger; it appears to turn it off.

These areas of the hypothalamus stimulate hunger or fullness because they are sensitive to hormones in the blood that signal these two states. The empty stomach secretes a hormone called **ghrelin**, which signals hunger and stimulates appetite. **Leptin** is the hormone that reduces appetite. This hormone is secreted by fat cells when there are adequate fat stores in order to decrease hunger.

The brain also monitors levels of **glucose** (sugar) in the blood. When we eat, glucose levels in the blood increase. When blood sugar is low, we feel hunger. **Insulin** is the hormone that converts glucose into energy that the body can use. This hormone keeps levels of glucose in the body balanced. This is one of the mechanisms that maintains the body's **metabolism**, the process that converts the food we ingest to energy that the body can use. If you recall, metabolism is regulated by the thyroid gland, ensuring that our body maintains a state of homeostasis, or balance.

ENVIRONMENTAL FACTORS

Our body's physiological processes are only one part of hunger. Environmental influences also have a large effect on the motivation to eat. Taste preferences and available food are two such sources of influence. You might be more motivated to eat your favorite food and less motivated to eat something you hate. Culture can have a large influence on food preferences, making foods that are more familiar, more desirable. Exposure to food cues – like a commercial for rich, chocolate ice cream – can also stimulate desire for it.

Seeing your favorite food in a cafeteria line might open up your appetite.

Some people also find motivation to eat while experiencing certain emotions, such as sadness, stress, or boredom, even when there is not a physical need for food. Research has demonstrated that people eat more after the completion of stressful tasks (Epel et al., 2001). One study also demonstrated the effect of dieting on desire and consumption of certain foods (Stirling & Yeomans, 2004). They found that when presented with food forbidden by the diet, people showed an increase in desire and consumption of these foods.

What motivates us to diet in the first place? This is another environmental factor that influences our eating habits: body image. One study found that when people are in front of a large mirror, they eat less, because the mirror makes them more self-focused (Sentyrz & Bushman, 1998). Though this self-awareness mechanism can prevent overeating in situations when the body does not need food, excessive focus on body image can lead to disordered eating.

EATING DISORDERS

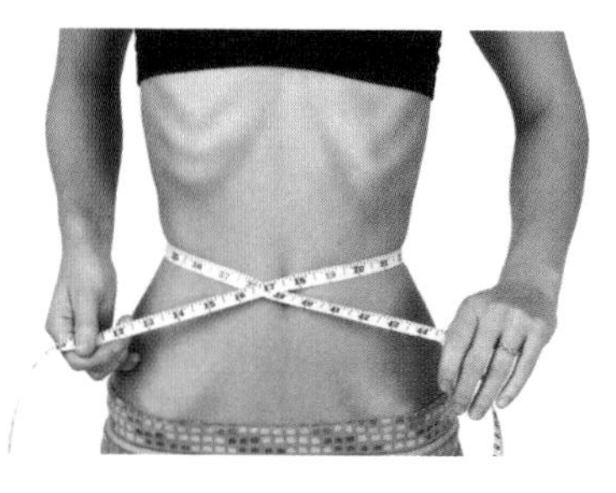

For someone suffering from anorexia, no amount of weight loss is enough.

Anorexia nervosa is an eating disorder in which individuals go to extreme lengths to lose weight and feel they are overweight even though they are actually underweight. The defining characteristics of the disorder involve intense fear of being obese, disturbance of body image, and restrictive eating leading to significantly low body weight. The severity of the disorder is determined by how low the individual's Body Mass Index (BMI) is. A person suffering from anorexia would have a BMI indicating that he or she is underweight for what is normal and appropriate for his or her height.

Bulimia nervosa is another common eating disorder that involves episodes of binge eating – periods when an individual consumes large amounts of food – and purging behaviors, to prevent weight gain. During binge eating episodes, a person feels a lack of control over his or her food intake. Purging behaviors can include vomiting, using laxatives and diuretics, fasting, or excessive exercise.

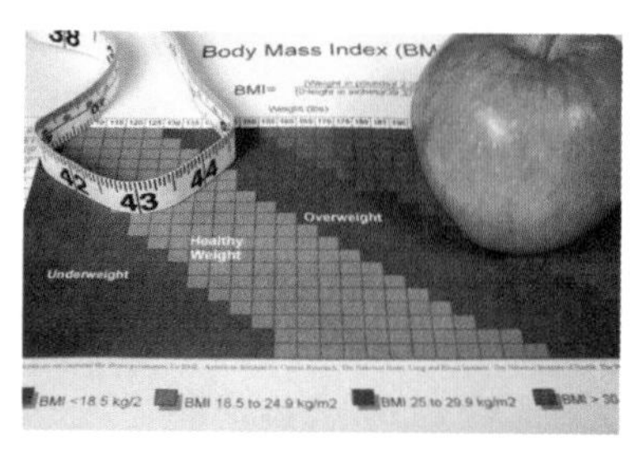

Your BMI allows you to see if you are within a healthy weight range for your height.

Though both of these eating disorders tend to be more prevalent in females, cases of anorexia and bulimia are found in males, as well. The media is one factor that is consistently incriminated in the development of eating disorders. Models and actors in television and movies are constantly portraying the message that beautiful people are thin (and that attractive men are muscular and fit). The internalization of these messages can lead to the development of eating disorders. Furthermore, large bodies of research have found that peer and family influence have a major effect on disordered eating (Quiles et al., 2013). Daily interactions with others can influence dieting behavior, body dissatisfaction, and bulimic symptoms.

With the release of the *DSM-5* (2013), **binge-eating disorder** is being recognized for the first time as an eating disorder. Binge-eating disorder involves recurring episodes of binge eating and distress associated with how much one is eating. This disorder is sometimes linked to one of the biggest health problems in the United States: obesity. Obesity is an unhealthy excess of body fat, and it is a problem that is associated with increased risk for hypertension, stroke, diabetes, and heart disease.

Developing a healthy lifestyle is not about being thin; it is about eating the right nutrients, cutting toxins like alcohol and smoking, and optimizing your body's normal functions.

The causes of obesity are complex and multi-faceted. Some people have a genetic predisposition to obesity, making it very easy for them to gain weight and difficult to lose it. One theory, called the **set point theory**, suggests that our bodies have a pre-set weight that it naturally maintains (Liebel et al., 1995). According to this theory, our metabolic rate changes in response to how much we eat in order to maintain that weight. This is why dieting can sometimes be ineffective and can lead to sharp fluctuations in weight. When we diet and eat fewer calories than are needed to maintain our set weight, our metabolism slows, burning fewer calories in order to preserve energy. Thyroid dysfunctions can also lead to excessive, unwanted weight gain. In addition, lifestyle factors are major contributors to obesity. In American culture, there is no shortage of unhealthy and highly caloric foods that are heavily marketed and readily available. Lack of exercise to burn consumed calories can also lead to obesity.

The ease and availability of fast food combined with our busy lifestyles can lead to greater consumption of unhealthy foods.

In addition to the health risks associated with obesity, social stigma plagues obese individuals. Being overweight is associated with negative stereotypes such as laziness and lower socioeconomic status. Many obese individuals experience discrimination in employment, salary determinations, and housing, some of which is greater than ethnic and gender discrimination (Roehling et al., 2007).

All these complex factors contribute to increasing obesity and disordered eating, making it difficult to come up with any one universal solution to these problems.

SEXUAL MOTIVATION

Sex plays an important role in mating in all animals; it is necessary to ensure the propagation of a species. However, in humans, psychological factors are stronger motivations for sexual behavior than mating.

William H. Masters and Virginia E. Johnson (1966) spearheaded a large-scale study of the human sexual response, in which they observed over 10,000 complete sexual responses. Based on this study, they were able to develop the **human sexual response cycle**, which organizes the phases that comprise the sexual act. They found that while people differ in what kinds of stimulation is arousing, the physical response is similar across individuals. During the first phase of the human sexual response cycle, the *excitement phase*, arousal begins and blood circulates into the genitals. Males experience an erection and females experience vaginal lubrication and swelling of the clitoris. This engorgement continues into the *plateau phase*, during which arousal remains elevated and genital secretions increase. During the *orgasmic phase* arousal level reaches its peak, when the male ejaculates and the female's pelvic muscles contract. Following orgasm, in the *resolution phase*, excitement levels decrease to normal, along with heart rate, blood pressure, and breathing.

This cycle differs between genders. Notably, men experience a *refractory period* following orgasm during which they cannot achieve another orgasm. On the other hand, women can experience another orgasm with further stimulation. Masters and Johnson's research allowed for the identification of dysfunctions in the sexual response.

During orgasm, the hormone *oxytocin* is released, leading to sensations of emotional well-being. This rewarding sensation could be an important motivator of sexual behavior in humans. Animals also secrete substances called *pheromones* that signal sexual readiness to potential partners. Hormones like *testosterone* have also been shown to correlate with sexual desire in men and women (Meston & Frohlich, 2000). However the effect of these substances on humans is not as pronounced as it is in non-human animals.

In humans, sex is highly motivated by psychosocial factors. The things that arouse one person may differ wildly from what arouses another, including what individuals find attractive. Studies on gender differences in mate preferences have shown that women are affected by status, not attractiveness, and men are affected by physical attractiveness, not status (Kenrick & Keefe, 1992). Men and women also demonstrate differences in sexual behavior. Men report thinking about and desiring sex more often than women and rate their sex drives as higher than women's sex drives (Peplau, 2003).

Sexual behavior is also influenced significantly by culture and ideas about morality and sexual appropriateness. For many, sexual motivation is an expression of behavior they have learned and experienced in the past.

SEXUAL ORIENTATION

Pride parades all over the world celebrate sexual diversity.

Theories of sexual motivation that emphasize reproductive behavior fail to capture the spectrum of **sexual orientation**, which refers to the gender a person prefers for romantic and sexual intimacy. In one of the first studies of adult sexual behavior, Alfred Kinsey et al. (1948, 1953) suggested that sexuality is on a continuum. Researchers found that nearly 46% of males and between 6-14% of women had bisexual experiences with both genders, and that about 10% of males and 2-6% of females were predominantly homosexual – interested in partners of the same gender.

The origins of sexual orientation have been the subject of debate in the United States and throughout the world. Though heterosexuality is acceptable across many different cultures, many view homosexuality and bisexuality as unacceptable and in some cases, even as condemnable. At the heart of the debate is the question: is homosexuality a learned choice or a biological phenomenon like being born male or female?

A large body of research has found support for genetic influence on sexual orientation. One study of identical twins, fraternal twins, and adopted siblings found that 52% percent of identical twins were both homosexual, compared to 22% of the fraternal twins and only 11% of adopted siblings (Bailey & Pillard, 1991). Another study, using neuroimaging techniques, found that heterosexual men and homosexual women, who are both attracted to women, seem to be more neurologically similar to each other; likewise, homosexual men appear more neurologically similar to heterosexual women (Savic & Lindstrom, 2008). Though these studies do not completely rule out the influence of learning and experience on sexuality, they do imply strong biological mechanisms behind differences in sexual orientation.

SOCIAL MOTIVATIONS

Consistent with Maslow's hierarchy of motivations, aside from our basic biological needs, we experience strong needs for belonging and achievement.

LOVE AND BELONGING

One of the most basic needs is the social motive to belong. Humans are driven to form intimate and long-lasting interpersonal relationships. In fact, social isolation has been strongly related to unhappiness and is negatively correlated with feelings of well-being (Baumesiter, 1991). Even non-human animals demonstrate a need for closeness, as illustrated by the classic experiments of Harry Harlow (1958). He found that when newborn monkeys were separated from their mothers and given two "surrogate mothers" made of cloth and wire, respectively, the monkeys clung to the cloth mother. This was true even though the wire mother was the one with the bottle that would allow the monkey to nurse. Even though the wire mother fulfilled the physiological need for food, the baby monkeys gravitated toward the soft cloth mother, indicating an intense need for closeness. For humans, this need is demonstrated in our willingness to form and maintain friendships and in the time and effort we invest in others.

Harlow's monkeys demonstrated the need for soft touch over their physiological needs like feeding. They would cling to the cloth mother in search of physical closeness.

Our motivation to belong also makes us very sensitive to signs of rejection. In one study, participants played a computer game where a ball was tossed, believing that the other players in the game were real people who continuously skipped them when tossing the ball (Eisenberger et al., 2003). Researchers found that when excluded from the ball toss, participants showed increased activity in parts of the brain normally associated with unpleasantness and pain. The need to belong is strong, indeed, if failure to fulfill that need is felt in the brain like physical pain.

ACHIEVEMENT

What drives someone to succeed, to excel, and to feel accomplished in the world? If anyone has ever asked you why you are enrolled in a higher education program, you've probably pondered this question.

Research has shown that some people are particularly driven to succeed at challenging tasks, by being persistent and innovative (Murray, 1938; McClelland et al., 1953). People with a high need to achieve tend to get better grades in school and have more success in their careers.

Culturally, the need for achievement can vary depending on the expectations for achievement from family and society. For example, research has shown that Asian-Americans place a higher degree of importance on education as a means to upward mobility (Sue & Okazaki, 1990). This culturally-valued need for achievement may not be present in other individuals raised in a families and communities that do not value education as much.

EMOTION

All the motivations already discussed in this chapter can be associated with a specific emotion or set of emotions. We seek out love because love makes us happy. We eat and have sex because they are satisfying. We seek out achievement because it makes us feel a sense of pride. Behind most, if not all, motivations of behavior are emotions. Emotions, like motivations, can be very complex and involve not only a specific feeling, but physical arousal and visible behavior that identify the emotion. For example, think about the last time you were surprised. What were all the things you felt? Or the things you did to show your surprise?

THEORIES OF EMOTION

Different theories have been proposed to explain our emotional experiences. One early theory called the **James-Lange theory** suggests that emotional experience is an interpretation of physiological changes in the body (see Figure 8.2). According to this theory, any stimulus that produces an emotion must first have an effect on the body. For instance, if you are walking alone in the woods and you see a bear, you would probably start perspiring, feel your heart beating faster, and experience dryness of the mouth. These physiological changes would be interpreted as fear.

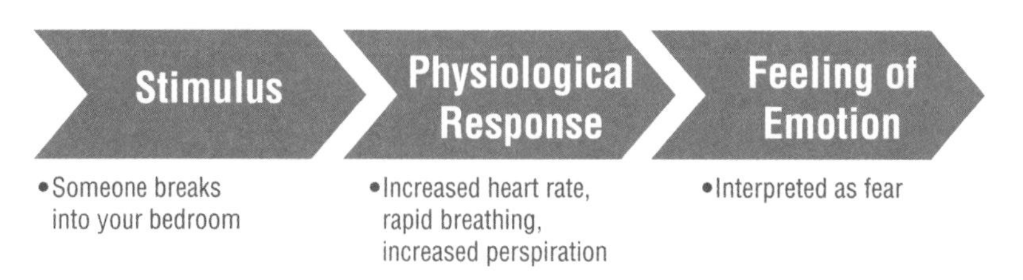

Figure 8.2: James-Lange theory of emotion.

Can you spot any flaws in this theory? Many psychologists have. Isn't the physiological response to many different emotions the same? Doesn't your heart beat faster when you are extremely joyous or angry? This theory does not do well in explaining how the brain differentiates between distinct emotions given that the physiological response to any emotionally arousing stimulus is quite similar. And does an emotional response really require the presence of a physiological response? Information about bodily sensations, like heart rate, is relayed to the brain from the peripheral nervous system. If this theory were correct, then people with spinal cord injuries that cut off sensations to the rest of the body should not feel emotion, which is obviously not the case (Chwalisz, et al., 1988).

Another theory of emotion, known as the **Cannon-Bard theory**, agrees that physiological responses play an important role in emotions, but rejects the idea that physiology alone can explain emotional responses. Instead, the Cannon-Bard theory argues that any event that can produce an emotion triggers both a physiological response and the conscious experience of emotion simultaneously (Cannon, 1929: see Figure 8.3). The two are independent, so neither relies on the other, unlike the James-Lange theory which speculates that the emotion depends on the physiological response.

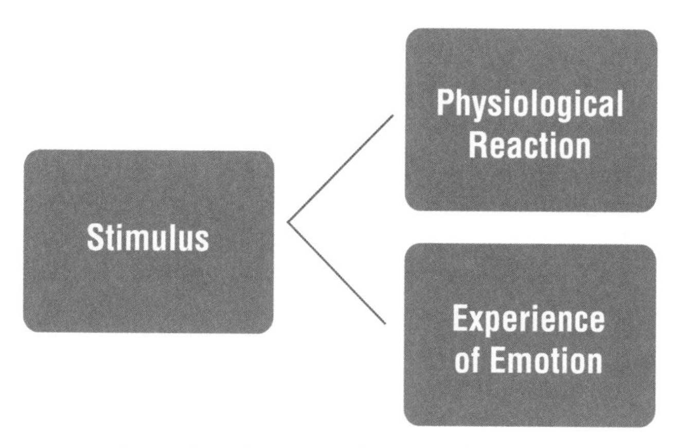

Figure 8.3: Cannon-Bard Theory of emotion.

Cognitive psychologists put their own spin on the interpretation of emotion. One theory called the *two-factor theory* by Schacter and Singer (1962) explains the experience of emotion as a two-factor process. They agreed that physiological reactions play a big role in emotion, which is one part of the process. The other consists of the environmental cues that we interpret to arrive at an emotional response. The cognitive appraisal part of this theory has been criticized by psychologists who believe that emotion and cognition are two separate entities and argue that some emotions are instinctual and do not require thinking to be experienced. Think about the last time you saw road kill or stumbled across a gory movie scene while looking for something to watch on TV. Do you really need to think about what you are seeing in order to feel disgusted? Though this theory certainly could account for many emotional responses, like guilt, which worsens the more you dwell on it; some emotions are, indeed, separate from cognition.

UNIVERSALITY OF EMOTION

There have been many attempts to identify *primary emotions* – that is, emotions that are seen in every culture. One of the largest studies in the field was conducted by Paul Ekman et al. (1987). Ekman included participants from 10 different countries in his research. He believed that emotions are discreet, measurable, and physiologically distinct. His research demonstrated that, indeed, people of many different cultures were able to identify emotions based on facial expressions alone. This led researchers to classify six basic emotions: anger, disgust, fear, happiness, sadness, and surprise. In his study, he found that facial expressions corresponding to these emotions could be identified by people of any culture, even those where they could not have been learned through media.

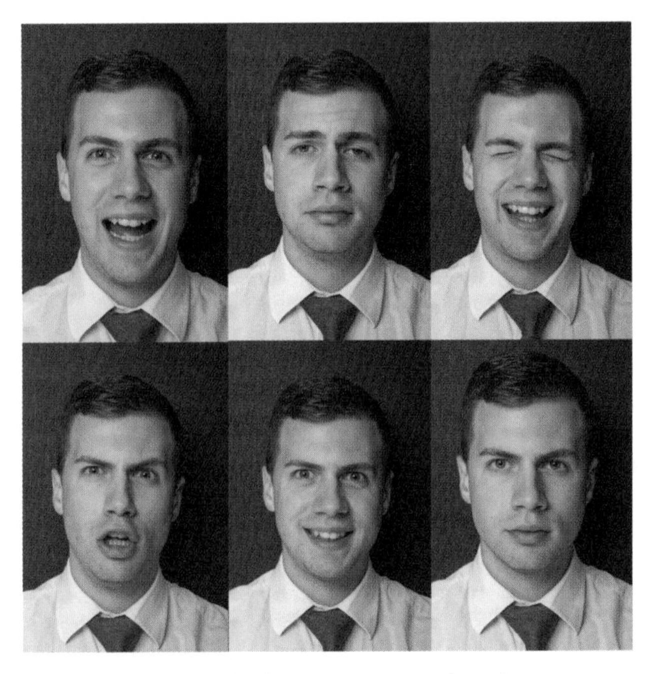

Most people can easily discern an emotion from the expression on someone's face.

Continued research in the area led Ekman to expand the list of basic emotions, to include: amusement, contempt, contentment, embarrassment, excitement, guilt, pride, relief, satisfaction, sensory pleasure, and shame (Ekman, 1999). This line of research was also expanded to measuring nonverbal communication. He found that facial muscular movements associated with the basic emotions, like the muscles involved in smiling or frowning, could be reliably identified empirically.

COMMUNICATING EMOTION

Even though the experience of many emotions can be considered universal, the *expression* of emotion can significantly differ between individuals and from culture to culture. Think about how you communicate emotion. How do you scold your child for not cleaning up after himself? Do you raise your voice? Do you put your arms on your hips or tap your foot? All of these nuances signal your underlying emotion.

Voice quality can communicate a lot of information about how you feel, even in times when you are trying to obscure it. Your voice might get a little louder when you are losing your patience, even if you are trying to keep your cool. A sad voice might crack; a scared voice might sound shaky. Aside from being able to communicate verbally that you are upset, angry, or happy, the tone of your voice can convey the same information.

Yelling can be an obvious sign that someone is upset or angry.

In addition, your body language communicates a whole lot about how you are feeling. Think again about what you do when you are angry. You will notice that a lot of your responses involve nonverbal communication, including gestures, posture, and explicit acts that may convey emotion. For example, when in an uncomfortable situation, people might exhibit defensive body language such as arm crossing, eyebrow raising, or leaning away. Of course, behavior that communicates emotion can be much more obvious, like slamming a door to communicate anger, or giving a long hug to communicate affection.

The way the gentleman on the left has his arms crossed and the way the gentleman on the right is leaning away from him indicate that the two of them might not be enjoying this conversation.

GENDER DIFFERENCES IN EMOTION

Conventional wisdom will tell you that women are more emotional than men. Psychological researchers have attempted to use empirical evidence to address the issue, often finding that emotional responses do differ somewhat between men and women.

Studies have shown that men are more likely to inhibit emotional expression than women, particularly with emotions like sympathy, sadness, empathy, and distress (Brody & Hall, 2000). This finding suggests that perhaps it is not that men experience less emotion than women necessarily, but that they inhibit themselves from expressing emotions that might be considered more feminine and less manly.

Research has also shown that women and men tend to react differently to the same situation (Fischer, et al., 2004). The study, which analyzed differences in six emotions from people in 37 different countries, found that women are more likely to react to events with sadness and fear while men are more likely to report anger in response to the same event. Researchers found that men tend to react more outwardly whereas women react more inwardly, turning anger against themselves.

CULTURAL DIFFERENCES IN EMOTION

The findings of gender differences in emotion are also influenced by culture. Fischer et al. (2004) attribute the fact that women report feeling more powerless emotions, such as sadness and fear, to women's status and gender roles in many countries.

However, cultural differences go far beyond gender. Despite the research by Ekman and colleagues showing that many emotions are inborn and expressed the same way universally, there are many cultural factors that affect the expression of emotion, called **display rules** (Ekman & Friesen, 1975). For example, in many Hispanic and European cultures, it is acceptable (and even expected!) for people to kiss each other on the cheek as a greeting. This practice is not common for many Americans, who might opt instead to wave or shake hands, as is customary in many U. S. states. In Indian culture, people demonstrate a ritualized display called the "tongue bite" used to express embarrassment, a practice which has no significant meaning to people in the U.S. (Haidt et al., 1999). In certain instances, merely the presence of another has been shown to inhibit spontaneous expression of emotion in a variety of situations (Matsumo, 1980). These influences of culture on emotional expression cannot be understated and can be critical in identifying the emotions of people from different cultures.

Two young Buddhist monks meet and salute in a temple in Cambodia.

CHAPTER 8 REVIEW QUESTIONS

1. Which of these are learned from experience or conditioning?

    a. Instincts

    b. Primary drives

    c. Secondary drives

    d. Both A and C

2. Kelly always loved doing her homework. Then her mother started making her allowance dependent on how many hours a day she spent working on her homework, and now she does not enjoy it as much as she used to. Which of these is Kelly demonstrating?

    a. Intrinsic motivation

    b. Extrinsic motivation

    c. Overjustification effect

    d. Self-actualization

3. According to Maslow's hierarchy of needs, the need for love and belonging would arise after satisfying ______________________ and before ______________________.

    a. self-actualization; esteem needs

    b. physiological needs; self-actualization

c. safety needs; physiological needs

d. esteem needs; safety needs

4. ______________________ is an eating disorder which motivates individuals go to extreme lengths to lose weight and feel they are overweight even when they are underweight.

5. According to the ____________________________, emotions are a result of physiological changes in the body.

a. James-Lange theory

b. Cannon-Bard theory

c. Two-factor theory

d. None of these

6. Who was/were the researcher(s) associated with identifying basic emotions present in all cultures?

a. James-Lange

b. Schacter & Singer

c. Cannon-Bard

d. Ekman

7. Which of these is not considered a basic emotion?

    a. Disgust

    b. Anger

    c. Excitement

    d. All of these

8. Cultural norms about when, where, and how one should express emotion are called ______________________________.

9. T/F. Men and women show little difference in how they experience and express emotion.

10. Emotion is often communicated:

    a. Through body language

    b. Even when attempts are made to obscure it

    c. A and B

    d. None of these

CHAPTER 9

DEVELOPMENT THROUGH THE LIFE SPAN

THE AREA OF **developmental psychology** is concerned with the changes humans undergo throughout life. Human development begins prenatally, or before birth, and continues into old age. At every stage of life, there are significant changes in a vast number of physical and psychological processes. Human development has an effect on virtually every topic in psychology including intelligence, personality, cognition, social interactions, and biological processes.

STUDYING DEVELOPMENT

Development is unique in that it is a process that changes over time, so developmental psychologists have special research methods they use to study these changes. Whereas other psychologists can study a variable – like reaction time or cognitive ability – the key variable in developmental psychology is change. Developmental psychologists want to see how different aspects change over time as we age.

One way to test age-related changes is to perform a **longitudinal study**, which follows the same group of people, observing the same variable as they age. For instance, imagine studying mathematical ability over the life span. A longitudinal design would involve selecting a group of participants to study at age 12, then testing them again at age 25, and then again at age 50 and age 75. This would allow you to see how mathematical ability evolves and changes over the lifespan. Since this method uses the same participants, there are no confounding variables introduced from individual differences. However, the method is not without its drawbacks. For one, longitudinal studies can be very long and expensive. Another drawback is participant attrition; that is, the loss of participants over the years as a result of lack of interest, losing touch with researchers, or death. If attrition is very high, the sample size could be reduced to a point where the results are no longer statistically significant.

For these reasons, psychologists sometimes opt for **cross-sectional studies.** This design allows researchers to observe different people of varying ages all at the same time. Using the same variable as an example – mathematical ability – researchers can examine 12 year olds, 25 year olds, 50 year olds, and 75 year olds, simultaneously. This eliminates the problems brought about by participants dropping out several years into the study, and it is much more cost effective. However, it introduces individual differences as well as *cohort* differences, the differences between people born and raised in different periods. To understand cohort differences, imagine you were studying how age relates to the stigmatization of AIDS/HIV patients. You might find that older people tend to stigmatize the disease more, but age alone cannot account for the differences. Wouldn't the perceptions of people born in the 50s and 60s who were around for the discovery of the disease differ somewhat from that of people born in the 1990s and 2000s? This would be considered a cohort effect.

PRENATAL DEVELOPMENT

From the moment of conception until birth, a single cell develops into a baby. Fertilization occurs when a woman's egg is united with a sperm. The fertilized egg, called the *zygote*, contains genetic material from each parent. If you recall from Chapter 2, we receive 23 chromosomes from each parent, meaning we have equal amounts of DNA from each one.

After fertilization, the cell begins dividing rapidly, with each new cell containing the same genetic material as the first. The cells begin to specialize in order to become the organs, skin, muscles, and bones that make up the human body. This developing organism is called an *embryo* until about eight weeks after fertilization, when it becomes a *fetus*. By the end of the embryonic period, the cells of the body have developed their specific functions, at which point the organism begins to grow. The fetal period lasts until birth and is a period of incredible growth. Organs continue to develop during this time until they become functional.

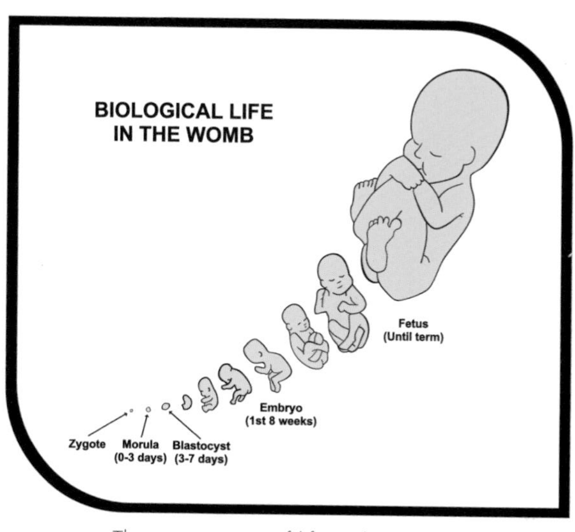

The progression of life in the womb.

During this prenatal period, the child is nourished by the mother through the placenta and umbilical cord, which connect the fetus to the mother's uterine wall. This connection allows the developing baby to receive nutrients and remove waste. This is a **critical period**, in which environmental influence can have major impacts on the baby's development. Substances like drugs, chemicals, or viruses – known collectively as *teratogens* – can be passed on to the baby and have devastating effects on his or her development. These substances can lead to serious, permanent developmental and neurological problems, like **fetal alcohol syndrome (FAS)**, which encompasses the physical and cognitive defects associated with alcohol consumption during pregnancy.

DEVELOPMENT IN INFANCY AND CHILDHOOD

After birth, the child begins another chapter of development as a newborn, or a *neonate*. All newborns are born with an innate set of reflexes that help them survive: rooting, sucking, grasping, swallowing, and stepping. Babies instinctually demonstrate *rooting*, which is a tendency to turn their heads and open their mouths in response to stimulation of the cheek. This reflex is designed to help the baby find the mother's nipple in order to eat. Babies also instinctually suck anything put into their mouths and swallow when they feel stimulation in the backs of their mouths. Together, these reflexes allow newborns to obtain the nutrients they need to grow. Babies also demonstrate the ability to grasp objects with their hands. This tendency underscores the importance of baby-proofing a household. Without knowing whether things are safe to eat or not, children will instinctively grab anything they can get their

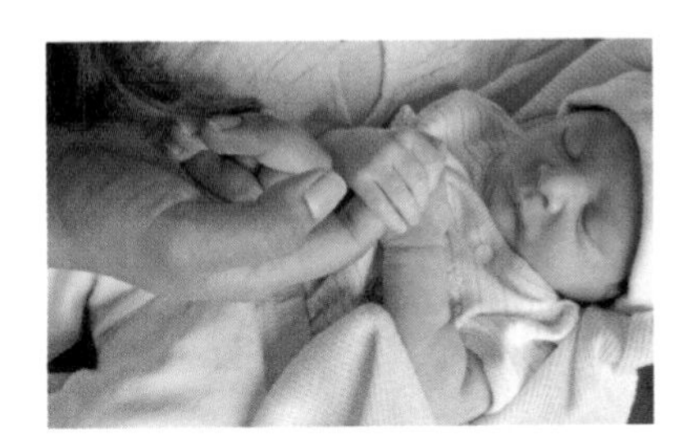

Grasping is one of the innate reflexes babies are born with.

hands on and put it in their mouths. Finally, newborns have a built-in step reflex, which are the stepping motions they make when their feet touch a stable, flat surface. This reflex, a precursor to eventual walking, predisposes the child to put one foot in front of the other to achieve forward motion. At birth, these reflexes are used to test the health of newborn babies, and the absence of these can indicate neurological problems (Majnemer at al., 1992).

Newborns, like their adult counterparts, vary considerably in their reactions to stimulation. This is known as a **temperament**. In the same way as some adults are quick to anger while others are more easy-going, some are shy and some are outgoing, babies have their own innate patterns of behavior. Psychologists have identified three types of temperaments: easy, difficult, and slow to warm up (Thomas & Chess, 1977). Babies that are *difficult* tend to be innately irritable and hard to please, often reacting negatively in new situations. They are naturally more prone to negative emotional reactions and tend to be fussy. These are the types of babies that keep you up all night or cry for the entire duration of a flight. By contrast, babies with *easy* temperaments are cheerful, relaxed, and adaptable. They are easy to please and are not very picky, and they tend to find some enjoyment in novel situations. *Slow to warm up* children can be fussy and withdrawn in new situations and around new people but with repeated exposure to them, they become more positive. They can be less active than others, as though more reserved. Throughout the life span, these temperaments are shaped by the child's environment to become full-blown personalities.

At birth, newborns have nearly fully developed senses. The sense of touch is the best developed, followed by the sense of smell. Taste is also fully developed and infants show a preference for sweet and salty foods, and a dislike for sour and bitter tastes as evidenced by the grimaces they make while eating (Ganchrow, et al., 1983). Hearing and sight take a little longer to develop fully, though they are functional at birth. For the first few months of life, vision is fuzzy and babies tend to have poor color vision (Adams, 1987). However, newborns demonstrate visual preferences from birth, determined by the time they spend looking at certain stimuli, especially human faces (Fantz, 1961).

COGNITIVE DEVELOPMENT

One of the most well-known developmental psychologists is Jean Piaget (1896-1980), who advanced a comprehensive theory of cognitive development. He believed that children learn by creating concepts, called **schemas**, as they experience new situations. For instance, if an infant saw an apple for the first time, she would create a schema for what an apple looks like. Through the process of *assimilation*, she would incorporate new knowledge into existing schemas, which is why a child might see an orange and call it an apple. The process of *accommodation* involves changing existing concepts. So if a parent corrects the child, the child would accommodate her existing schema of an apple to exclude similar items like oranges. Using these processes, children are able to form increasingly complex concepts that help them understand the world.

According to Piaget, as children grow, their thinking evolves and passes through four distinct stages (Piaget, 1952, 1983).

- Sensorimotor Stage

This is the first stage in Piaget's theory and it lasts from birth until about two years of age. In this stage, newborns are exploring the world for the first time, using their sensory abilities and physical contact. Their understanding of their surroundings is largely limited to what they can see. They do not think about concepts or objects that are not presently visible. One major cognitive milestone of this stage is the development of **object permanence**. Before reaching this milestone, children seem to forget about objects, like toys, that are removed from sight. After the sense of object permanence has developed, children will search for hidden objects, indicating that they are able to think about objects that are not in their presence.

- Preoperational Stage

During the second stage of cognitive development, the preoperational stage, their ability to form mental representations of objects improves. This stage lasts from age 2 to about age 7, encompassing the preschool and kindergarten years. During this time, children no longer rely as heavily on sensory and motor abilities to explore the world; instead, they rely more on their imaginations. They are able to use representative thought to play pretend, allowing them to see blankets and pillows as a fortress, and to make snacks and serve tea to their dolls using only gestures.

Imagination becomes very important in the preoperational stage of development.

Though their capabilities are vastly improved, they still lack several of the skills that are central to adult thinking, like logic and reasoning. Children are also limited by **egocentrism**, the false belief that everyone knows, thinks, and feels the same way they do. This is why you might see a child cover their own eyes in a game of hide-and-seek, falsely believing that if they cannot see, that means others do not see them.

- Concrete Operational Stage

The third stage of cognitive development is called the concrete operational stage, and it typically lasts from about age 7 until age 11. This is an important stage in which children begin to develop some key abilities of cognition, including the ability to *conserve*. Before age 7, children tend to be driven by the way things look, ignoring other relevant information. One of Piaget's experiments showed this deficiency in thought by presenting children two identical glasses, filled to the same capacity with liquid. Children shown the glasses accurately state that both have the same amount of liquid. However, when Piaget emptied out one of the glasses into a taller, thinner glass – making the level of liquid appear higher – they tend to believe that the taller glass has more liquid. For children at the preoperational stage, if it looks like more, it is more. If you have children of your own, you have probably had to defuse many arguments caused by one child believing that the other got a larger portion of something simply because his sibling's plate looks like it has more. By the end of the concrete operational stage, children stop making this error because they come to understand the principles of *conservation*; the amount of liquid stays the same regardless of the shape and size of the container it is poured into.

This girl is simulating a test of conservation. Her perception of the amount of liquid in each glass is changed simply by the shape of the glass. The tall glass looks like it holds more because it is thinner, but it holds the same amount of liquid as the short glass.

During this stage, children also begin to form more complex concepts, allowing for higher-order classifications using the basic principles of assimilation and accommodation. For example, a young child may be able to identify a variety of different fruits including apples, oranges, and bananas, without being able to group them all mentally into the higher-order category of fruits. As thinking develops during the concrete operational stage, children are able to understand increasingly complex concepts. Despite the development of these important skills, they are still limited in certain aspects of logic and reasoning that are not developed until the fourth and final stage of development.

- Formal Operational Stage

At about age 12, until adulthood, adolescents begin to use logic and reasoning to solve problems, including entirely hypothetical problems. They are able to think about different possibilities and even some impossibilities, like what the world would be like if men gave birth instead of women. With this developmental landmark, people come to a point where they can make educated deductions based on limited information. Piaget did not believe everyone would be capable of thinking at this level, theorizing that some adults use more practical, concrete solutions to problem solving than others. One study demonstrated that, indeed, only about half of adults function at the formal operational level (Sutherland, 1992).

Influential as it has been, Piaget's theory is not without its critics. Many believe that the stages are not necessarily reached in the order or time frame that Piaget suggests, arguing that at older ages, children seem to reach several of these cognitive milestones much sooner than Piaget suggested (Gopnik, 1996). Nonetheless, his theory is one of the most complete and widely held theories of cognitive development.

SOCIAL DEVELOPMENT

Humans are social creatures and interacting with others is a process that begins at birth and lasts throughout the life span. We are surrounded by other people our entire lives, and during this time, we develop a variety of important relationships that can affect subsequent social relations.

The first significant relationship people have is with their caregiver, with whom they form an **attachment**, or an emotional bond. This may be a mother, or father, or someone else entirely. It is the person that the newborn perceives as his caregiver. This bond can be seen as early as 6 months, and tends to intensify over the next couple of years (Bowlby, 1969, 1973, 1980). Children will cling to the caregivers and react positively to their appearance. By contrast, babies will also begin to exhibit **stranger anxiety** when they are approached by an unfamiliar person; this anxiety is characterized by fearful responses.

Psychologists believe that children differ in their levels of attachment to their caregivers, with some children demonstrating more close attachment than others. In order to differentiate between the types, a test was designed called the *strange situation procedure*, in which a mother leaves her child alone in a playroom and a stranger enters and attempts to play with the child until the mother returns (Ainsworth & Bell, 1970). The children in the study demonstrated four types of attachment: secure, avoidant, ambivalent/anxious, and disorganized (See Table 9.1). In addition to typical child behavior differing for each attachment type, researchers found that the corresponding caregiver characteristics also had significant differences.

Attachment Type	Child Behavior	Caregiver Behavior
Secure	• Feels safe in exploring environment • Distressed at caregiver's departure • Comforted at caregiver's return	• Responds to child's needs • Reacts to child's requests
Avoidant	• Shows no distress when caregiver departs • Shows little response when caregiver returns • Ignores or turns away • Treats stranger the same as caregiver	• Has little or no response to distressed child • Encourages independence • Discourages crying
Ambivalent / Anxious	• Clings to caregiver • Distressed by separation • Ambivalent and/or angry upon return • Resists contact even when they seek it out	• Responses to child are inconsistent • Responds to increased attachment from child
Disorganized	• Freezes or rocks • Lacks coherent type of attachment	• Abusive toward the child • Frightened or frightening behavior

Table 9.1: Attachment styles and patterns of child and caregiver behavior.

Securely attached children adjust well to the strange situation procedure. They are happy with the parent present, feeling secure enough to explore their surroundings. When the parent leaves, they are distressed, but return to a happy mood when the parents return. They are then able to continue exploring the playroom contently, using the caregiver as a secure base. This type of attachment develops through consistent caregiver attention to the needs of the child. The children are soothed and comforted by their caregiver's presence allowing them to feel safe going out of their comfort zones. Securely attached children trust that if anything were to go wrong in their curious exploration, their caregivers would save them from potential harm.

Children with avoidant attachment styles seem unconcerned or disinterested in both the caregiver and the stranger. They appear to treat the stranger the same way they treat the caregiver, showing very little response and even turning away or ignoring them. The caregivers with avoidant infants tended to be unresponsive and cold, in contrast to caregivers of secure infants, who tended to be more loving, warm, and sensitive to their needs. This attachment style suggests that the child is aloof and disinterested, in kind with the behavior of their caregiver.

Ambivalent/anxious infants tended to have mixed feelings about their caregiver, while demonstrating clinging behaviors and unwillingness to explore the room. Like the securely attached children, these children appeared to be distressed when left alone without the caregiver, but, in contrast, they were very difficult to soothe when the mother returned, exhibiting ambivalence in their response – as though torn between being angry and being clingy. Though they demanded to be picked up by the caregiver, they pushed them away or kicked them upon their return. Mothers of ambivalent/anxious infants tended to be responsive but inconsistent and insensitive to the baby's actions. This inconsistency is reflected in the child's emotional reaction.

Finally, children with a disorganized attachment style appeared unable to decide how to react to the caregiver's leaving and subsequent return. The children would approach the caregiver but sometimes with their eyes turned away, as if afraid to make eye contact. The mothers of babies with disorganized attachment were found to be abusive or neglectful when interacting with their children. This interaction leaves the child unsure of how to feel about the caregiver; the caregiver is the only person the child can rely on to save him from threatening situations and at the same time, these caregivers are themselves frightening or threatening.

These differences in attachment have been shown to have an effect on adult relationships. According to developmental research, children that have secure attachment to their caregivers tend to have more successful peer relationships than children who exhibited other attachment types as a child (Pastor, 1981). Our adult romantic relationships also tend to closely mirror these early caregiver relationships (Hazan & Shaver, 1987). That is, we seek out similarities in adult relationships to those that we had at an early age. People who had a cold and distant father report having adult relationships with partners who are similarly cold and distant. By contrast, people who perceived their mothers as respectful and accepting, would more frequently report having relationships with accepting and respectful partners.

ERIKSON'S STAGES OF PSYCHOSOCIAL DEVELOPMENT

One theory of psychosocial development that encompasses the entire lifespan was proposed by Erik Erikson, who believed that as we age, we progress through different stages of psychosocial development (Erikson, 1959). He divided up the life span into eight major phases and he believed that as we pass through each one, we experience an emotional crisis that must be successfully resolved for healthy development (See Table 9.2). Unsuccessful resolutions of each stage lead to unhealthy development.

Stage	Age	Crisis
Trust versus Mistrust	**Infant** Birth to 1 year	Learning to trust or mistrust the world based on whether their needs are met
Autonomy versus Shame and Doubt	**Toddler** 1 to 3 years	Realizing one is independent and can direct their own actions
Initiative versus Guilt	**Preschooler** 3 to 5 years	Taking responsibilty and feeling capable of initiative
Industry versus Inferiority	**Elementary School Age** 5 to 12 years	Learning new skills and cooperation with others
Identity versus Role Confusion	**Adolescence** 13 years to early 20s	Defining who you are and what you want to be: occupation, beliefs and attitudes
Intimacy versus Isolation	**Early Adulthood** 20s and 30s	Satisfying need for intimate relationships
Generativity versus Stagnation	**Middle Adulthood** 40s and 50s	Being creative, productive and finding meaning in life
Ego Integrity versus Despair	**Late Adulthood** Late 60s and beyond	Attaining wisdom and viewing life as satisfying and worth living

Table 9.2: Erikson's Stages of Psychosocial Development.

The first four stages of development according to Erikson, occur during infancy and childhood, and successful or unsuccessful completion of each crisis has different implications for personality in adulthood. For example, during the first stage of life, depending on our relationship with our caregiver, we either learn to *trust or mistrust* others. If our needs are largely met by our caregiver, we learn to be trusting and expect life to be good. When our needs are not met and our caregiver ignores or abuses us, we learn to distrust our surroundings.

At the second stage of development, *autonomy versus shame and doubt*, the child aims to achieve a level of control of his life and feel independent. Successful completion of this stage leads children to feel confident and autonomous, allowing them to securely make choices as they get older. On the other hand, those who are not able to develop a solid sense of control tend to feel self-doubt and inadequacy. After the resolution of this stage, children continue attempting to exert control over their environment, this time through social relationships in the *initiative versus guilt* stage. For instance, a child at this stage may influence other preschoolers to build a giant sandcastle, which makes him feel capable of taking initiative and directing others. Children who are not able to plan and accomplish tasks or whose parents are dismissive of their efforts may feel embarrassed to have taken the initiative, resulting in shame and self-doubt.

These desires to succeed and feel pride in their accomplishments continue progressing in the fourth stage of development: *industry versus inferiority*. When children are around elementary school age, they are very concerned with receiving praise for their hard work. That is why many children bring home their drawings and assignments to show off to mom and dad. When children are commended for their efforts, they feel industrious and productive, allowing them to continue seeking success. When their efforts are disregarded or dismissed, children begin to develop a sense of inferiority – that nothing they do will ever be good enough.

As we progress in our discussion of development through adulthood, we will discuss Erikson's remaining psychosocial stages and the implication of the conflicts that arise at each one.

ADOLESCENCE

The period of adolescence brings about many important changes, including important physical changes. During this period, adolescents grow to their adult height and they experience *puberty*, the onset of sexual maturation. In females, this is marked by the start of *menstruation*, while males develop mature sperm cells and enlarged testes and penises. Sexual maturation also brings about the development of secondary sexual characteristics like pubic hair and breast development in girls, and a deepening voice and facial hair in boys.

The capacity to reproduce brings about many issues for teenagers like teen pregnancy. Research shows that nearly half of all teenagers are sexually active (Brenner at al., 2002). Teen birth rates have declined in the U.S. by one-third since the early 1990s. However, the U.S. still has the highest rate of teen births in developed countries, with 42 per 1,000 girls, nearly double that of the UK, which ranks second (Martin, et al., 2010). This underscores the importance of sex education and family planning.

SOCIAL DEVELOPMENT

According to Erikson, the time of adolescence is marked by the crisis of *identity versus role confusion*. Teenagers must establish their values, beliefs, and goals in order to form a healthy sense of self. However, this time can be a turbulent one. Many teenagers feel pressure to conform to their peers in order to be liked and can be devastated when they do not fit in. Many adolescents tend to form small groups with their peers, called cliques. Whereas some friend groups encourage independent thinking that is necessary in order to form a personal identity, other relationships may have the opposite effect and stifle the person's ability to express himself openly. Many teenagers conform to the values and beliefs of their peers, simply to avoid being excluded. Adolescents also begin dating during this time, and exploring intimacy and sexuality.

For many adolescents, self-esteem can decline in part because of dissatisfaction with appearance (Altabe & Thompson, 1994). Low self-esteem can also be linked to social isolation and bullying, an increasing problem in the United States. Teen bullying can involve direct attacks like violence, intimidation, teasing and taunting, name-calling, as well as more subtle activities like spreading rumors (Nansel, et al., 2001). These are just some of the factors that contribute to the disproportionately large rates of depression and suicide among adolescents. Suicide is the third leading cause of death among adolescents (Mental Health America, 2013).

Rejection can lead to depression and lower self-esteem for many adolescents who want to feel like they belong.

In some cases, severe neglect, rejection and abandonment lead to gun violence, as seen in cases like the shootings in Columbine, Virginia Tech, Sandy Hook Elementary School, and the Colorado movie theater. When incidents like these occur, people wonder what might cause someone to commit such an atrocity. It may be brought on by anger toward peers associated with social isolation. The draw of infamy could also be a motivating factor. Many cite untreated mental health issues related to a lack of resources. However, research has been unable to identify psychological variables that could predict aggressive behavior. Some predicted variables like low self-esteem do not correlate with propensity to carry out aggressive behaviors (Bushman & Baumeister, 1998). Research has, however, linked availability and accessibility of guns to aggression, because the mere presence of guns actually increases

School shootings are becoming more and more commonplace in our society. Some people point to the availability of guns, while others blame lack of access to psychological help.

levels of testosterone and propensity to aggress (Klinesmith, Kasser, & McAndrew, 2006). In addition, it has been correlated with lack of adult supervision, lack of support, and lack of emotional attachments (Garbarino, 1999).

MORAL DEVELOPMENT

One major psychological advance in adolescence is the deepened understanding of right and wrong. According to one developmental psychologist, our understanding of morality passes through three distinct stages as we age. Kohlberg (1973) believed that young children see morality at a *preconventional* level, with the consequences of behavior determining their ideas of right and wrong. A child in the preconventional stage might not see stealing as wrong if he steals a toy from his sibling and does not get caught, because the behavior brought about no negative consequences.

Older children and adolescents progress to *conventional* morality, where they conform to social norms about right and wrong. Moral decisions are motivated by maintaining social order and meeting interpersonal obligations. For example, established laws should be followed because that is what society believes is right. According to Kohlberg, many adults maintain a conventional level of morality.

Some adults progress to *postconventional* morality, where moral decisions are driven by personal principles of right and wrong, which may run counter to societal norms. To those with postconventional moral guidelines, actions are justified if they are for the greater good. Many civil rights activists, like Martin Luther King, Jr., would be considered to have reached this level of morality, because he took a stance for human rights and equality even at a time when it was not the societal norm.

ADULTHOOD

The challenges of adulthood and old age are not as predictable as those of childhood and adolescence. However, according to many psychologists, including Erikson, there are some experiences that all adults face at some point in their lives. Continuing with his psychosocial stages theory, Erikson believed that certain conflicts arise that must be resolved as we grow old.

YOUNG ADULTHOOD

After adolescence, many young adults seek out long-term romantic partners. According to Erikson, this behavior aims to resolve the major challenge of the twenties and thirties, *intimacy versus isolation*. People that succeed learn how to form and maintain satisfying intimate relationships. Those who do not feel isolated and lonely. Establishing intimacy can be more difficult for people that have unsuccessfully resolved previous stages of life (Erikson, 1968). For example, a woman who has a poorly established identity – or sense of self – may have more trouble forming commitment.

For many, a happy, fulfilling romantic relationship ends in marriage, though there has been a decline in the number of adults getting married from 1970 to 2010. People are also trending toward marrying later in life. The median age for first time marriages is 28.3 for men and 25.8 for women (Wilcox & Marquardt, 2011). Many couples opt to cohabitate outside of marriage, even raising children together.

MIDDLE ADULTHOOD

Aside from family and relationships, many adults seek out fulfilling and meaningful careers. This reflects our resolution of the seventh psychosocial stage of life: *generativity versus stagnation*. According to Erikson, we seek to resolve the middle adulthood stage of life with productive, creative endeavors for the benefit of ourselves, our families, and future generations. For example, for some, saving up to buy a home can be a source of fulfillment and pride. For others, getting a coveted position in their careers can help them succeed in this stage.

Those who fail to do these things may feel like they have done nothing worthwhile in their lives or for their children and future

It is never too late to pick up a new hobby.

generations. This feeling of stagnation can lead to a **midlife crisis**, during which people seek out a major change to their careers, lifestyles, or relationships, if they are feeling stuck in a rut in their current situation. It is not uncommon for adults to return to school, pick up a hobby, or seek out more fulfilling relationships in hopes of adding more meaning to their lives. This type of self-evaluation at this stage gives some adults an opportunity to turn things around while there is still time to do so – to do things they can be proud of later in life.

Physically, middle adulthood is a time when our reproductive organs start functioning more inconsistently. Women go through **menopause**, the cessation of the menstrual cycle and ovulation. Males also experience a drop in several hormones, like testosterone, which lowers their reproductive abilities. This is the body's natural way of signaling that we are too old to reproduce. This, by no means, implies that life is over. As we will discuss below, there is still a lot of development left in older adults.

LATE ADULTHOOD

Late adulthood is a time when many look back on their lives and decide whether they feel fulfilled overall and whether they believed their lives were worthwhile. This is a period that Erikson calls *ego integrity versus despair*. Those who reach wisdom and tranquility, believing they are fulfilled, will live happily and not fear death. They are able to enjoy the fruits of their labor once they reach retirement age and watch their children and grandchildren grow old. By contrast, those that do not successfully resolve the crisis of this stage may feel like their lives are empty, void of meaning, and they will fear death. As with other psychosocial stages, the resolution of one has an effect on subsequent stages. So someone who at midlife felt stagnant and did not take the opportunity to change his own course, would probably reach this stage and feel a lot of despair.

Physically, people undergo more severe changes in this stage than any other stage of adulthood. Skin begins to wrinkle, hair turns gray or begins to fall out, and senses like hearing and vision may decline. Height also begins to decrease, with people losing about half an inch of height every 10 years after age 40.

COGNITION IN ADULTHOOD

Overall, intellectual abilities do not decline with age. However, speed of processing and memory do decline and tend to be the most noticeable changes in middle age and late adulthood. Compared to young people, adults bring a wealth of knowledge and life experience to problems. They are able to think more freely than young adults, who tend to have more literal and formal thinking, and certain abilities such as vocabulary and verbal memory actually improve into the sixties.

Keeping your brain active by solving Sudoku puzzles or crosswords can help you maintain higher mental functioning well into old age.

In addition, people who exercise their mental abilities with exercises like crossword puzzles maintain higher mental function in old age. Research has shown that mental activity, like reading, taking classes, going to plays, and participating in physical activities, reduces the likelihood of developing disorders such as Alzheimer's disease (Ball et al., 2002). **Alzheimer's disease** causes changes to the brain resulting in a dramatic loss of cognitive abilities. It usually begins with minor memory loss, like the inability to recall names or words or misplacing items around the home. As it progresses, the changes become more dramatic and sufferers can go through long periods not recognizing their families or being able to find their way home. Eventually, they may lose the ability to handle the activities of daily life.

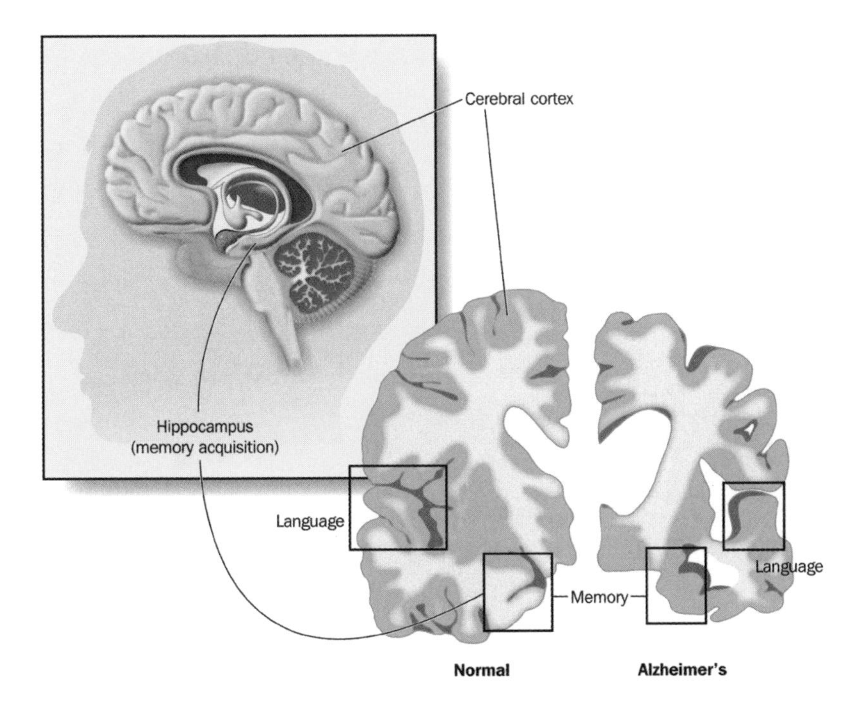

Many parts of the of the brain are affected in people with Alzheimer's including the area of the brain involved in memory and language, which leads to the cognitive deficits caused by the disease.

FACING DEATH

Death can be a difficult idea to cope with, though surprisingly, it is a greater concern for people in middle adulthood than in later adulthood (Bengston et al., 1977). Consistent with Erikson's theory, those who feel like they have achieved their goals in life are less likely to fear death (Neimeyer & Chapman, 1980/1981).

Nonetheless, facing the end of life can be a difficult experience. Based on a large-scale study of dying people of all ages, Kubler-Ross (1969) identified five distinct stages people pass through in reacting to their own impending death. First, people experience *denial*, refusing to believe their fate. In the *anger* stage, people are angry because they are unable to change things, and they are resentful of people who are still healthy. This anger can sometimes be directed at family members or medical staff, leading them to lash out, sometimes accusing others of trying to kill them.

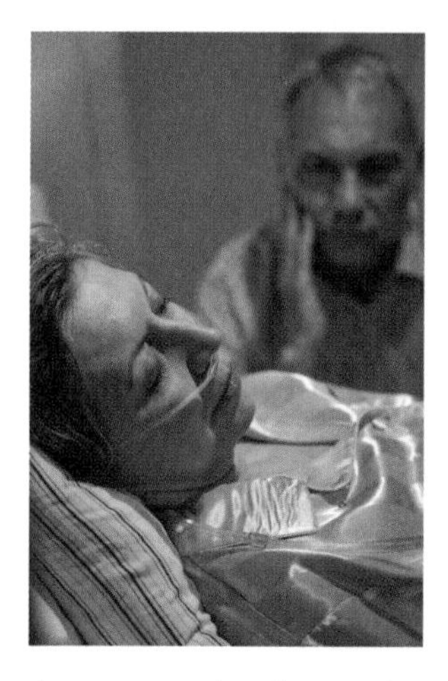

Accepting death can be difficult for anyone involved.

The next stage is *bargaining*, in which people try to make a deal to stay alive, sometimes with doctors or with a higher power. For instance, they may ask God to grant them another few years, in exchange for charity and goodwill. When this fails, people experience *depression*. During this time, people lament their losses including loss of freedom, family, and the inability to correct their mistakes in life. Once they reach this point in life where there is nothing they can do to change the course of their lives, they experience many regrets. Finally, there is *acceptance*, at which point, people understand that death is inevitable and accept it.

Not all people go through all the stages, either because of lack of time, or because of individual differences. Some do not experience these in the order Kubler-Ross suggests, and many psychologists believe that the process is more unique and unpredictable due to factors like life history, personality, and the course of a terminal condition (Kastenbaum & Costa, 1977). Despite these criticisms, Kubler-Ross was the first to investigate a topic that many researchers avoid, making the experience of death a little bit more understandable.

CHAPTER 9 REVIEW QUESTIONS

1. The area of ______________________________ is concerned with the changes we undergo throughout life.

2. Dr. Duenas is trying to find out how visual acuity changes over the lifespan. In her study, groups of 20 year olds, 40 year olds, and 60 year olds perform visual tasks and their performances are compared. What kind of developmental study is this?

    a. Longitudinal study

    b. Cross sectional study

    c. None of these; this is not a developmental study

    d. It is a combination of both a and b.

3. Which of these is not a newborn reflex?

    a. Rooting

    b. Stepping

    c. Spitting up

    d. Swallowing

4. A child that cannot yet understand that when a glass of milk is poured into a differently shaped glass, the amount of milk does not change is probably in the ______________________ ______________________ stage of cognitive development.

a. Concrete operational

b. Sensory-motor

c. Preoperational

d. A or B

e. B or C

5. Match the attachment pattern to child behavior in the strange situation:

a. Secure	_____ Treats strangers the same as caregiver
b. Avoidant	_____ Freezes or rocks
c. Ambivalent/anxious	_____ Comforted when caregiver returns
d. Disorganized	_____ Angry when caregiver returns

6. At which stage of Erikson's psychosocial development does a person define whom she is and what she wants to be?

    a. Trust versus mistrust

    b. Ego integrity versus despair

    c. Identity versus role confusion

    d. Generativity versus stagnation

7. Beth does not cross red lights because it is against the law. What level of morality is most probable for her?

a. Conventional

b. Postconventional

c. Preconventional

d. Quasiconventional

8. T/F. Cognitive abilities decline with age.

9. ____________________ causes changes to the brain resulting in dramatic loss of cognitive abilities.

10. According to Kubler-Ross, we go through five stages when facing own impending death. Which stage involves refusing to accept that death is imminent?

    a. Anger

    b. Acceptance

    c. Depression

    d. Denial

CHAPTER 10

PERSONALITY

HOW WOULD YOU DESCRIBE your personality? What words would you use? Are you outgoing? Friendly? Talkative? Shy? While these are all examples of personality, they do not exactly represent the concept of personality itself; they represent specific variations of personality. **Personality**, itself, is the way individuals tend to think, act, and feel throughout life that develops as they age and tends to be resistant to change. Most people that are stubborn or shy cannot simply stop being that way from one day to the next. Those patterns of behavior tend to be very pervasive across situations.

The descriptions you probably used to describe yourself are known as **personality traits**, specific ways in which people can differ from one another. One's personality, as a whole, might be considered a collection of traits. If you are shy, that is certainly not the only personality trait you possess. You may also be kind-hearted, helpful, curious, or optimistic. In addition you may have more or less any of any one trait. You may be extremely shy, or only a bit shy, or only shy in certain situations. The unique combination of different traits makes you who you are.

So how is it that people become a certain way or another? What explains personality and how does it develop? This is a question that psychologists have had a hard time answering because there is so much variation in personality from person to person that it makes it a difficult construct to measure scientifically. Different perspectives have different approaches to the study of personality:

- The *psychodynamic perspective* focuses on how the unconscious drives the development of personality.
- The *behavioral and social cognitive perspectives* identify the ways in which the environment shapes behavior and how a person's own cognitions and interpretations of his behavior shape personality.
- The *humanistic perspective* focuses on our conscious choices and experiences and how they shape us.
- Finally, the *trait perspective* aims to simply describe different characteristics of personality, without necessarily explaining their origin.

PSYCHODYNAMIC PERSPECTIVE

As summed up above, Sigmund Freud developed a psychodynamic theory of personality, referred to as the **psychoanalytic theory**, which presumes that our behavior is determined by unconscious factors of which we are unaware. He developed a psychotherapy technique called **psychoanalysis** in tandem with his theory, which seeks to uncover and resolve unconscious conflicts. Without our awareness, our instincts, drives, and fears underlie our behavior.

Sigmund Freud, 1856-1939.

FREUD'S PERSONALITY STRUCTURE

Freud theorized that the mind was divided into several realms: some that are within our awareness and some that are not. In the *conscious mind*, we are fully aware of our current thoughts and our experiences. Many psychologists of different perspectives would agree with this part of his theory. The second realm of the mind is the *preconscious mind*, which represents all the information that is just outside of awareness but that can be easily brought forth into awareness. Memories that are not in your immediate awareness, like the plot of a movie you watched last weekend – but that you could recall if you were asked to – would be considered preconscious.

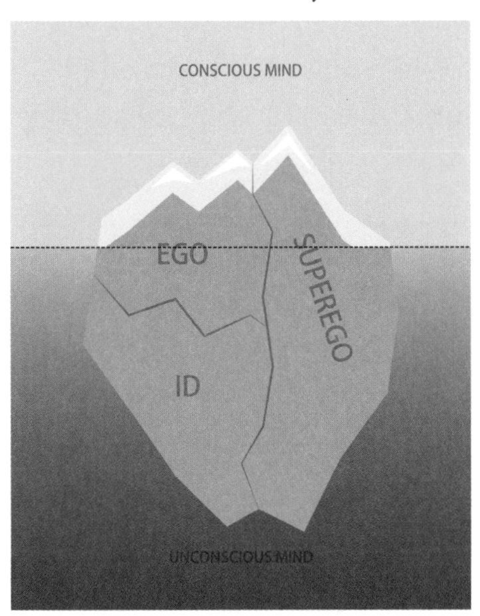

Freud's iceberg model of personality.

Finally, there is the *unconscious mind*, which is what truly separates psychodynamic psychology from other perspectives. The information in the unconscious mind is kept hidden from oneself and emerges only in dreams and behavior that is driven by these hidden motives. To Freud, this was the most important contributing factor in human behavior and personality.

Freud also believed that personality itself was divided into three separate parts that interact with each other: the id, the ego, and the superego. Each of these parts lies at a different level of awareness or consciousness.

The **id** would be considered the primitive part of personality and is the only one present in infants. The id is completely unconscious and seeks to satisfy primary drives such as hunger, thirst, and pleasure. Like infants that are demanding, illogical, impulsive, and fussy, the id does not care how its needs are met as long as they are. This is what Freud called the **pleasure principle**: the id seeks immediate satisfaction regardless of the cost or consequence.

Naturally, behaving this way can be reckless and dangerous. The id needs another part of personality to anchor it to reality: the ego. The **ego** is the part of the personality that is logical, rational, and responsible for interacting with reality. Whereas the id has no concept of obstacles and constraints, the ego does because it operates on the reality principle. Using the **reality principle,** the ego attempts to satisfy the demands of the id in a way that is realistic and that minimizes negative consequences.

Imagine, for example, that you are interested in getting the latest, largest flat screen TV on the market. The id's need for satisfaction would probably ignore cost – the most obvious obstacle to satisfying that need. Of course, you could obtain the TV by stealing it or maxing out your credit card, but both of those options have major negative consequences. The ego, operating on the reality principle, would probably find a solution to this problem that prevents those consequences while still satisfying the needs of the id. For example, you might save up – even if it takes a few weeks or months – in order to be able to afford the TV, and satisfy the id.

The ego might not necessarily lead us to make the most moral decisions, as long as they are logical. For example, imagine a teenager coming home after soccer practice wanting to snack while his mom is preparing dinner. The ego might deny the teen the snack, but only while the mother is looking, knowing that the negative consequence is that she would get mad and scold him. However, if the mother leaves the room and the consequence can be avoided, there is no reason not to indulge. In these types of situations, a third part of personality is involved in our actions: the superego. The **superego** is the part of personality that functions as a moral center or as the conscience. Think about the superego as the voice inside your head that makes you feel guilty when you do not do the right thing – when you cheat, steal, or lie. The superego forms when children are a little older and understand the difference between right and wrong. So even if, realistically, the teen could probably sneak a bite behind his mother's back, the superego might prevent that behavior to avoid feeling bad about the behavior later.

When the desires of the id become overwhelming, the ego and the superego work to control these unconscious desires.

Together these three metaphorical structures work to influence behavior. Because they each pull a person in different directions, when one gets its way but not the other, it can cause a great deal of tension. To relieve this tension, people use defense mechanisms to reduce the stress that the interplay between the id, ego, and superego causes.

PERSONALITY DEVELOPMENT ACCORDING TO FREUD

Now that we know how the psychoanalytic personality is structured, let's discuss how it actually forms. If you recall Erikson's theory from the previous chapter, you can probably easily imagine how certain personality traits can arise from the resolution of each of the psychosocial stages. For instance, an infant who did not trust her caregiver growing up would be more likely to grow up to be the kind of person that is less trusting and more suspicious of others.

In a similar way, Freud believed personality developed very early in stages of development all children and adolescents pass through, which he called **psychosexual stages**. At each stage, children focus their sexual energy on specific erogenous zones, areas that produce pleasurable feelings, and the resolution of each one results in different personality characteristics (Freud, 1954). When there is conflict at any of the stages, it can result in a *fixation*, which leads to the development of personality traits and behavior associated with that particular stage.

1. The first stage is the **oral stage**, which lasts from birth until about 18 months of age. During this stage, the mouth is the erogenous zone and children relieve sexual tension by putting things into their mouths, sucking, and swallowing, as well as biting and chewing when their teeth have grown in. Weaning, as the mother stops breast feeding, is the most important experience during this stage. When a child is weaned from his mother's breast, he can experience conflict. A child that successfully passes through this stage gains a sense of independence. A child that does not may develop dependent and immature behaviors. A child fixated at this stage may also develop oral behaviors in adulthood, like nail biting, smoking, or overeating, that provide oral stimulation. When oral needs are denied at this stage, the personality can become hostile, aggressive, and pessimistic.

2. At the second stage, the **anal stage**, which lasts from 18 months to 3 years, the anus is the primary source of pleasure. During this time, children are toilet training, which becomes the main conflict-causing experience. The way in which they resolve the conflict leads to the development of different patterns of behaviors. Children must balance the desires of the id and ego, with the id demanding gratification by eliminating waste immediately, and the ego preventing this so that it is done cleanly and properly. Children might rebel by refusing to go to the toilet altogether, leading to *anal retentive* adult personalities, which are orderly, stingy, and neat. Others might develop an *anal expulsive* personality, which begins when children defecate purposefully; as adults, they become sloppy, unorganized and messy. Successful resolution would result in the child having self-control as an adult.

Freud's theory of psychosexual development presumes that children obtain pleasure from defecating during the anal stage.

3. The **phallic stage**, lasting from 3 to 6 years of age, is marked by curiosity and interest in the genitals. Children become aware of the differences in their bodies and those of members of the opposite sex. During this stage, children develop a strong attachment to the opposite sex parent and become jealous of the same sex parent. In boys, this is called the **Oedipus complex**, a strong jealousy of their fathers because of their sexual attraction to their mothers. The name comes from a story in Greek mythology in which a character killed his father and married his mother. Freud also believed that during this

stage, girls realize that they have different genitalia than their male counterparts and develop penis envy. Fixation at this stage can lead to promiscuity and vanity in adulthood.

4. The next stage is the **latency stage**, at which point children lose interest in sexual behavior altogether, and they play primarily with members of the same gender. You'll recognize children in this stage when girls begin to think that boys are yucky and boys begin to think that girls have "cooties." This stage lasts from about age 6 until puberty. The habits and traits learned during the previous four stages become more firmly established. This is a stage that influences our ability to get along with others as adults, as sexual energy is directed toward activities that are socially acceptable like school, hobbies, and forming friendships with peers.

5. When children hit puberty, they enter the last psychosexual stage, the **genital stage**. At this stage, repressed sexual feelings emerge once again, and they are directed toward their peers. Adolescents and adults are focused on having a sexual relationship with a partner. This can give people an opportunity to resolve any unresolved conflicts from the previous psychosexual stages. The difference is that sexuality now involves other people. Ensuing difficulties at this stage can result in immature love or failure to form relationships in the future.

This theory of psychosexual development is one of Freud's most criticized. Many suggest that the theory reflects his own perverse fixation on human sexuality, stated as a scientific generalization. Many female psychologists deride his views as being sexist for suggesting that women feel inferior to men from a young age and are envious of the phallus. From a scientific perspective, the theory is founded primarily on observation, lacking the support of stringent research methodology. His conclusions about personality were based on interpretations of conversations with patients and the content of their dreams, making it simple for him to fit their experiences into the interpretations he was seeking. Nonetheless, the theory was very influential and stimulated a lot of interest in research and personality development.

NEO-FREUDIAN PSYCHODYNAMIC THEORISTS

Several other psychoanalytic psychologists modified Freud's original theories to form their own perspectives on personality. These are referred to as *Neo-Freudian*, or "new" psychoanalysts.

- Carl Jung

Carl Jung agreed with Freud in the belief that we have an unconscious mind. However, he believed it was composed of much more than our own personal memories and urges. According to Jung, aside from the *personal unconscious*, we also have a **collective unconscious**, which are memories that are shared by all humans (Jung, 1933). These collective memories, fears, and ideas seem to recur in many different cultures in folktales. He called these collective memories **archetypes**. Examples of archetypes include our established ideas about a father figure, or femininity and masculinity. These concepts are pervasive among species and form the collective unconscious. For instance, even a child born without a mother has a very clear idea of what

The idea of masculinity remains stable even in changing environments. This, Jung theorized, is a result of archetypes that are pervasive in our collective unconscious.

a mother is – nurturing, caring, and warm. Even without personal experience, these concepts are very clear to all people.

- Alfred Adler

Another psychologist whose theory is rooted in psychoanalysis is Alfred Adler, who believed that individuals were constantly attempting to overcome physical weaknesses and feelings of inferiority, a process known as **compensation** (Adler, 1954). Adler believed that as children, we constantly feel inferior to more powerful adults, which drives our behaviors, emotions, and thoughts. We want to be strong, intelligent, and capable, just as the adults in our lives are. Instead, we are dependent and helpless without the adults around us so we feel inferior. Instead of seeking pleasure, as Freud theorized, we seek superiority.

For some, becoming fixated on feelings of inferiority can lead to an **inferiority complex**, an internalization of these feelings that can be paralyzing. This complex might occur if a person experiences repeated failures in life, reinforcing the idea that this person is inferior. For others, these feelings lead to growth and development. That is, they compensate for the ways in which they feel inferior to achieve a state of superiority and fulfillment. These ideas would later form the basis for humanistic psychology.

BEHAVIORAL AND SOCIAL COGNITIVE PERSPECTIVE

Behaviorists, as you have seen throughout the book, are only concerned with behaviors that can be observed. Personality, according to them, is merely a set of learned responses, or habits (Dollard & Miller, 1950). These habits have been learned over time and become our automatic responses. For example, children who are disciplined harshly by a parent might learn to avoid punishment by being quiet and keeping to themselves; thus, developing into adults that exhibit patterns of shyness.

However, many psychologists do not believe that conditioning alone can explain the development of behavior patterns. Social learning psychologists have their own views of personality that emphasize the influences of others in the environment, as well as individual expectancies of success and failure. We undoubtedly learn by observing and modeling the behavior of those around us. However, we do not indiscriminately mimic the behaviors we see. In the social cognitive view, modeling is moderated by cognitive processes – in other words, what we think and how we interpret the behavior of others. This explains why some children of parents that are heavy drinkers follow in their footsteps, while others see it as reprehensible and grow up to avoid using alcohol altogether. The difference between one outcome and another is simply the individual's assessment and perception of their parents' behavior.

RECIPROCAL DETERMINISM AND SELF-EFFICACY

Albert Bandura, whom you may remember as the researcher behind the famous Bobo doll experiment, had a theory about personality based on these principles. He believed that patterns of behavior were influenced by three distinct factors: the environment, the behavior, and personal or cognitive factors that people learn from their experiences, a concept he called **reciprocal determinism** (Bandura, 1986; Figure 10.1). The reinforcers of a behavior are part of the environment, and they interact with the behavior itself, and with the beliefs and expectancies that each person brings into a situation.

To illustrate the theory of reciprocal determinism, let's use high-speed driving as an example of a behavior. Environmental factors related to high-speed driving usually highlight negative consequences. Driving at high speeds can lead to getting pulled over and getting a ticket. Even if it does not happen to us personally, we sometimes see people getting pulled over for such behavior. In addition, it increases the probability of an accident. Driving at high speeds led to the death of actor, Paul Walker, and coverage of such incidents as well as accidents we see on the road act as environmental deterrents to that behavior.

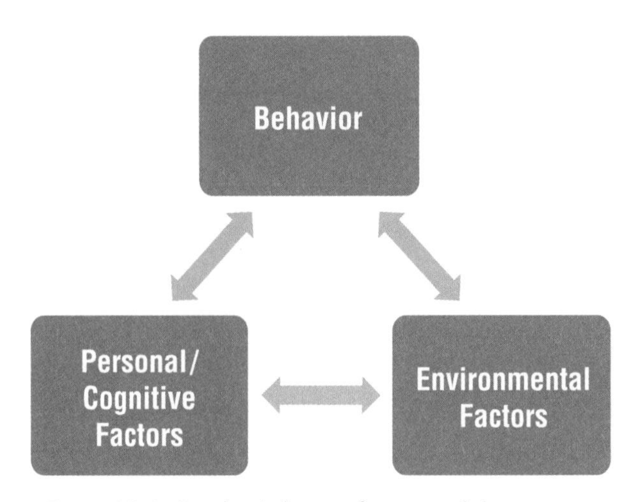

Figure 10.1: Bandura's theory of reciprocal determinism.

Of course, personal factors play a very important part in that equation, as well. People who believe that driving fast will help them get to where they need to go much faster, or who believe their own chances of getting into an accident are low, may still drive at high speeds. On the other hand, someone who has previously gotten into an accident may not be so confident in his own driving ability and may tend to drive more cautiously.

One example of expectancy is known as **self-efficacy**, and it is crucial in determining behavior. According to Bandura, we have expectancies about how likely we are to succeed in a specific task. Succeeding gives us a sense of high self-efficacy, while failing is likely to create a sense of low self-efficacy. Bandura (1998) believed that those with high self-efficacy are more likely to persist because they expect to succeed. If you are good at music and you play a variety of different instruments, you would probably not hesitate to try to learn how to play a new one. But would you apply to be a contestant on *The Voice* if you think you cannot sing?

To illustrate how Bandura's self-efficacy variable interacts with the other two variables of the reciprocal determinism model, imagine walking into a gym class and being asked if you will volunteer to do 20 push-ups in front of your classmates. The setting, including the people in it, makes up the environment; the intimidating gym teacher with his whistle and other classmates who will mock you or cheer you on are all part of the environment. The behavior itself is the task at hand – the 20 push-ups. Your level of self-efficacy – in other words, personal characteristics and expectancies about how easy or difficult it will be to complete – will influence the other two. A person with high self-efficacy, believing she will succeed, would probably be less likely to back down from the challenge. Whereas a person with low self-efficacy, who probably expects negative remarks from his classmates, will be less likely to volunteer.

LOCUS OF CONTROL

The idea that people are motivated to seek out activities and perform behaviors that are reinforcing also influenced Julian Rotter's theory of personality. According to Rotter (1954), personality is a set of potential responses to situations. We generally tend to repeat responses that led to positive consequences in the past and avoid behaviors that did not. Like Bandura, he believed that a person's decision to perform some behavior is based on the expectancy of whether or not that person will succeed, and the reinforcement value of the task. We are simply not motivated to do everything that we know we can complete successfully unless there is an attractive incentive, or a high reinforcement value. For example, radio stations often have giveaway contests that require listeners to call in and participate. Imagine you hear a promotion for a contest that involves solving a series of puzzles to win tickets for a concert you do not want to see. Even if you are confident in your ability to correctly solve the puzzle, you probably would not call in because the prize does not interest you. In other words, the reinforcement value is not high enough.

According to Rotter, one important expectancy is what he called

locus of control – the view that one does or does not have control over what happens to them. People with an *internal* locus of control tend to believe that they are in control of their own fate. For example, a basketball player with an internal locus of control would believe that he won because he is skilled. By contrast, those with an *external* locus of control believe that their lives are controlled by external factors like fate, luck, or other people. A basketball player with an external locus of control might believe that he won the game because the other team was not playing their best, or because he got lucky. Rotter suggests that people with an internal locus of control tend to be more motivated, whereas those with an external locus of control give up quickly and can easily feel learned helplessness.

To illustrate why this is, let's compare two hypothetical students in an introductory psychology course. Jenny believes that her success in the course depends on factors outside her control. When she gets a bad grade, she complains that the teacher does not like her. When she gets a good grade, she claims that the test was very easy. Her classmate, Ellen, believes that her success depends on her effort. She knows that if she works hard and studies, she will do well on her exams, regardless of the difficulty of the exam or of her teacher's opinion of her. Jenny is demonstrating an external locus of control, and is probably more likely to give up if she gets a bad grade, because she believes she has no power to change it. On the other hand, Ellen is more likely to work hard because when all is said and done, she will take responsibility for her own success or failure.

Thinking that your success depends on your effort allows you to take control of your own life.

HUMANISTIC PERSPECTIVE

Humanistic psychology takes a slightly different stance on personality, emphasizing positive motivation and personal growth instead of experiences that may have been influential in the past. In other words, they believe that everyone is responsible for themselves and how they behave.

One of the most well-known and influential humanistic psychologists, Carl Rogers (1961), believed that personality develops and is shaped by our attempts to become fulfilled and capable in all the ways that we have the potential to be. He believed that everyone has a **self-actualizing tendency**, which makes us strive to reach this potential. In this process, he states that many of us develop a **self-concept**, based on what we know about ourselves and what other people say about us. We also have an **ideal self**, which represents the person we strive to be. For example, you may hold a self-concept that you are a helpful and altruistic person. Your ideal self is one that has accomplished a significant positive change in the world. This is something that would obviously take a lot of dedication to volunteering and charity work and would probably take years to accomplish. When a person's ideal self finally matches his actual self closely, that person becomes what Rogers called a **fully functioning person**. Fully-functioning people accurately perceive themselves and the world, and trust themselves to do what is in their own best interests. They are open to new experiences and live in the moment. In achieving their goal of becoming their ideal selves, they would be fulfilled.

Sometimes our self-concept differs drastically from our ideal self.

One of Roger's most important contributions to the field was the concept of **unconditional positive regard**. He defined this idea as love and respect that is not linked to specific behavior. In his theory, unconditional positive regard was crucial to becoming a fully functional individual because it allows you to love and respect yourself and to pursue things in life that are good for you. This is contrasted with *conditional positive regard,* which is dependent on behaving the way others want you to.

For example, being raised in a family that is warm, loving, and respectful regardless of your career choices would free you to explore any career or lifestyle that you might find fulfilling, without having to worry about how it would be perceived by your parents. On the other hand, children who are expected from a very young age to follow their parents' footsteps and become doctors or lawyers, feel that their family's acceptance and love are dependent on this. Their ability to explore their talents and passions is limited, which can make them deeply unhappy. Homosexual children with homophobic families would also have more difficulty achieving fulfillment, because they may feel like they are not accepted for who they are.

The concept of unconditional positive regard has become invaluable in all types of psychotherapy as a way to create rapport between the client and the therapist. Knowing that a therapist will not judge or lose respect for you regardless of what you share makes it easier to open up and explore different aspects of yourself. Research has linked positive regard with therapeutic success (Farber & Lane, 2001).

CRITICISMS OF THE HUMANISTIC PERSPECTIVE

One of the biggest criticisms of this perspective is that it is overly positive and that it does little to explain the negative aspects of human nature. How does one become a violent criminal or a terrorist? Humanistic psychology would not be able to provide the answer. Furthermore, humanistic psychology – like psychodynamic theories – can be difficult to test scientifically and is sometimes considered a more philosophical than scientific viewpoint. Others also argue that it promotes self-centeredness that is characteristic of Western perspectives but does not easily fit other cultures.

TRAIT PERSPECTIVE

Unlike all the aforementioned theories, the *trait perspective* is unconcerned with how personalities develop; it merely summarizes what traits differentiate one person from another. There is a long list of adjectives that can be used to describe people's personalities. One way psychologists narrowed it down was using a statistical technique called a *factor analysis*, which creates clusters of related items. For example, someone might be described as outgoing, talkative, and sociable – all traits that are linked by a single underlying factor: *extraversion* (Cattell, 1990). In this way, long lists of traits could be narrowed down to what Cattell called *source traits*, which represent basic traits that underlie the more visible characteristics.

This number of source traits was reduced by personality researchers to create a five factor model, or the **Big Five** (Botwin & Buss, 1989). These five personality trait dimensions are believed to accurately capture the concept of human personality. These trait dimensions are on a continuum so one can exhibit different degrees of each one. The five can be easily remembered by using the acronym OCEAN:

- Openness
  - This refers to a person's openness to new experiences and their willingness to try new things. Those who do not like change and who tend to be more traditional would probably score low on this trait dimension. Those who do not conform and that seek out novel experiences would score high. On one end of the spectrum would be someone who is uncomfortable with new experiences, does not like to travel, or explore ideas that they find unusual. They prefer the

tried-and-true practical endeavors. On the other end would be the kind of person who will "try anything once. Twice if I like it. Three times to make sure." (Mae West)

- Conscientiousness
    - This trait dimension captures a person's degree of organization, motivation, and dutifulness. For example, a person that is organized, punctual, and reliable would be highly conscientious while someone that has trouble maintaining appointments and is forgetful and disorganized would not be considered very conscientious. Highly conscious individuals tend to be successful because they are persistent. However, excessive conscientiousness can make people workaholics and strict perfectionists. On the other hand, those that lack conscientiousness may be less driven to succeed, disorganized, and may be perceived as unreliable by others.
- Extroversion

Extroverts are outgoing and enjoy the company of others.

    - Extroversion refers to whether a person is energized and stimulated by the external or the internal world. Those who are extroverted tend to be very outgoing and sociable, taking pleasure in activities that surround them with other people. By contrast, those who are not very extroverted, also known as introverts, tend to prefer more solitary activities and are reserved and quiet. Where an extrovert might get energy from social situations, introverts can find them exhausting. Misconceptions about introverts may lead to the belief that they are depressed, but they simply prefer to be alone; excessive social activity may be draining to them.

- Agreeableness
  - This dimension describes one's emotional style, particularly in relating to others. Those high on agreeableness are kind, helpful, easygoing, trusting, and forgiving. These people tend to be liked by most because of their consideration and good nature. Those low on this dimension can be cynical and hard to get along with, finding fault in everything. They may be more self-serving, to the detriment of other people, and suspicious of the motives of others.
- Neuroticism
  - Neuroticism refers to emotional stability or instability. Highly neurotic individuals tend to worry excessively or be moody. Neurotic people also tend to be quicker to intense emotional reactions – even when faced with relatively minor stressors – than those that are more emotionally stable. Those that score low on this dimension are even-tempered and calm. They are less likely to get upset over minor incidents, which make them better able to deal with stressful situations.

According to many theorists, these five traits can accurately describe the personality of anyone, under the assumption that everyone falls somewhere in each of these dimensions.

ASSESSMENT OF PERSONALITY

Now that we've discussed different theoretical perspectives on how personality can develop and how it can differ from individual to individual, let's turn our attention to how personality is measured. Like many psychological tests, personality assessments are used to measure the way we behave, think, and feel. There are many different ways in which this information can be ascertained.

1. Interviews

One of these is the interview. An interview would be similar to a conversation where the goal is to obtain information about someone's personality. Therapists can ask questions or let the conversation flow naturally. With structured interviews, the questions tend to be pre-determined so that the topics discussed are always fixed, regardless of who is being interviewed. On the other hand, the content of unstructured interviews may vary depending on where the conversation goes.

Though interviews can be helpful, they can also be problematic. Like any self-report test, interviews are susceptible to falsification. Not unlike a job interview, people might be motivated to provide the answers that they think the interviewers want to hear, or that might make them look good, even if they are not actually representative of their actual personalities.

2. Behavioral Assessments

Personality can also be studied by observing behavior, instead of just discussing it. Many times, what we *think* we might do in a hypothetical situation is markedly different from what we *actually* do if placed in that situation. Behavioral assessments allow researchers to observe the actual behavior. One such assessment is called **direct observation**, and it involves observing someone's behavior in the setting in which it naturally occurs, like school or work. For example, child psychologists might sit in a classroom and observe whether a child is distractible and off-task, and whether the child cooperates with others.

This assessment has its own problems, however, beginning with the observer effect. Would you take a personal phone call at work if your boss was sitting across from you? Even if you are the type of person that makes personal calls at work, the answer is probably no, because you know you are being observed. The same is true of behavioral assessments, in which the subject is aware that he is being watched; he is more likely to make sure he is on his best behavior. In addition, it is important to remember that just because a behavior did not occur in the period that the person was being observed does not mean that it never occurs.

3. Personality inventories

Another way to assess personality, especially in the realm of research is to use personality inventories. These are questionnaires, also known as objective tests because they contain pre-determined questions that require one of a limited number of answers. For research, these are preferred because they permit psychologists to obtain the same information from many different people, allowing them to compare differences between them. In these inventories, the questions are standardized – everyone gets the same ones – and the responses are limited, unlike open ended interview questions, which may provide vastly different information about different individuals.

There are many different specific personality inventories designed to measure particular traits. Many companies require these personality tests as part of the hiring process, in order to narrow down specific qualities they are seeking in a candidate, like honesty, organization, and motivation. One example is a test called the NEO-PI-R, which has been developed to assess personality using the Big Five personality traits (Costa & McCrae, 1992). One of the most widely used personality inventories is the **Minnesota Multiphasic Personality Inventory (MMPI-2)**, which tests for abnormal behavior patterns in personality (Butcher & Rouse, 1996). Respondents are asked to agree or disagree with statements like "I wish I could be as happy as others seem to be" or "I believe I am being plotted against."

Aside from the advantage that these inventories are standardized and it is easy to compare one person to another, these tests eliminate observer or interviewer bias that can affect results of behavioral and interview assessments. However, these tests can be faked, with respondents purposefully answering questions in a way that promotes a certain personality type. They can be very long which might cause people to start answering randomly or not carefully consider all the answers. Furthermore, they depend on people having good enough self-awareness to accurately assess their own thoughts and behaviors.

4. Projective Tests

Projective tests were designed for use by psychoanalysts who want to uncover the hidden conflicts and wishes that unconsciously affect behavior. They rely on the human tendency to "project" the unconscious onto ambiguous stimuli. Unlike personality inventories, there are unlimited numbers of responses that can be provided to a projective test because test-takers are free to respond any way they want. In doing so, they give meaning to something that has no inherent meaning and thus, give the psychologist insight into their innermost thoughts and feelings.

One of the most famous projective tests is the *Rorschach inkblot test*, in which test-takers are shown a series of patterns of ink and asked to share what they see in the inkblots. The psychologist must then interpret these responses in order to glean information about a person's personality. The *Thematic Apperception Test (TAT)* is another projective test in which people are asked to tell a story about a series of pictures depicting ambiguous situations (Morgan & Murray, 1935).

Though these tests do theoretically prevent falsification and allow test-takers to demonstrate the true determinants of their behaviors, they are plagued with issues of *reliability* and *validity* – whether or not they are accurately measuring personality. For one, projective tests have no standard grading scales so the psychologist is free to interpret responses in any number ways. This opens the door to examiner bias. What if the interpretation of responses is biased by the interviewer's own personality? And how much might two psychologists agree in their interpretations of the same person? Despite these legitimate concerns, many psychologists still use projective tests as a way to gain insight into motives and feelings that are generally beneath a person's awareness. It remains one of the many tools that are available for personality assessment.

Though the aim of many projective personality tests is for the test-taker to interpret the ambiguous stimulus, the examiner's bias can enter into the interpretation of that response.

CHAPTER 10 REVIEW QUESTIONS

1. According to the ______________________________, the id seeks immediate satisfaction regardless of the cost or consequences.

2. Which of these theorists believed in the existence of a collective unconscious?

   a. Sigmund Freud

   b. Carl Jung

   c. Carl Rogers

   d. Alfred Adler

3. Personality, according to Freud is composed of three parts. What are they?______________________________

   ____

   ____

4. According to Bandura, when we succeed in doing the things that we attempt to do, we develop:

   a. A fixation

   b. Inferiority complex

   c. Self-efficacy

   d. Extraversion

5. Carl Rogers is responsible for the concept of:

    a. Locus of control

    b. Unconditional positive regard

    c. Self-efficacy

    d. Compensation

6. A person that worries excessively and is very cynical and suspicious of others is probably:

    a. High on neuroticism and low on extraversion

    b. Low on openness and high on neuroticism

    c. High on agreeableness and high on conscientiousness

    d. High on neuroticism and low on agreeableness

7. Harrison likes everything to be stable and unchanging. He holds traditional values and is wary of new experiences. Which of these would most likely be true about him?

    a. He is low on openness

    b. He is low on extraversion

    c. He is low on agreeableness

    d. He is high on neuroticism

8. Personality inventories are advantageous in all these ways, except:

    a. They are standardized.

    b. They allow researchers to compare results between people.

    c. They are not susceptible to experimenter bias.

    d. They prevent lying.

9. Which of these involves observing people in a natural setting?

    a. Thematic Apperception Test

    b. Interview

    c. Direct observation

    d. Personality inventory

10. T/F. Behaviorists tend to use projective tests of personality.

CHAPTER 11

SOCIAL PSYCHOLOGY

WHILE PERSONALITY PSYCHOLOGISTS study how our own characteristics, thoughts, and feelings predict our behavior, social psychologists believe that these fixed traits alone cannot account for all behavior. Social psychologists believe in the power of the situation and the influence that others have on us regardless of our personality characteristics, and the supporting research is pretty compelling. **Social psychology** scientifically studies how we are influenced by the presence of others. As we will see in the ensuing pages, the person-situation debate mentioned in Chapter 1 heavily influences the research topics in the field of social psychology.

SOCIAL INFLUENCE

One of the major areas of study in social psychology is that of social influence. **Social influence** is the process by which other people can affect our thoughts, feelings, and behavior – even when the presence of others is merely imagined. Social influence can take many forms, like conformity, compliance, and obedience. Whether intentional or not, other people are constantly affecting your decisions, thoughts, and behavior.

CONFORMITY

When you are in a restaurant for the first time with a novel ordering system, how do you figure out what to do? You probably observe others and do what they do. If everyone is standing in one line, you are likely to stand behind them and watch the people ordering ahead of you to see how they behave in the situation; and more likely than not, you would probably do the exact same thing. This is the process of **conformity**, changing one's own behavior to match that of those around you.

How would you react to seeing a group of people all looking up at something? Would you ignore it and keep walking? Would you be curious to see what they're looking at?

Unwittingly, we sometimes conform to silly behaviors. In one study, Cialdini (2001) had confederates – people acting as part of an experiment that appear like a passerby – look up into the sky on a crowded street corner. Before long, other people walking by began looking up at the sky to try to see what they were looking at. The experiment had to be terminated because there were so many people in the street that they were obstructing traffic. This experiment illustrates that even without any explicit request, the average person will change their behavior just because they see others all doing the same.

The line-test experiment, developed by Solomon Asch (1951), is one of the most famous studies in conformity. In the classic test, he placed seven participants in a room where they were told they would be participating in an experiment of visual judgments. They were shown a single line on a white card, and then another card with three lines of different lengths (See Figure 11.1). Their task was to verbally state which of the three lines matched the length of the single line. Of course, this was not the real purpose of the test. There was only one real participant and the others were confederates who had been instructed to repeatedly give the wrong answer. The real test was whether the true participant would conform to the group and give the obviously wrong answer. Researchers found that over one-third of participants did conform to the group and provided the wrong answers, with 75% of participants conforming at least once.

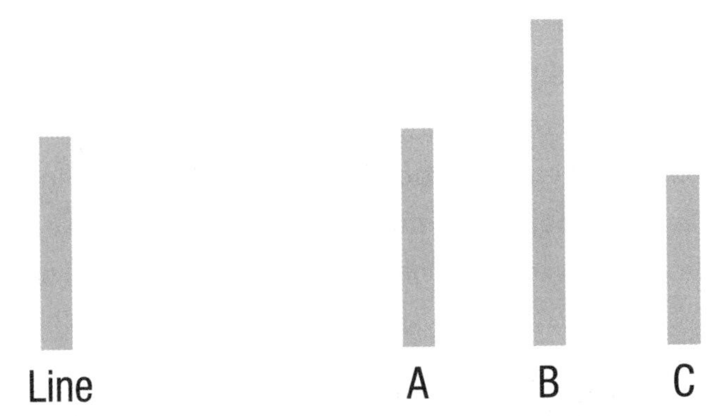

Figure 11.1: In the Asch (1951) experiment, participants were shown a single line (left) and then asked to pick which of the lines on the right matched the length of the first line. What would you do if you were a participant in this study and all the other participants replied C, instead of A?

Once established that people tend to conform in social situations, Asch set out to answer the question: why? What circumstances affect the rate of conformity? In several studies using the same paradigm, he found several factors that increased or decreased conformity (Asch, 1956). The size of the group appeared to matter; conformity increased in correlation with the number of confederates giving the same wrong response, with the rate of conformity leveling off at four. Whether or not the group's decision was unanimous also affected the rate of conformity. When there was at least one other person dissenting from the group's answer, conformity dropped. In difficult and ambiguous tasks, conformity increased because participants were less sure of the correct answer, so they deferred to the answer of the majority.

COMPLIANCE

Social influence is not only limited to the ways in which we conform, but the ways in which we comply. **Compliance** is when people change their behavior when another asks them to do something. This area of social psychology is central to the purpose of marketing and advertising: how to get you to buy what advertisers are selling. There are several techniques that have been shown to increase compliance in others. If these have been used on you, you might recognize them.

Companies invest a lot of money into advertising which will increase the chances that you will comply with their request: to buy their product.

The first is the *foot-in-the-door* technique, which relies on the idea that once people have complied with a minor request, they are much more likely to agree to a larger request. Another way to think of it is, literally and figuratively, the fact that once you get a foot in the door, you are more likely to get it open. Imagine, for instance, that you need a friend to help you move. Many people will make up some excuse to avoid this daunting task. What if you ask him to simply help you move a coffee table? That does not seem so bad and is more likely to get him to comply. Now imagine that when your friend gets to your apartment, you tell him, "Since you're already here, do you mind moving my sofa, and lamps, and all the boxes, too?" This is the foot-in-the-door technique, and you'll probably find that you successfully conned your friend into helping you move. He may not be happy about it, but he'll probably do it.

Researchers believe that the success of the foot-in-the-door technique relies on the need for people to remain consistent (Cialdini et al., 1995). Once you've already committed to something, like helping, you do not want to back out and appear unhelpful and inconsistent in your behavior. This is why many charities ask you to sign a petition before asking you for money. Signing a petition is a minor request but it is much more likely to get them a monetary donation from you later.

Another technique used by salespeople and sneaky friends is the *door-in-the-face* technique (Cialdini et al., 1975). This one works in the opposite way as the *foot-in-the-door*, because the large request comes first. Imagine the same scenario as above where you are asking someone for help moving. This is a large request that is likely to get denied. If you follow it up with a minor request that takes less time and effort – like moving a nightstand – you are much more likely to get compliance. Street vendors commonly use techniques like this – asking for a very high, unrealistic price for an item – expecting you to give a lower offer. So they might offer you a carpet for $300 that is only worth $100, knowing you probably will not buy it for that much. If you bargain and get it down to the actual value of the carpet, you feel like you got a good deal and they make a sale.

When the price is negotiable, count on salespeople to use tactics like the door-in-the-face or the lowball technique to get more money out of you.

Finally, there is the *lowball technique*, which hinges on the idea that when people commit, they are more likely to follow through with their commitment even if the cost, monetary or otherwise, increases (Bator & Cialdini, 2006). For example, imagine that you are interested in buying a car and you see a low price written on the window of a brand new sedan. So you stop at the dealership, take it for a test drive and decide the price is within your budget and agree to buy it. When you sit down to do the paperwork, the car salesman lets you know that power locks and windows do not come standard; they will be another $1000. He also informs you that, though the car you drove had a navigation system and sunroof, those features will also incur an added cost. If you want all the features and specs of the car you test drove, it is going to cost you several thousand dollars more than the price they advertised. Would you still buy it? The answer, according to social psychologists, is probably yes, because you have already made a commitment to buy and most people go through with their commitments, even if the cost increases considerably.

Would you disobey your drill sergeant?

OBEDIENCE

Another important tool of social influence is **obedience**. Unlike compliance, in which anyone can make a request, obedience is a direct order from an authority figure. Teachers, police officers, bosses, and army sergeants all wield a social power that allows them the right to demand behavior.

Just how much influence does this power exert? If your boss asked you to kill someone, would you? What if your boss is your commanding officer in the Army? Social psychologist Stanley Milgram (1964) sought to find answers to these very questions and in doing so, designed one of psychology's most famous (and infamous) experiments.

Participants in Milgram's study were told the purpose of the study was to see the effect of punishment on learning. The participant and a confederate were "randomly assigned" to the role of learner and teacher. The real participant was always assigned the role of teacher with the confederate always playing the part of the learner. The learner was strapped to a chair that delivered a shock whenever the person answered a question wrong. The teacher, of course, was the one that had to flip the switch. The teacher was seated in front of a huge machine that determined the voltage of the shocks being delivered and they were instructed to increase the level of shock by 15 volts, all the way to the maximum of 450 volts, every time the learner got a question wrong.

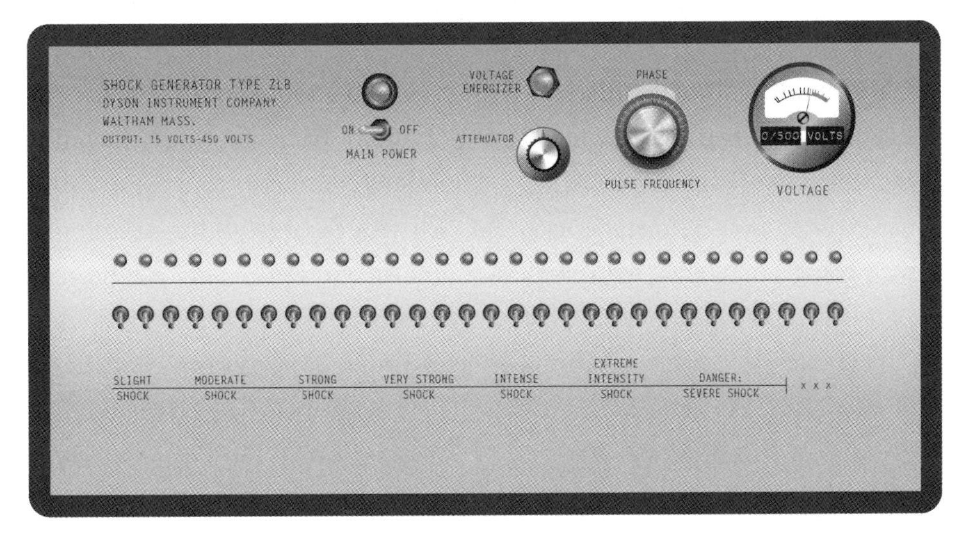

What would you do if you were seated in front of the shock machine and asked to deliver shocks to other participants? Would you go all the way to 450 volts?

The learner followed a script of protests and complaints in response to the increasing severity of the shock, until eventually their screams gave way to complete silence, at which point the teacher was instructed to treat no answer as a wrong answer and continue the procedure. During the duration of the study, the experimenter – serving as the authority figure in the experiment – prodded the teacher to continue delivering the shocks despite hesitation and concern about the learner's safety.

Prior to the study, college students and psychologists alike agreed that less than 1% of participants would go all the way and administer 450 volts of shock to another person. Everyone was quite surprised (shocked, if you will) to find that 65% of the participants in the study did. The study has generated plenty of controversy from those in disbelief of the results, as well as those with ethical concerns who believe that participants were put through undue stress. Indeed, under modern ethical guidelines for psychological testing on human subjects, a study like this would not be allowed. In particular, because research participation must be voluntarily and a participant must feel like they are allowed to quit at any time – a right which the original study seemingly denied. In addition, because the true nature of the experiment was obscured, participants would not be able to consent to such a task, largely unaware of the actual risks (or perceived risks, in this case) that it entailed.

Nonetheless, the study made a very important contribution to psychology, spurning hundreds of follow-up studies to try to explain and replicate the data. Many wondered if the original group of participants was disproportionately composed of aggressive, sadistic, or more dependent and easily controlled people. Replications of the procedure consistently found between 61 and 66% obedience, regardless of the people in the sample (Blass, 1999). Later research also analyzed the personalities of the original participants to see if any trait or group of traits could predict greater obedience, finding none (Blass, 1991). Most average people, regardless of personality, will obey commands from an authority figure, even in extreme cases such as this where such obedience can cause potentially lethal harm to another.

The implications of this study can be seen in real life. People, particularly those in the military, are constantly faced with morally ambiguous situations that may be contrary to their own personal beliefs and the value they place on human life. But the power of an authority figure can be so great that despite potential misgivings, people may still commit violent and regrettable acts. Some psychologists, including Milgram himself, have used the Holocaust as an example of this tendency to obey, presuming that not every German soldier could have been evil, but that they were ordinary people carrying out their jobs on the orders of someone much more powerful than they were (Miller, 2004). Other theorists see this as an unnecessary generalization, believing that Nazi officers voluntarily committed those acts and suggesting otherwise is akin to justifying their behavior. Like other topics in the person-situation debate, valid points are presented on each side.

SOCIAL COGNITION

Not only is our own behavior altered by other people, but the way we perceive other people influences *our* behavior towards *them*. The area of **social cognition** focuses on exactly that, our perceptions of others and our explanations of their behavior.

ATTITUDES

Our **attitudes** are learned tendencies to respond in certain ways to ideas, objects, situations, or people. These are developed over time with experience and can color our behavior when placed in certain situations. In fact, even before we experience new situations, our preexisting attitudes can make us come into these situations with our minds already made up, positively or negatively.

Attitudes are made up of three different components: feelings, behaviors, and thoughts. For example, what is your attitude about the President or about exercising? Can you think of how these three components are interwoven? You might like exercise because you find it fun (feelings), and you probably know that it is good for your health (thoughts), so you exercise every morning (behavior).

You probably have an established attitude about the members of Congress.

It turns out that attitudes are surprisingly poor predictors of actual behavior. Often, people say they will do one thing but do another (Wicker, 1971). For instance, you might support breast cancer research but not donate time or money to the cause. This is in part because stronger attitudes are more likely to elicit consistent behavior than weaker ones. Someone who lost a family member to breast cancer is probably more likely to behave in line with her attitude, because it is more significant to her.

COGNITIVE DISSONANCE

When attitudes clash with behavior, it can cause a great deal of tension.

This emotional discomfort is called **cognitive dissonance**, and it usually results in a change to either the behavior or the attitude in order to relieve the tension (Festinger, 1957). This can occur when people feel that something they've done was immoral, illogical, or irrational. For example: "I knew I should not have stayed up so late last night" causes dissonance if you did. Dissonance is simply an inconsistency, or disagreement, in thought.

When confronted with this dissonance, people are motivated to change one of the circumstances in order to reduce or eliminate the tension. They can do this by either changing their behavior to match their attitude or changing the attitude to justify the behavior. In one classic experiment by Festinger and Carlsmith (1959), results showed how powerful cognitive dissonance can be in attitude change. In the study, participants were given a long, boring task of sorting items and turning pegs. After an hour, the researchers gave them some money to tell the incoming participant that the task was enjoyable. Some of the participants were paid only $1 to convince the other participant it was fun, and others were given $20. After doing so, participants were asked to rate how much they themselves liked the task.

Many researchers at the time, as you might be thinking yourself, assumed that those paid $20 would like the task more because they had greater reinforcement. Surprisingly, the opposite was true. Those that were only paid $1 to lie to the incoming participant actually convinced themselves that the task was fun. Cognitive dissonance can explain these findings. Those that were only paid $1 lied to the participant for almost no incentive, which produces discomfort. So convincing themselves that the task fun – meaning they did not actually lie – reduced that tension. On the other hand, those paid $20 experienced no dissonance at all, because the money was enough justification for the lie. They could be honest with themselves and the researchers about how much they enjoyed the task – very little – with no accompanying psychological discomfort.

When cash is given for a task, you do not have to internally justify your participation in the task; it has been justified by the money.

This might seem like an unrealistic change of opinion, but from time to time, this has probably happened to you, as well. For example, imagine a situation in which you have an old childhood friend that you do not have very much in common with anymore, but whom you still have lunch with occasionally. Seeing her always ends up annoying you somehow, and your spouse is always asking, "Why do you even bother seeing her if you dislike her so much?" This would probably cause a good bit of dissonance. On the one hand, you have a negative attitude about your friend but on the other, you do spend valuable time with her. The tension caused by this situation is likely to lead to one of two actions. You will either stop seeing your friend altogether, effectively ending the friendship, or you'll change your attitude in order to justify the friendship. "She's not so bad and we've known each other since we were kids!"

PERSUASION

Aside from the desire for internal cognitive consistency, our attitudes can be changed purposefully by other people, through the process of **persuasion**. Hopeful presidential candidates, salespeople, and motivational speakers are all interested in swaying your opinions, beliefs, or behaviors in their favor. But there are many factors outside of the content of the message that affect how likely it is to be persuasive.

First, consider the *source*. If you see a magazine article about invading aliens on the cover of *National Enquirer*, you are not likely to believe it. However, if the same story was on CNN, you would probably be more likely to take notice. This is because you would have analyzed the credibility of your source. Why do you think that so many toothpaste commercials suggest that 5 out of 6 dentists prefer their brand? Because dentists are experts on oral health! You are more likely to be persuaded by the opinion of an expert than a commercial actor. Research supports the idea that you are more likely to give credence to people you perceive to be experts or trustworthy (Eagly & Chaiken, 1993).

The message itself and how it is presented are also important factors in persuasion. Would you be persuaded to buy a beer after seeing an ad in the newspaper that contains nothing but a paragraph of information about how the beer is brewed? Or is it more convincing to watch a commercial of beautiful people dancing and drinking beer?

A depiction of people hanging out and enjoying a few beers is likely to make you thirsty for your local pub.

When information is a little more important than what beer to order at the bar, a persuasive message is one that presents both sides of an argument (Crowley & Hoyer, 1994). This occurs because speakers are more likely to be seen as trustworthy and unbiased if they do not obscure the other side of the argument.

The characteristics of the audience are also a significant factor in the success of persuasive tactics. This is the hardest element of persuasion to control because individual differences can be unexpected. For instance, research has shown that people younger in age are more susceptible to persuasion than older individuals (Visser & Krosnick, 1998). The audience factor is probably a big part of the reason why they do not advertise feminine products on SpikeTV. Even if you cannot always control who your audience is, knowing demographics can help you tailor your message in the right way.

FORMING IMPRESSIONS

Organizing the information we know about other people can be a complex process. When we meet others for the first time, we have to process a large amount of information about them and we tend to mentally classify them into a pre-established category, or a **schema**. Schemas organize our expectations and beliefs about different groups of people. If you recall from Chapter 7, categorizing new information using concepts is a cornerstone of our thinking. Socially, we do the same thing. If we have had several experiences with doctors that are narcissistic, we come to believe that anyone we meet in that social category is narcissistic, as well.

The information we notice and remember about people is framed by the schema that we have created for them. As in memory, when we form impressions, there is a *primacy effect*: first impressions are the most important. The way in which a person dresses and behaves upon first meeting is likely to be more influential in your opinion of him than any subsequent behavior. So if the first time you met someone, he was having a bad day and was rude or standoffish, that impression is likely to persist even after several subsequent interactions where he was perfectly pleasant and polite.

Impressions can also be completely distorted by expectations of people before even meeting them; they can even bring about the behavior one expects, a phenomenon called the **self-fulfilling prophecy**. Consider the research of Snyder & Swann (1978), in which participants were pitted against each other in a competitive game. Some participants were led to believe that their partners were hostile, leading them to treat them badly. The other participants, in turn, responded in a hostile manner, as well; thus bringing about the behavior that was expected in the first place. The self-fulfilling prophecy is also seen in the classroom, where a teacher's expectations of what she considers to be successful students ends up making those students more successful, in part because of the way the teacher treats them (Harris & Rosenthal, 1985). A teacher is much more likely to push a child harder to succeed if she has a pre-established idea that the student is intelligent and has potential. On the other hand, the teacher is more likely to accept mediocre work and not be as exigent of students that she expects to perform poorly. This treatment results in precisely the outcomes the teacher expects.

STEREOTYPES

Social categorization can also lead to the formation of **stereotypes**, the belief that all members of a particular social category share the same characteristics. Stereotypes can lead to negative inferences about people in certain social groups like gender, race, occupation, and culture, to name a few. When people are guided by stereotypes, they are likely to misjudge what other people are like and sometimes, treat them differently. However, stereotypes can be useful in organizing and categorizing information about other people. One just has to avoid making unnecessary, or negative, assumptions about people without giving them a chance to demonstrate what they are really like.

ATTRIBUTIONS OF BEHAVIOR

Social cognition also involves making **attributions**, or explanations, about why other people behave the way they do. Many of us wonder why people act the way they do (some of us do it for a living!), particularly when we cannot understand or relate to the behavior. For instance, someone who habitually makes plans, only to cancel them at the last minute would cause many friends and acquaintances to wonder why that is. This would lead them to make attributions, which may or may not be correct. Attribution theory was developed by Fritz Heider (1958) who believed that we tend to make one of two kinds of explanations for behavior: internal and external.

External causes are those that are due to situational factors, like the weather, traffic, and opportunities. Your friend may have cancelled on your dinner plans because she got a flat tire on her way home from work. This would be an external attribution. Internal causes are those that one would attribute to characteristics of the individual, like personality. If you assume that your friend cancels plans because she has no intention or desire to keep them and she is an inconsiderate friend, you are making an internal attribution. Every behavior has some sort of internal or external cause and it is in our nature to make assumptions about what they are.

The kind of attribution we make about behavior tends to depend on whose behavior we are observing. Generally speaking, people tend to fall prey to the **fundamental attribution error**, and attribute the behavior of others to internal causes, without considering the potential situational factors influencing their actions (Jones & Harris, 1967). If someone cuts you off in traffic, you are likely to angrily label the person as reckless or a bad driver. If you are adhering to stereotypes, you might even assume it is a young male behind the wheel. However, there are a variety of reasons why one might do something like that, having nothing to do with inherent characteristics of the driver's personality. What if he was rushing to the hospital to see the birth of his child?

When it comes to explaining our own behavior, we are much more likely to make external, situational attributions. You probably would not walk in late to class and tell the instructor, "Sorry, I was late because I'm irresponsible," which is an internal attribution. Instead, you probably ran into traffic or got stuck at work.

Part of the reason why we tend to attribute the behavior of others to internal factors but our own to external factors is the *actor-observer bias*. If you are observing yourself and attributing your own behavior, you are the actor, and you have an understanding of all the circumstances around you that might influence that behavior. Often, these circumstances are not known to someone simply observing your behavior. As mere observers of others' behavior, we do not see all the possible situational influences; instead, we see only the person. If you get into an elevator and attempt to make conversation with another person who looks annoyed and is ignoring you, you might get the impression that he is rude and unfriendly, because all you know is his behavior. However, that person might have just lost his job or found out that he has a terminal illness, so he is too distracted by his problem to make small talk. But how could you possibly know that?

Attributions can also lead to victim-blaming due to a way of thinking called the **just world hypothesis** (Lerner, 1980). This is the belief that people tend to get what they deserve because human behavior leads to fitting consequences. If you do good things, good things happen to you. If you do bad things, bad things happen to you. Most people do not want to believe that bad things happen to good people so when faced with such a situation, they will try to justify ways and reasons in which the person's behavior brought about their own bad fortune. One reason for this, psychologists suggest, is because it is comforting to believe that no such thing

Victim blaming is common in rape cases, causing some to suggest that victims were inciting the assault by dressing or behaving provocatively.

could ever happen to us (Dalbert, 2001). We would rather believe it only happened to *them* because they were walking alone at night, associating with the wrong people, or dressed a certain way – things *we* never do. This is a way of obtaining distance between ourselves and the victim. However, the reality is, bad fortune could happen to anyone.

SOCIAL INTERACTION

Social psychologists also seek to understand interactions, good and bad, between people; this is known as *social interaction* – why we love, why we hate, and how we behave towards others. They study the variables that influence prejudices, attraction, aggression, and altruism.

PREJUDICE AND DISCRIMINATION

A **prejudice** is an unfairly negative, stereotyped attitude about members of a social group. For instance, a business owner who believes that Latinos are lazy and more likely to steal from his business, holds a prejudicial view of Latinos. When these prejudices result in unequal treatment of a person simply because he belongs to a particular group, it is called **discrimination**. If that same business owner refused to interview anyone with a Hispanic last name, he would be discriminating. Though many laws exist that can prevent discriminatory behavior, prejudicial attitudes cannot be eliminated.

Prejudice and discrimination can occur against any individual that belongs or is perceived to belong to a particular social group, whether in age, race, gender, sexual orientation, or religious affiliation, to name a few. The two do not always have to occur together. One can disguise prejudices, not openly discriminating against others, while still holding negative opinions of them. Conversely, it is also possible to engage in discriminatory behaviors without being prejudiced. For example, a hiring manager might choose not to hire a qualified woman because she is pregnant, even though he does not hold negative views of pregnant women.

EXPLAINING PREJUDICE AND DISCRIMINATION

Research on prejudices and discriminatory behavior have found that people tend to easily align themselves to those with whom they identify – the in-group – and prejudice and discrimination towards the out-group tends to follow (Brewer, 2001). Intergroup conflicts tend to be more pronounced when groups are fighting for the same common resource such as jobs. This leads to *scapegoating*, the blaming of an out-group or members of an out-group for frustrations of members of the in-group.

One theory associated with this phenomenon is the **frustration-aggression theory** that suggests that prejudices are the result of people's frustrations over their own negative circumstances (Allport, 1954; Smith & Mackie, 2005). For example, the prejudiced view that immigrants take the jobs that belong to Americans is easily explained by this theory. Everyone is fighting for employment and when someone in the in-group has failed and is frustrated, they take out their anger and frustration on unsuspecting out-group members who are employed.

The immigration debate is a hot button issue, with some believing that immigrants deserve the opportunity to live in the United States and others believing that allowing them to do so is a detriment to the country.

Other views suggest that those with authoritarian personality types tend to show more prejudicial behavior because they tend to be extremely traditional and can be hostile to others that represent a shift from their social norms or values (Altemeyer, 2004). Their prejudice arises from their cynical, suspicious view of people they perceive as different, manifesting itself as prejudices and discriminatory behavior. So if a Muslim family moves in next door to someone with an authoritarian personality, he may perceive the family negatively, simply because they are from a culture different than his own.

These prejudices are diminished when members from different groups must cooperate in pursuit of a common goal (Aronson et al., 1978). When everyone in the group is vital to reaching a goal, people are more likely form close relationships with members of the out-group. In-groups and out-groups can be formed in any almost any situation regardless of differences between the groups. You may have seen this at work. Your particular department may hold prejudicial attitudes about people in other departments and vice versa. In one study, this was also demonstrated with boys at summer camp (Sherif et al., 1961). Researchers split the boys up upon their arrival at camp into two groups; the groups were often competing against each other in games and activities for prizes that only one team could win. Naturally, this led both groups of boys to develop prejudiced attitudes towards the boys in the competing group, leading to hostility and aggression. However, when the groups were working together toward a common goal, like banding together to pay for a movie to watch, these prejudicial attitudes were reduced.

THE RULES OF ATTRACTION

Social interactions also relate to the way we become romantically linked to other people. What is it that attracts us to one another? Interpersonal attraction is determined by several different characteristics; research on attraction has found proximity, similarity, and physical attractiveness to be key factors in attraction.

What characteristics do you think attract you to other people? The research may surprise you.

The first is *physical attractiveness*, which has been shown to influence our decision to get to know people better, though other factors become more important later in relationships (Eagly et al., 1991). In initial attraction, people assume that those that are physically attractive are superior in other areas as well, such as intelligence, happiness, and success. Another line of attractiveness research suggests that people are more likely to form relationships with someone who is equally as attractive as themselves (Feingold, 1988). Often, when partners differ significantly in physical attractiveness, the less attractive partners have compensating qualities, like wealth. Logically, it would make sense for people to be attracted to others of similar attractiveness. When we do not, it creates a sense of disparity in the relationship. We feel more secure when we are on a level playing field.

Another important factor in determining attraction is *proximity*, referring to actual physical distance. Those that work together or live near each other are more likely to be attracted to each other than those that do not because they have more chances to interact. One theory about why this is the case stems from the **mere exposure effect**, the idea that repeated exposure to a stimuli breeds liking (Zajonc, 2001). This is the same reason why songs on the radio grow on you if you hear them a few times. Attraction to people works the same way, and people choose friends and romantic partners from those around them.

Attraction also depends on *similarity*. People tend to prefer those who are similar to them in some way, whether in attitudes, beliefs, or interests (Hartfield & Rapson, 1992). Psychologists suggest this is because being around people who share our beliefs and attitudes validates them. This makes common sense since we like to be around people who enjoy the same activities we do, and it can be frustrating to be around those that have fundamentally different values. You might be wondering: what about the phrase "opposites attract"? Is that not true? Relationships with others that have complementary qualities – that balance each other out – can be very successful. However, research supports the idea that similarity is a stronger force in bringing people together and helping them stay together.

Having differences in lifestyles, opinions, and interests can lead to a lot of fighting in relationships.

Finally, most people like others who like them back, an idea called *reciprocity of liking* (Curtis & Miller, 1986). This concept is tied to the self-fulfilling prophecy. When we believe that someone likes us, we tend to like and treat them well, leading to reciprocated liking.

HELPING BEHAVIOR

Prosocial behavior is any behavior that benefits others. One example of prosocial behavior is **altruism**, which occurs when we help someone with no expectation of reward, simply for the sake of helping. Altruistic behaviors include donating to a charity or helping a stranger. So what exactly makes someone helpful and altruistic?

If you saw a woman trapped in a car after a bad accident, you would probably get down and see if she needs help, right? Many of us like to believe that we are fundamentally good and kind, so you probably believe that you would. But as you should have already learned by now, what you think you will do and what you actually do may be very different.

Take the case of Kitty Genovese, a woman who was assaulted in an apartment complex parking lot and left for nearly a half hour until the assailant returned and stabbed her to death. According to police, there were at least 38 people who heard or saw the attack and none reported it to the police until after she was killed (Rosenthal, 1964). You might be wondering, what kind of horrible, disturbed people would let that happen in plain sight without so much as dialing 911; but remember, you would be making an internal attribution without considering the external circumstances.

According to social psychologists, the external circumstances that lead to the decision not to help is called the **bystander effect**, a finding that shows that the greater the number of observed bystanders, the less likely people are to help (Darley & Latane, 1968). If only one person witnesses an emergency, that person is much more likely to help, because he feels the full weight of responsibility. The likelihood of helping decreases with each new bystander, because responsibility for helping is diffused across all bystanders. "I don't need to call 911, surely someone else already has." If you have ever had training in Basic Life Support (BLS) or Cardiopulmonary Resuscitation (CPR), one of the first things you are taught

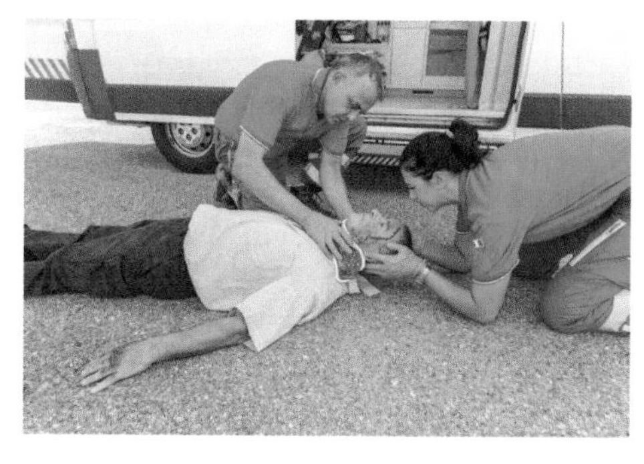

The training procedure for Basic Life Support teaches practitioners to prevent the bystander effect by giving someone the responsibility of calling the police for help.

is to point at someone in the vicinity and tell them to call 911. This is meant to prevent the bystander effect. Most people will help if they feel or are assigned a personal responsibility, but without it, they tend to assume that someone else is doing something about it so they do not have to.

In all, Darley and Latane (1968) identified five steps we take when deciding whether or not to help:

1. Noticing an emergency.
2. Interpreting the situation as an emergency.

   "Is she screaming because she's in trouble or is she horsing around with her friend?"
3. Taking responsibility for helping.
4. Planning a course of action – determining how to help.

   "Should I call the police or intervene myself?"
5. Taking action.

Sometimes the interpretation of the situation is also biased by how others react. If others who are witnessing the same event do not interpret it as an emergency, we will be less likely to. So if a group of people are on a train and there is a suspicious package in the corner but no one else is reacting to it, it might lead you to believe that it is probably not a danger. In general, the costs of helping – like for example, potential danger to self – should not outweigh the rewards of helping. When they do, people are unlikely to get involved to help. For example, if you are in a store that is getting robbed by masked gunmen, you are probably not going to try to help the cashier, because it poses a threat to you. In this case, running out of the store and calling the police is a safer course of action.

CHAPTER 11 REVIEW QUESTIONS

1. ____________________ is the process by which other people can affect our thoughts, feelings, and behaviors.

    a. Social influence

    b. Social interaction

    c. Social cognition

    d. None of these

2. Karen asked her sister to help her clean the house. Her sister agreed and in doing so demonstrated:

    a. Obedience

    b. Compliance

    c. Conformity

    d. Prejudice

3. Eloise believes that a good diet is important, but she has a candy bar after lunch every day. Her behavior is likely to create cognitive dissonance leading her to:

    a. stop eating candy bars.

    b. justify eating candy bars as a reward for adhering to her diet.

    c. conclude that a good diet is not that important as long as you have an active lifestyle.

    d. Any of these

4. T/F. If the person delivering a persuasive message is perceived as an expert, people are not as likely to be persuaded by the message because they will not understand them.

5. Jackie's neighbor, Danny, got shot and killed in front of a pawn shop. Jackie assumed that he must have been involved in shady dealings that got him killed, because of:

    a. Prejudice
    b. Just world hypothesis
    c. Fundamental attribution error
    d. Self-fulfilling prophecy

6. William and Leilani work next door to one another. They often pass each other in the hall and make conversation. According to the ________________________ they are ______________ likely to be attracted to each other.

    a. Mere exposure effect; less
    b. Mere exposure effect; more
    c. Self-fulfilling prophecy; more
    d. Self-fulfilling prophecy; less

7. ____________________________ is when we help someone with no expectation of reward, simply for the sake of helping.

8. T/F. Prejudice can occur as a result of categorizing people into in-groups and out-groups.

9. According to research on attribution, when a classmate gets straight A's on all of his assignments, most people would:

    a. Assume he cheated.

    b. Think he is lucky.

    c. Think he is really smart.

    d. Be jealous.

10. T/F. The more people are around in an emergency, the faster one is likely to help.

CHAPTER 12

ABNORMAL PSYCHOLOGY

WHEN YOU FIRST ENROLLED in a psychology class, you probably assumed the entire class would be about "crazy people" and "insane" behavior, and what makes people hear voices and have multiple personalities. The area in psychology primarily concerned with this kind of abnormal behavior is **psychopathology**. Psychopathologists study the minds of people who suffer from mental disorders to attempt to determine how they differ from the minds of those who do not. They also aim to find a way to predict psychological disorders in order to prevent their occurrence. The line between normal and abnormal, disordered behavior can often be blurred. What exactly makes behavior abnormal? What is normal, anyway?

DEFINING ABNORMALITY

Discriminating between abnormal and normal behavior is not as simple as one would think. There are many different ways to define abnormality, each having different implications for psychopathology.

Statistically, the term abnormal is used to mean rare and infrequent. For example, take the distinction of intellectual disability, as discussed in Chapter 7. Since the majority of people have average intelligence, those with much higher IQ's are considered abnormal, statistically – because they are rarer. That does not mean that a person with an IQ of 150 is mentally disordered. The problem with a statistical definition of abnormality is that one must have a clear idea of what constitutes the norm.

Another way to understand abnormality would be to think of it as a behavior that violates social norms. For example, if you walked into an elevator and someone was in there facing the back instead of the door, you might consider that behavior abnormal because it is violating a standard social norm. Sometimes, bizarre behavior that violates social norms can be indicative of psychological distress. If someone is a recluse, living in the woods and avoiding all human contact, he may also be labeled abnormal, and could perhaps meet the diagnostic criteria for social phobia or schizotypal personality disorder, which is characterized by social isolation. But what about a monk taking a vow of silence and living in seclusion in pursuit of spiritual enlightenment? Would that behavior be considered abnormal?

Try it yourself! Get into a crowded elevator and face the back wall to see the reactions of those around you.

Context, in this case, is key.

Abnormality can also be defined on a personal level when a person is experiencing significant discomfort as a result of a behavior or thought that departs from his own norm. For example, a woman that develops a fear of driving, when she has spent her whole life doing so, would consider her own state of anxiety distressing and abnormal. This behavior would also be considered **maladaptive**, meaning that it does not allow the person to live her life completely.

Mental health professionals normally analyze behavior in terms of how maladaptive it is. In other words, how it might prevent someone from living a full and healthy life. Most people tend to seek treatment when they consider their own behavior maladaptive or distressing. Often, at this point, people have developed a **psychological disorder**, a pattern of behavior that causes distress and affects their ability to function in daily life. Psychological disorders may prevent otherwise normal people from building and maintaining relationships, holding jobs, or even simply taking care of themselves.

PERSPECTIVES OF PSYCHOLOGICAL DISORDERS

Historically, psychological disorders were seen as having significantly different causes than we believe today. Archeologists have found human skulls, dating back to 3000 B. C., with holes cut into them as part of a process called *trepanning*, which was believed to release the demons of people that were behaving strangely (Gross, 1999). In the time of the Greeks, it was believed that mental illnesses were the result of imbalances in the body's vital fluids: phlegm, black bile, blood, and yellow bile. These were known as the four humors and were believed to have an effect on personality, behavior, and overall health. Later still, the people of the Middle Ages, believed that spiritual possession was the reason for abnormality and they believed that exorcisms would cast out the demons and cure the patient (Lewis, 1995).

Over time, there was a departure from these perspectives, and the mentally ill were placed in asylums, where conditions were often deplorable and did little to improve patients' mental health. As the understanding of psychological disorders and their causes have evolved, so have the treatments. The etiology, or study of the cause of a disorder, has progressed across several different lines of research, most of which we have already discussed. Each of these models – psychodynamic, cognitive, behavioral, biological, and biopsychosocial – lend credible explanations for the causes of psychological disorders.

CONTEMPORARY MODELS OF ABNORMALITY

One prevalent perspective of psychological disorders is the *biological model*, which maintains that psychological disorders are largely due to physical, genetic, or medical causes (Gamwell & Tomes, 1995). According to this model, many disorders – like depression, anxiety, and schizophrenia – are caused by malfunctioning physical processes in the body, such as chemical imbalances, or genetics. Psychologists in the field often cite genetic research that suggests that some disorders are more likely in people who have family members with the disorder. The study of key neurotransmitters, such as dopamine and serotonin, is also relevant to biological psychology, as imbalances of such chemicals can lead to the development of depressive disorders. Abnormalities in brain structures are sometimes linked to the development of psychological disorders. Psychiatrists and others who hold a biological perspective tend to favor biological treatments such as medication or surgery; however, many psychologists believe medication only controls symptoms without solving the underlying problem.

Psychodynamic psychologists would probably agree with that criticism. The *psychodynamic model*, as championed by Freudian psychologists, holds that abnormal behavior arises when someone represses unconscious thoughts and memories from childhood. When these unconscious concerns and urges try to resurface, they manifest themselves as psychological disorders. For example, a cold, neglecting parent may lead a person to develop low self-esteem and depression, because of the ego's inability to obtain attention and praise in childhood. As you will see later, according to psychodynamic psychologists, the solution is to uncover the hidden secrets of the unconscious. In other words, once one is able to uncover the root of the disorder, one can work through the problematic experiences or neuroses.

Behaviorists have their own take on the development of psychological disorders. In what is known as the behavioral model, they theorize that abnormal behavior is learned over time, the same way all learning occurs (Skinner, 1971). For example, Munchausen syndrome and Munchausen syndrome by proxy (diagnosed as *factitious disorder imposed on self* and *factitious disorder imposed on another* in the *DSM-5*) are disorders characterized by feigning disease or illness in oneself or their one's children in order to draw attention and sympathy to oneself. According to behaviorists, the development of this factitious disorder is due to the reinforcement of sympathy, attention, and reassurance which results from faking illness. In other words, the more attention the afflicted person receives from doctors, family, and friends, the more likely she is to continue feigning illness.

The *cognitive perspective*, never too far behind, is the idea that people develop abnormal behavior as a result of negative and illogical thoughts and beliefs. For example, someone that believes he is worthless and that the world would be better off without him is likely to develop depressive symptoms as a result of this thinking. Recent times have seen, more and more, a merging of cognitive and behavioral research to form the *cognitive-behavioral model*. The historically competing perspectives, when united explain psychological disorders from both internal, cognitive factors and external, learning factors. From this joint perspective, one could sum up the etiology of a phobia as a combination of irrational beliefs about the danger of an object or situation, and a learned tendency to avoid that object or situation.

The *diathesis-stress model* takes into account biological predispositions (diatheses) as well as stressful life circumstances that could lead to the development of disorders. This model considers the fact that not every person with a genetic predisposition to depression or schizophrenia will develop the disorder. Life circumstances play a role, as well. For instance, a person who had two alcoholic parents may already be predisposed to addiction. If that person got divorced or lost his job, it might trigger him to develop an alcohol problem.

The most comprehensive of all models is the *biopsychosocial model* or the *systems model*, which takes into account biological factors, like genetics and chemical imbalances, as well as a person's psychological state, and external stressors in the environment. This model continues the growing trend to move away from defining psychology in black-and-white terms. It holds that many different factors can cause the same problem for different people. For instance, a genetic predisposition to schizophrenia combined with being reared in a dangerous, threatening environment could potentially lead to the development of the disorder. However, the person's own coping mechanisms and psychological tendencies must also be taken into account. If this person deals well with stress, there is less chance of the disorder developing.

CLASSIFYING MENTAL DISORDERS

Since the publication of the first edition in 1952, psychologists have relied on the *Diagnostic and Statistical Manual of Mental Disorders (DSM)* to classify and diagnose psychological disorders. With each revision, disorders have been added, renamed, and re-categorized. In some cases, with greater understanding of psychological conditions, some have been removed altogether. Now in its 5th edition, the manual has shifted from a categorical approach, identifying the presence or absence of a disorder, to a more dimensional approach, in which disorders are considered as continuous dimensions. This way, some manifestations of a disorder are diagnosed as very slight deviations from normal behavior and others as more severe and debilitating (DSM-5; American Psychiatric Association, 2013). Instead of simply diagnosing someone as having depression or not having depression, psychologists are able to specify the severity of the depression, from mild to severe, depending on how many symptoms a person meets.

The Diagnostic and Statistical Manual of Mental Disorders, currently in its fifth edition, is widely used by psychologists and other mental health professionals to diagnose mental disorders.

The *DSM-5* describes over 300 psychological disorders in its 22 chapters, like depressive disorders and dissociative disorders. Each disorder is listed along with its diagnostic criteria, including symptoms and severity ratings. Normally, certain criteria, including symptomatic criteria or length of the episode, must be met for diagnosis. The manual also contains statistical information about the prevalence of each disorder including demographic information to aid in diagnosis. The appendix of the manual contains information about disorders not yet classified in the body of the manual but that require further study. This ensures the continual growth and evolution of psychological diagnosis, which is reflected in each new edition.

DEPRESSIVE DISORDERS

Depressive disorders are illnesses that involve depression, or overwhelming sadness, as their prevalent symptom. These are some of the most common types of psychological disorders, affecting 9.5%

of the U.S. population (National Institute of Mental Health, 2010).

Though several different disorders fall under this category, *major depressive disorder* is the most well-known. A diagnosis of major depressive disorder requires depressed mood or loss of interest and pleasure from enjoyable activities for at least two weeks. These predominant criteria must be accompanied by other symptoms related to depression including insomnia, fatigue, feelings of worthlessness, and recurrent thoughts of death or suicidal ideation. Typically, suicidal ideation stems from feelings of hopelessness, which cause people to believe that they will never feel happy or enjoy life again. People suffering from depression might isolate themselves from their friends, stop playing sports or exercising, and stop partaking in the pastimes they enjoy. In severe cases, they may not leave their beds or homes, dwelling on their sadness.

Another depressive disorder with similar symptoms is *persistent depressive disorder (dysthymia)* which is characterized by long-term depression for at least two years that can vary in terms of severity. Historically, the disorder, previously known simply as dysthymia, was seen as a persistent, less severe depression. The reclassification in the *DSM-5* allows for a diagnosis of the disorder as mild, moderate, or severe; this means it is no longer only persistent, mild depression, but can be used to diagnose a long-term, severe depression.

The cause of depressive disorders tends to vary depending on whom you ask. Behaviorists believe that depression is linked to learned helplessness (Seligman, 1975). Like the dogs in Seligman & Maier's study (1967), people learn to let life metaphorically shock them, seeking no relief and no way to improve their well-being. Cognitive psychologists hold the view that people's own negative thinking spirals into depression and despair (Beck, 1979). Biological researchers suggest that imbalances of brain chemicals like serotonin, norepinephrine, and dopamine, which regulate mood, are the cause of depressive disorders. Consequently, drugs affecting these chemicals and their neurotransmitters are used to treat depressive disorders (Cohen, 1997).

BIPOLAR AND RELATED DISORDERS

Previously categorized along with depressive disorders as mood disorders, in the *DSM-5*, bipolar disorders are separated into their own category. While depressive disorders are characterized by a downward shift in mood, **bipolar disorders** involve both depression and mania, which is an upward change in mood. Mania is a period of abnormally elevated mood including symptoms such as elevated self-esteem, decreased need for sleep, excessive talkativeness, racing thoughts, distractibility, and excessive goal-directed activity, particularly activity with potential for negative consequences. People in a manic episode may take risks, like promiscuous sexual behavior, or partaking in criminal activity such as breaking and entering or theft. This is partly due to an increase in impulsive behavior combined with a decrease in judgment.

A manic episode results in a sharp upward shift in mood that is abnormal and excessive.

A person with bipolar disorder commonly cycles between the extreme highs of mania and the extreme lows of depression. There are two types of bipolar disorders: *bipolar I*, which involves a manic episode lasting at least 7 days; and *bipolar II*, which involves a hypomanic episode, lasting at least 4 days. A hypomanic episode is less severe than a manic episode.

Cyclothymic disorder is a related disorder in which an individual exhibits symptoms of mania and depression but do not meet the criteria for a hypomanic or major depressive episode. For example, someone who presents with a history of depressive episodes and exhibits manic episodes for only one or two days at a time, or with insufficient symptoms to be diagnosed as mania, would be diagnosed with cyclothymic disorder and not bipolar disorder.

Bipolar disorders have a highly genetic component. Having a relative with bipolar disorder makes your chances of having it as well up to 20 times higher than those without relatives suffering from the disorder (MacKinnon, Jamison, & DePaulo, 1997).

ANXIETY DISORDERS

In the *DSM-5*, disorders previously categorized as anxiety disorders, like obsessive-compulsive disorder and posttraumatic stress disorder, were removed from the category and placed in their own category. The remaining anxiety disorders are: specific phobia, social anxiety disorder (social phobia), panic disorder, agoraphobia, and generalized anxiety disorder.

GENERALIZED ANXIETY DISORDER

Generalized anxiety disorder (GAD) is marked by unexplained, excessive worry not linked to anything in particular. Sufferers find their worry is difficult to control and the anxiety can be about anything at all, even insignificant events. For example, a person might worry about getting to work on time, even if she is not late. When she arrives at work and does not have to worry about that anymore, she might worry about being told by her boss that some assignment she worked on is not good enough. If her spouse or child does not a return her phone call right away, she may assume he was in an accident. The anxiety is not related to any one thing and can persist throughout the day about a variety of concerns. Those with GAD tend to experience problems with sleep, as well as fatigue, irritability, and difficulty concentrating. The excessive worry can lead to frequent bouts of insomnia, resulting in the drowsiness, irritability, and lack of concentration that are characteristic of sleep deprivation.

PANIC DISORDER AND AGORAPHOBIA

Panic disorder develops when people who are prone to panic attacks develop a fear of having another one. A **panic attack** is a brief period of overwhelming fear or terror that is accompanied by several different symptoms including increased heart rate, sweating, shaking, chest pain, abdominal distress, feelings of losing control and dying, and chills or hot flashes. Panic attacks typically begin suddenly and can peak in intensity within minutes, though they can last longer than that. The experience can be so intense that many people who have a panic attack for the first time go to the hospital, believing they are having a heart attack.

Panic attacks alone do not constitute panic disorder. Many adults have had one or more panic attacks throughout their lives without developing the disorder. Diagnostic criteria require that panic attacks be followed by at least a month of worry or concern about having another panic attack or significant maladaptive change in behavior to avoid having panic attacks. For example, a person may avoid exercise, which increases physiological arousal similar to the way a panic attack does, because he is afraid of having a panic attack the gym.

A related condition is **agoraphobia**, which causes individuals to avoid certain situations where they might not receive help if they develop panic symptoms. People with agoraphobia might avoid using public transportation, driving over bridges, going in shops and theatres,

People with agoraphobia sometimes end up housebound because they are afraid to leave the only place they perceive as safe.

or being in crowds. Many of them do not like to be alone in public and cling to people they consider "safe" in order to venture out of their homes. In cases of severe agoraphobia, sufferers refuse to leave their home or a room in their home that they consider safe.

In many people with panic disorder, agoraphobia develops because they begin to avoid situations in which they have previously had a panic attack. As a result of this natural human response to avoid situations that make us uncomfortable, panic disorder and agoraphobia frequently occur together.

PHOBIC DISORDERS

Some of the most common anxiety disorders are **phobias**, unreasonable and excessive fears of specific objects or situations. People with specific phobias experience immediate fear and anxiety at the presence – and sometimes simply the thought – of the feared object or situation. Typically, people make efforts to avoid the situation or object that they fear, which is how people's lives can become significantly affected. A person scared of doctors might experience serious health problems because of the refusal to see a doctor.

"Visualize yourself not falling off the wall."

Many phobias develop as a result of negative and traumatizing experiences.

Phobias are generally classified as four different types: animal type, natural environment type (including heights and water), blood-injection injury type, and situational type (including examples such as fear of elevators and fear of flying). Animal phobias are one of the most common, including fear of spiders, snakes, or dogs.

Social anxiety disorder (social phobia) is another phobic disorder which is marked by excessive fear surrounding social situations. Social phobia involves the fear that others are negatively evaluating them. The most common type of social phobia is fear of public speaking, which affects many people at least to some degree. As with specific phobias, individuals with social phobia tend to avoid social situations to prevent symptoms of anxiety. A variety of different situations can be stressful for someone with social phobia including meeting new people, being called on in class, giving a presentation at work, attending parties, using public restrooms, and even eating or writing in public. As we discussed in Chapter 4, social phobia has been linked to alcohol abuse because alcohol reduces the symptoms of anxiety (it is a nervous system depressant, remember?) and because it is readily available in many social situations (Burke & Stephens, 1999; Schneier et al., 1989).

Public speaking is the most common kind of social phobia.

OBSESSIVE-COMPULSIVE DISORDERS

When you go to the grocery store, you are probably accustomed to pressing the button on your car key to lock the door before heading inside. Occasionally, after you are inside, you second guess whether or not you actually locked the car. For some, this concern might be so great that they would actually go outside and lock it again just to be sure. Others probably just reassure themselves that they probably did lock it and go about their shopping.

For people with **obsessive-compulsive disorder (OCD)**, it is not that easy. For them, these *obsessions*, or persistent thoughts, cause extreme anxiety and the only way to relieve that anxiety is to perform certain *compulsive behaviors*. The urge to perform these behaviors becomes so strong that the compulsions become ritualistic. For example, a person with an overwhelming fear of leaving the car door unlocked might lock and unlock every door of the car several times before they feel satisfied. The disorder tends to worsen with time because the compulsions remove the anxiety caused by the obsessions, leading to the creation of more and more intricate compulsive behaviors and rituals.

Behaviorists would agree that the compulsions provide negative reinforcement because they reduce anxiety, making them more likely to repeat such behavior. Simply put, if you feel like your hands are dirty, it feels good to wash them. If you *always* feel like your hands are dirty, as is the case with many individuals with OCD, then you feel compelled to wash your hands excessively. To meet diagnostic criteria for the disorder, the obsessions or compulsions must be significantly time consuming, taking up at least one hour per day.

Compulsive hand washing is a common symptom of obsessive-compulsive disorder.

Other obsessive compulsive disorders include *hoarding disorder*, *trichotillomania*, and *excoriation disorder*. Hoarding disorder is a disorder in which people have trouble discarding possessions. The idea of throwing anything away can cause them a great deal of stress and being surrounded by their material possessions gives them a sense of security and relieves their anxiety. Trichotillomania is a disorder that causes people to pull out their hair when stressed. Many people with this disorder end up with bald spots on their eyebrows and scalp from excessive hair pulling. Excoriation disorder is characterized by recurrent skin picking, resulting in lesions. With many of these disorders, people report an uncontrollable urge to engage in these behaviors despite attempts to stop.

SOMATIC SYMPTOM AND RELATED DISORDERS

Somatic symptom disorders, previously called somatoform disorders, are characterized by symptoms of physical illness that cause significant distress or disruption of daily life, resulting from excessive time and energy devoted to the symptoms. In somatic symptom disorder, these symptoms may or may not be associated with a real medical condition. The disorder requires that a person have persistent symptoms for at least 6 months in order to be diagnosed. Typically, doctors rule out likely medical disorders before diagnosing someone with this mental disorder. What makes it a psychological problem is the excessive worry and distress over the physical symptoms.

One of the related somatic symptom disorders is *illness anxiety disorder*, previously known as hypochondriasis. This disorder involves persistent preoccupation with having or getting a serious illness. People with illness anxiety disorder do not exhibit symptoms –if they did, they would be diagnosed with somatic symptom disorder; they merely experience a high degree of anxiety about their health, sometimes leading them to repeatedly go to the doctor in search of an illness they think they may have. A hypochondriac tends to self-diagnose frequently, assuming minor occurrences like occasional fatigue are an indication that they have a serious, perhaps, life-threatening illness. Sometimes, convinced that they have an illness they do not have, they may seek out different specialists and diagnostic tests, even after they have seen a doctor.

Conversion disorder is another disorder in this category, involving symptoms of voluntary motor or sensory function that cannot be explained by a medical condition. A person with conversion disorder might complain of blindness or paralysis, despite showing no medical cause for these symptoms.

Factitious disorder is also categorized as a somatic symptom disorder. This disorder is marked by falsification of medical symptoms or self-induced disease or injury. Factitious disorder is the current diagnostic name for the well-known Munchausen syndrome. *Factitious disorder imposed on self* is a pattern of behavior in which a person fakes or induces symptoms in themselves. *Factitious disorder imposed on another* involves the faking or inducing of medical symptoms on someone else, typically a child.

DISSOCIATIVE DISORDERS

Dissociative disorders are those characterized by disintegration – or separation – of a person's consciousness, memory, identity, emotion, perception, or behavior. By definition, to dissociate means to separate so all the disorders in this category involve a separation of one or more of these features from the person.

One example of a dissociative disorder *is dissociative amnesia*, which causes individuals to suddenly forget parts of their lives as a result of emotional trauma. The gaps in memory vary from being as little as hours to as long as years. The forgetfulness brought on by dissociative amnesia cannot be attributed to normal forgetfulness. Sometimes people do not even know who they are, forgetting everything about their identity including name and birthday. Usually memory begins to return in under a week.

People with *dissociative fugue*, in addition to losing memory of their identity, travel long distances from home and often assume new identities. Previously, this was categorized as its own disorder, but as of the *DSM-5*, it is a specifier for dissociative amnesia. Typically fugue states only occur once in a lifetime. Often, people suffering from a fugue state recover their memory all at once, sometimes forgetting the fugue period altogether.

As dramatic as that might sound, it still does not compare to the severity of **dissociative identity disorder**, which you would probably recognize by its old name: multiple personality disorder. People suffering from dissociative identity disorder (DID) experience several distinct identities each with their own unique characteristics, including different genders, preferences, talents, and mannerisms. Stressful circumstances can lead to a shift into another identity. The course of the disorder can vary and sometimes the identities know of each other, but sometimes they do not. The person suffering from DID tends to have gaps in memory when an *alter*, or another identity, has control. Sometimes, she will discover evidence of actions she does not remember doing, like new clothes she does not remember buying.

Dissociative identity disorder can result in the creation of multiple identities, some of which can vary dramatically in their personalities, talents, preferences and motivations.

A prevalent theory of the cause of dissociative disorders is that dissociating helps people separate themselves from the memory and awareness of some traumatic experience, like child abuse (Dorathy, 2001). In other words, the disorder acts as a coping mechanism, allowing one to obtain distance from traumatizing experiences. In some cases, this manifests as periods of memory loss, as in the case with dissociative amnesia. In other cases, the person's very identity is dissociated into multiple different alters.

SEXUAL DYSFUNCTIONS AND PARAPHILIC DISORDERS

The *DSM-5* includes a section on **sexual dysfunctions**, including delayed ejaculation, erectile disorder, and female orgasmic disorder, among others. All of these disorders are marked by some impairment or loss of function in the sexual response. Some of these, like *erectile disorder* and *female sexual interest/arousal disorder*, involve the inability to become sexually aroused. These disorders are typically diagnosed when the problem is recurrent and impairs the ability to hold a normal sexual relationship. Others, like *orgasmic disorders* involve the inability to reach orgasm. For men, the opposite problem would be *premature ejaculation*.

Another category of psychological disorders are **paraphilic disorders**, which used to be categorized under the umbrella of sexual disorders, but has been separated into its own category in the *DSM-5*. Paraphilic disorders are sexual behaviors and interests that are persistent, intense, and cause distress to an individual or risk of harm to the self or others. The manual attempts to demedicalize and destigmatize unusual sexual preferences and behaviors, provided they are not distressing or detrimental to the self or others. Included as paraphilic disorders are: *voyeurism*, which is the desire to spy on others engaging in private, sexual activities; *exhibitionism*, which is the exposure of genitals in public; *frotteurism*, involving touching or sexually rubbing against a nonconsenting individual; *sexual masochism*, which is interest in experiencing pain, suffering, and humiliation in order to be sexually aroused; *sexual sadism*, which is the desire to inflict pain; *fetishism*, which is the sexualizing of inanimate objects such as shoes to achieve arousal and orgasm; and *transvestic disorder*, which involves engaging in cross-dressing to be sexually aroused.

Pedophilia is a particularly serious paraphilia that involves the desire to engage in sexual activity with children under the age of 13. Like frotteurism, voyeurism, and exhibitionism, pedophilia is criminally punishable because of issues of consent. In each of these situations, the person who is the object of their sexual desires has not provided consent to such activities, which is where the pleasure lies for the one with a paraphilic disorder. However, if a consenting sadist and a consenting masochist want to re-enact scenes from *Fifty Shades of Grey* and neither finds it distressing, there is really nothing psychologically wrong with that.

GENDER DYSPHORIA

Gender dysphoria is defined as distress accompanying the incongruence between one's assigned gender and one's expressed gender. Children and adults express this incongruence by dressing like the opposite sex or, in the case of children, playing with toys characteristic of the other gender. Some people with gender dysphoria undergo surgical procedures to physically change their sex.

This is a particularly controversial disorder whose definition has been altered several times in response to widespread protests that gender is socially constructed and unrelated to biological sex, and that classifying it as disordered behavior is akin to the classification of homosexuality in *DSM-I and DSM-II*. (Homosexuality was later removed in the seventh printing of the *DSM-II*.) Thus, in the *DSM-5*, criteria for gender dysphoria emphasizes distress or impairment in areas of daily functioning, to destigmatize those who insist they are the opposite gender and feel no clinically significant distress as a result.

There is evidence that genetic variations, hormonal imbalances, and differences in brain structures are largely responsible for the development of gender dysphoria (Heylens, at al., 2012). For example, intersex (or hermaphroditic) children are born with chromosomes and sex characteristics, including genitalia, that cannot be clearly identified as male or female. When children are born intersex, doctors typically perform surgery to be able to classify them as one gender or the other. If doctors and the parents label and rear the child as a girl, that person may feel as though they were assigned the wrong gender, leading to the development of gender dysphoria. Sociocultural factors, like traumatic childhood experiences, may also play a role. In one famous case, a child whose penis was accidentally severed in infancy was raised as a female by his parents. This led to significant discomfort with his assigned gender and transition to male later in life (Colapinto, 2001).

SCHIZOPHRENIA

Schizophrenia is a severe disorder which renders an individual unable to distinguish what is real and what is not, due to hallucinations and bizarre or delusional thoughts and behaviors. Several key features characterize the disorder including delusions, hallucinations, disorganized thinking and behavior, and negative symptoms, such as flat affect and reduced energy. **Delusions** are false beliefs that people hold, refusing to accept evidence to the contrary. These delusions can involve several different themes, including the delusion that someone is after them or that they have exceptional abilities, wealth, or fame. **Hallucinations** are false sensory perceptions, which might cause people to hear voices or see things that are not actually there. Typically, hallucinations of touch, smell, or taste are not as common.

Disorganized thinking is another hallmark of schizophrenia. People exhibiting disorganized thinking have affected speech patterns and tend to switch from one topic to another or ramble incomprehensively. Motor movements can also be disorganized or abnormal. Catatonic activity, including maintaining rigid, odd postures or not reacting to the environment can also be caused by schizophrenia. *Negative symptoms*, such as flat affect or emotional expression, lack of speech, or lack of motivation represent another cluster of symptoms. Some clusters of symptoms may be more prominent than others in a person with schizophrenia, though that is not necessarily the case.

Research on the causes of the disorder tends to favor the biopsychosocial model, indicating that genetic and hormonal influences, as well as environmental stressors, can predict the development of the disorder. The chances of having schizophrenia if an identical sibling has it are 1 in 2, and 1 in 10 if a parent or non-identical sibling has it (Plomin, DeFries, McClearn, & McGuffin, 2000). Other research on the etiology of schizophrenia has linked it to lower production of dopamine in the brain. However, analysis of the research suggests that people with this biological predisposition to the disorder will not develop it unless exposed to severe stressors throughout life (Harrison, 1999).

PERSONALITY DISORDERS

As we already know, personality can differ in many ways. Some patterns of thinking and behaving are maladaptive, leading to their classification as **personality disorders**. These tend to be rigid and persistent throughout life – as personality tends to be – and are so severe that they interfere with normal social functioning. The *DSM-5* identifies ten distinct personality disorders, grouped into three clusters based on similarity (see Table 12.1). One cluster includes disorders that are characterized by odd or eccentric behavior. This includes paranoid personality disorder, schizoid personality disorder, and schizotypal personality. Another cluster groups personalities that are all dramatic, emotional or erratic such as antisocial personality, borderline personality , and narcissistic personality. Finally, personality disorders associated with anxiety or fear, such as avoidant, dependent, and obsessive-compulsive personality, are grouped into a third category.

Personality Disorder	Key Features
Paranoid Personality Disorder	Distrust and suspicion of others
Schizoid Personality Disorder	Lack of interest in social relationships
Schizotypal Personality Disorder	Reduced capacity for close relationships
Antisocial Personality Disorder	Harming others without remorse
Borderline Personality Disorder	Unstable mood, relationships and view of self
Histrionic Personality Disorder	Attention-seeking behavior
Narcissistic Personality Disorder	Inflated sense of self and excessive concern with themselves
Avoidant Personality Disorder	Social inhibition and hypersensitivity to negative evaluation
Dependent Personality Disorder	Excessive need for care and support from others
Obsessive-Compulsive Personality Disorder	Fixations with orderliness and perfectionism

Table 12.1: Personality disorders and their defining characteristics.

Those with *paranoid personality disorder* tend to be suspicious and mistrusting of others, under the assumption that others might be looking to deceive or harm them in some way. As a result, they behave in oddly secretive, guarded ways. They can be hostile because of their paranoia and tend to hold grudges for a long time, even when remarks or actions are benign.

Antisocial personality disorder is characterized by self-serving behavior at the expense of others. People with this disorder might cheat, lie, and sometimes hurt people, with little or no guilt or remorse over their behavior. Many criminals and killers can be classed as having antisocial personality disorder because of their lack of regard for human life.

Some theorists have argued that the popularity of social media like Facebook and Instagram have led to an increase in narcissistic qualities in the overall population.

People with *narcissistic personality disorder* have an elevated sense of self; believing they are more important, talented, and revered than others. They require constant attention and admiration from those around them and often lose interest in social relationships in which they are not the center of attention.

Many of these personality disorders tend to manifest themselves as social isolation; what differentiates each one are the causes of the isolation. For example, people with *schizoid personality disorder* do not desire close relationships and get no enjoyment out of them. They see no point in getting close and forming relationships with others. Those that are *schizotypal* tend to avoid relationships because of cognitive distortions and suspiciousness of others. They do not get close to others because it makes them uncomfortable. Someone with *avoidant personality disorder* is equally likely to be socially isolated but in this case, it results from fear of being disliked or rejected. Avoidant types tend to avoid relationships unless they are certain they are liked. They tend to be very sensitive to negative evaluation from others and might perceive it even when it is not present.

NEURODEVELOPMENTAL DISORDERS

Neurodevelopmental disorders are disorders that tend to have an onset in childhood, though many of them continue into adulthood, including autism spectrum disorders, attention-deficit hyperactivity disorder (ADHD), and intellectual disability.

Attention-deficit hyperactivity disorder (ADHD) involves an inability to concentrate and/or hyperactive or impulsive behavior that is inappropriate for one's age. Children with ADHD may find it difficult to concentrate on a task without getting distracted. As a result of the lack of concentration, they may find it difficult to organize and understand new information. This distractibility can also make them forgetful and cause them to lose things, such as toys or writing utensils. They may fidget or squirm when they need to sit still, which is why they experience behavioral problems at school. Children with ADHD may be disruptive to other children in the classroom.

Some argue that the diagnosis and treatment of ADHD is disproportionate to the actual presentation of the disorder in the population, believing that some parents and teachers use the diagnosis as an excuse to not have to discipline normal, energetic children. After all, many school children have trouble following directions, paying attention to tasks, and controlling their behavior. Between 1989 and 2001, the number of ADHD diagnoses increased 381 percent (Bruchmuller et al. 2012). Nonetheless, it remains a very real problem for those who suffer from it, one that may even persist into adulthood.

Another serious neurodevelopmental disorder is *autistic spectrum disorder*, which is characterized by impaired social functioning and rigid, repetitive behaviors. This disorder now encompasses *autism*, a disorder that is characterized by lack of social and communication skills. The new reclassification also encompasses milder versions of autism such as *Asperger's syndrome*, which would now be considered a mild form of autism spectrum disorder; and *social (pragmatic) communication disorder*, which is diagnosed when sufferers only demonstrate social difficulties but do not exhibit restricted, repetitive patterns of behaving.

Children with autistic spectrum disorder do not socialize with other children and tend to be very withdrawn, sometimes showing signs of distress in social situations. They often lack social intuition and may have trouble understanding nonverbal communication, social cues, or sarcasm. As a result, developing and maintaining friendships can be quite difficult. Children with autism also exhibit several types of behaviors, including repetitive movements like rocking and clapping; compulsive behaviors like organizing; ritualistic behavior involving activities that are performed every day; and limited focus to certain activities.

The mind of an autistic child is very complex. Autistic children often have a world of insight and talent that they do not know how to express.

Research has found that biological factors are important in the development of neurodevelopmental disorders. Twin studies have shown the highly heritable nature of ADHD, suggesting that genetics plays a role in about 75 percent of the cases (Faraone et al., 2005). Some studies have found support for the genetic transmission of autism and associations between the disorder and dysfunction in neural synapses (Bauxbaum, 2009; Levy et al., 2009).

CHAPTER 12 REVIEW QUESTIONS

1. When Danay was 8 years old, she was attacked by a dog and she has had an intense phobia of dogs ever since. Which of these perspectives would best explain the cause of her phobia?

    a. Psychodynamic

    b. Diathesis-stress

    c. Cognitive

    d. Biological

2. Leah is constantly worrying that she left the stove on, so she turns the dial on the stove around three times to make sure it is off. She is exhibiting:

    a. Obsessions but not compulsions

    b. Compulsions but not obsessions

    c. Compulsions caused by obsessions

    d. Obsessions caused by compulsions

3. Aeilyng tends to worry about everything. She obsesses for days and days about minor concerns, like what to get friends for their birthdays or how much traffic she might encounter on the way to work. Her worries tend to keep her up at night. She is most likely suffering from:

    a. Panic disorder

b. Obsessive-compulsive disorder

c. Generalized anxiety disorder

d. Social phobia

4. Raul is extremely excitable, coming up with elaborate plans and talking to his friends about them, only to change his mind after coming up with a better idea. He stays up for hours excited about his imagined future. He is likely experiencing:

    a. A manic state of bipolar disorder

    b. A depressive state of bipolar disorder

    c. A mixed state of bipolar disorder

    d. A major depressive episode

5. Sara has been hearing voices when she walks down the street. When she turns around, there is no one there. It sounds like several people talking directly to her. She is likely experiencing:

    a. A manic episode

    b. Dissociative disorder

    c. Bipolar disorder

    d. Schizophrenia

6. T/F. Disorders with genetic causes like ADHD and schizophrenia are always developed if anyone in your immediate family has it.

7. False perceptions of reality like those that are typical of schizophrenia are called ______________________________.

8. Which personality disorder is marked by an inability to trust people and the suspicion that others are out to get them?

    a. Schizoid

    b. Paranoid

    c. Antisocial

    d. Histrionic

9. Ariel woke up not remembering how he spent his evening. He has a watch on that he does not remember owning. When he looked in his wallet, he found the receipt for the watch, purchased the day before. What disorder is he likely experiencing?

    a. Bipolar disorder

    b. Major depressive disorder

    c. Anxiety disorder

    d. Dissociative disorder

10. T/F. Even though ADHD is typically seen in children, it can continue into adulthood.

CHAPTER 13

STRESS AND HEALTH

FROM THE MOMENT you wake up in the morning to the moment you get to bed at night, you are working to accomplish a variety of goals and constantly making decisions. If your alarm does not go off and you wake up with only an hour to get dressed, eat breakfast, and get to work, you must rush through these tasks to make it on time, or you can decide to call your boss to let him know you are coming in late. Once you arrive at the office, there are a host of tasks waiting for you to complete them. You may realize throughout the day that it will be impossible for you to complete everything you have to do that day, so you must prioritize to ensure that the most important items get done. If it happens to be pay day, you are probably rushing to the bank after work before it closes, and trying to decide the best route with the least traffic to get you there. When you get home, you must decide whether to cook or to order in. If your child came home from school and feels under the weather, you'll need to contemplate whether to call the doctor or wait until morning to see if the symptoms worsen. By the end of the day, a slew of unexpected (and often undesirable) surprises have come up that you've had to deal with. On a day like this, you may find it difficult to fall asleep.

The daily concerns of any adult can be stressful. Every decision or behavior poses some challenge, sometimes minor and fleeting, sometimes major and enduring. To effectively deal with life's challenges, we must solve the problems we encounter to reduce the stress they cause. Failure to do so can have serious, potentially life-threatening consequences.

WHAT IS STRESS?

Stress is the emotional, cognitive, and physical response to situations that are challenging or threatening. Physically, stress can cause a lot of irregularities including problems sleeping, fatigue, and common bodily ailments like colds. In the ensuing sections, we will see why. Emotionally, stress can cause anxiety, fear, irritability, and sometimes depression, as well as anger and frustration. These problems can be much more pronounced if the source of the stress, or the **stressor**, is more significant or harder to resolve.

For example, having the fire alarm go off while you make breakfast is a problem easily resolved by turning on the air extractor to let the smoke out of your kitchen. This is a stressor that will demand immediate action, but the tension and anxiety caused by it will abate quickly. On the other hand, having your house burn down because of a lit candle is a much bigger stressor, requiring long-term coping and complex solutions.

Catastrophes, such as losing your home in a fire, are a source of major stress.

Sometimes stressors can arise from within, such as the pressure to get a perfect score on the paper you submitted for class. There is no external force creating this threat. The stress comes from your own thinking and the standards you place on yourself. This example illustrates one of the primary psychological reasons why certain situations are stressful: pressure. **Pressure**, as we have seen above, can come from within, or it can be external, like a deadline to finish a project within a certain timeframe. When we feel the need to work harder or faster toward a certain goal, we are experiencing pressure to achieve a goal or standard. Another example of pressure is the pressure to be thin caused by exposure to models, actors, and musicians. This is a major source of stress for a lot of teenagers who work tirelessly to meet this often unattainable standard.

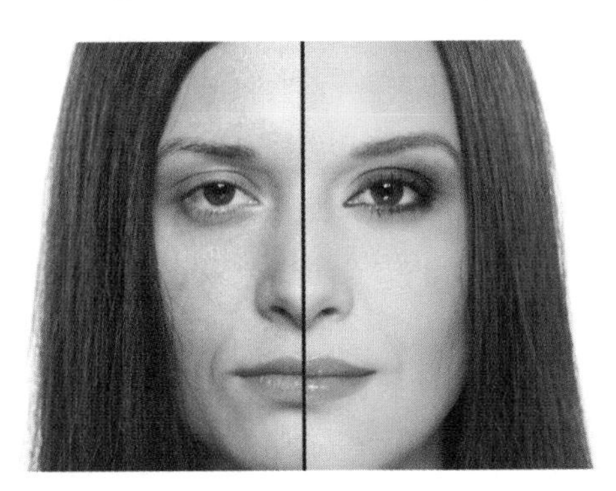
From a very young age, we are bombarded with images in periodicals of stick thin models with perfect hair, skin, and teeth. Though these photos are often Photoshopped to look perfect, this is the standard that is set for many adolescents for what is beautiful.

When we are unable to meet a desired goal, such as looking like a Victoria's Secret model, we experience **frustration**. Frustration can come from a number of different sources including failure, loss, rejection, or delay. For instance, imagine being a football player on a team with a perfect winning record, only to lose the final game of the season. This is a situation that would cause a great deal of frustration. Typically, when we are frustrated, we tend to either persist toward the goal – perhaps approaching it another way or trying again – or we aggress in order to take out our frustration. For example, a player on the team that lost their chance at a championship might take out his anger on the referee that he believed caused his team to lose the game. Another potential reaction to frustration is withdrawal: to quit a job, quit a team, or leave a partner.

Conflict is another major source of stress, and it occurs when one has different incompatible goals to choose from, whether they are psychological drives or external demands. There are different types of conflict depending on the nature of the opposing goals. In an *approach-approach conflict*, a person must choose between two desirable goals, like, for example, having to choose between two lovers or between two desirable job offers. You might be thinking: there are worse problems, right? But in both of these situations the stress comes from the fact that in making that decision, you are giving up something you wanted. Both of the goals have some attractive qualities – qualities that you want. So if you are involved in a love triangle worthy of daytime TV, you might end up choosing the man who is kind and treats you well over the man that is a little less considerate, but who has a much better sense of humor. No matter how happy you are with your final choice, you still had to give up that humor that you loved in the other man.

The opposite problem is an *avoidance-avoidance conflict*, which entails having to choose between two unpleasant or undesirable goals. Voting for president can often be an avoidance-avoidance conflict, where one must choose between "the lesser of two evils." When faced with a situation like this, many people choose to avoid or put off making a choice, like putting off a dentist visit when you have a cavity. The stress in this situation can be compounded after you've made your choice based on the outcome of that choice. For instance, if you are ordering food very late at night and the only thing open is a pizza place you hate, you would have to decide between ordering food you do not want or going to bed hungry. Either route you choose will probably lead to some post-decision dissatisfaction. If you order pizza and it makes you sick, you will probably wish you had just gone to bed without dinner. If you decide to go to bed and you are tossing and turning all night because your stomach will not stop grumbling, you will probably wish you had ordered pizza. In this case, as is the case with any of these conflicts, it is very easy to imagine what the alternative could have been.

A third type of conflict is an *approach-avoidance conflict*, which differs slightly from the first two in that the conflict regards one goal that is both repelling and attractive at the same time. This is true of a lot of situations in life that have both positive and negative aspects. Imagine landing a job that pays very well but requires you to move to a farm in South Dakota. For most people who have an established life and relationships in one place, it would be undesirable to leave it. This kind of conflict appears a lot in physically and emotionally abusive relationships, which is why it is so difficult for people to leave such relationships. No matter how bad the abuse may be, there are always characteristics of the abuser that are attractive to the victim, which is why she got into the relationship in the first place. Getting out of the abusive environment also means giving up those desirable aspects. Later on in the chapter, we will discuss further how to cope with a situation like this.

STRESS AND PERSONALITY

The key to what does and does not cause stress depends heavily on what you *perceive* to be challenging or stressful, and that perception can vary from person to person. If you are given a deadline that you know you can meet, you probably will not feel as much stress as someone given the same deadline that doubts his ability to complete the task. This has a lot to do with personality. For instance, someone who is on vacation who has created an hour-by-hour schedule of activities might experience a lot more stress if something in the schedule goes wrong than someone who prefers to go about their vacation with little to no planning. In the former case, something as minor as having to wait for a table for dinner might cause a great deal of stress because that person is probably thinking about how they are going to be late to the activities planned after dinner.

Psychologists have studied the link between certain traits and the propensity to experience and handle stress. One personality type that such research has linked to higher levels of stress is the Type A personality. Those with a Type A personality are very ambitious, driven, and hardworking, and tend to take on larger workloads, a characteristic that is associated with anxiety (Caplan & Kenneth, 1975). In fact, a study conducted on women found that those with a Type A personality reported feeling more nervousness in all situations, even those not work-related, compared to people with a Type B personality, who tend to experience less stress. (Dearborn & Hastings, 1987). Those with a Type B personality are not as affected by failure to succeed, and they work at a much lower stress level.

A second personality type that has been linked to greater levels of stress is one referred to as Type D, or distressed, personality. People with this personality type tend to experience greater levels of negative emotion, with a tendency to hide these emotions from people in social situations. Both of these tendencies have been shown to increase the chances of suffering from coronary heart disease (Sher, 2005). Researchers believe that the link between this personality type and risk of heart disease is the increased levels of *cortisol* caused by stress. If you recall from Chapter 2, *cortisol* – along with *epinephrine* and *norepinephrine* – is one of the hormones released by the adrenal glands in response to stress. Too much of this hormone causes increased blood pressure and a depressed immune system.

As we already know, personality is developed slowly as we age, and it can be very difficult to change. As such, people with these traits can have a predisposition to greater levels of stress and to long-term problems coping with it. However, realizing that you are more prone to stress, it would be useful to develop better coping and stress-prevention strategies so that stress does not become overwhelming.

HOW STRESS AFFECTS THE BODY

To better understand why stress-prone personalities are linked to such serious effects, let's discuss the mechanism by which stress acts on the body. Of course, not all stress is bad stress. A little bit of stress is healthy because it promotes motivated behavior, good health, and well-being. This is what psychologists call *eustress*. One theory of arousal suggests that people actually need stress, or arousal, in order to feel content (Zuckerman, 1994). Without some level of healthy stress, life would feel boring, mundane, and even a little meaningless. For example, healthy stress over a test would probably motivate you to study. Riding a rollercoaster and playing basketball are other examples of sources of eustress. They get your heart pumping and they are sources of excitement. Sports, like basketball, are also good for your health because they keeps you fit, as well.

Many people seek the thrill of rollercoaster rides because it gives them a rush without posing any real danger.

However, excessive stress, especially if it is prolonged, can spell trouble for your health and well-being. To understand why this is, we must think back to the fight-or-flight response and the nervous and endocrine systems. As you already know, the sympathetic nervous system and the adrenal glands are the parts of the body that react in response to stressful circumstances. In a stressful moment, your heart rate increases, breathing increases, digestion slows, blood rushes to your muscles, and you get the energy you need in order to act in response to the situation. The adrenal glands of the endocrine system secrete the right hormones, including norepinephrine and cortisol, to give you that burst of energy.

This is an evolutionary response that is supposed to increase the chances of survival. If our great, great ancestors experienced no physiological boost when encountering a woolly mammoth, they probably would not have lived very long and we would not be here. But with changing times, what one considers to be a dangerous, stress-inducing experience has changed quite a bit. Our ancestors in the Stone Age did not have iPhones or traffic lights. When we experience stress, even psychological stress, over such trivial things, we have the exact same physiological response as a caveman did running for his life from a wild beast. So when your gas light turns on in rush hour traffic or when your phone is about to die when you are shopping at the mall, your physiological response is commensurate with that of someone in an actually life-threatening situation. In the latter case, this is a great help in escaping that situation. In the former cases, it can be an abuse of your body's self-preservation mechanism.

Unfortunately, in our fast-paced world, many simple inconveniences become great sources of stress. And as those situations build up throughout the day, before you know it, your body has spent the entire day in an unnecessary state of alertness and anxiety. Psychologist Hans Selye (1956) identified a sequence of physiological reactions that we undergo when we experience stress, particularly with regards to the long-term consequences on the body. This is a sequence he called the **general adaptation syndrome (GAS)**.

1. **Alarm**: The first stage, as described above, is the nervous system and endocrine system response to a stressor. This activation

causes all the aforementioned effects on the body. This is the body's natural defense system. Typically, a simple stressor, like your gas light coming on can be easily resolved by filling up your tank. However, in certain situations, it is not that simple to fix a stress-inducing problem. For example, if you lost your job and you are having trouble finding a new one, returning your body back to its normal non-stressed levels is more difficult. In cases like these, when attempts to reduce the stress are unsuccessful, you pass into the second stage of adaptation.

2. **Resistance**: During this stage, the body becomes accustomed to the activity of the sympathetic nervous system and continues to release stress-related hormones. This also occurs when we have a lot of stressors affecting us simultaneously, even if they are all minor stressors. If you are running late and you get a lot of red lights, the entire drive will turn into a stressful experience. Even when that situation has passed, you may run into some issues at the office that need your attention, keeping your sympathetic nervous system active and your endocrine glands secreting stress hormones. As physical and psychological resources get used up, it becomes more difficult to resolve the problem, or problems, causing the stress.

3. **Exhaustion**. When there are no resources left, the person experiences exhaustion, which can lead to the formation of stress-related illnesses or burnout. Some physical symptoms of exhaustion may occur, like stomach problems. This is because the sympathetic nervous system inhibits the function of the digestive system. Chronic stress can lead to chronic digestive problems. People at this stage often turn to ineffective methods of coping, like drinking or drug use. These methods do not help improve the stress-causing situation and instead serve as a temporary escape from the stress.

According to Seyle, the prolonged secretion of stress hormones in the body is responsible for the most harmful, long-term effects of stress, such as ulcers and high blood pressure. Because stress is constantly drawing on the body's resources, it has a major effect on the immune system, similar to that of infection (Maier & Watkins, 1998). One study compared the amount of immune system chemicals that help fight off disease in students, finding that students under the stress of exams had significantly lower levels than those not under stress (Deinzer et al.,2000). This is because the hormones, like cortisol, that are meant to ensure your short-term survival are actually detrimental to your long-term survival by suppressing your immune system. Because of this effect on the immune system, stress causes the body to be more vulnerable to several major health problems including heart disease. Stress has been shown to put people at higher risk for heart attacks and strokes because it is associated with several of the risk factors for heart disease including obesity, high blood sugar, high triglycerides, and low levels of HDL – good cholesterol (Brunner et al., 2002).

Because stress can also lead to unhealthy behaviors like drinking, smoking, and eating high-fat, high calorie foods, it is also a risk factor for *diabetes*, which is an illness that causes high blood sugar. Diabetes is the result of the body's failure to produce enough insulin or to respond to available insulin, which impairs your ability to break down the food you consume (Surwit et al., 1992).

Diabetics are required to maintain a healthy diet and they need to monitor their glucose levels regularly because the body is not able to break it down.

SOURCES OF MAJOR STRESS

Aside from daily hassles, there are certain events in life that are sources of long-term, intense stress for most people. Many of these are stressful due to the fact that they are major life changes, and according to researchers, the bigger the change, the more stress it causes (Holmes & Rahe, 1967).

One source of major stress is unemployment. Losing your job could impair your ability to provide for yourself and your family and requires you to readjust your lifestyle, sometimes for a very long period of time. The stress caused by unemployment makes many other day-to-day activities much more stressful, like grocery shopping and paying bills. Researchers have found that adjusting to unemployment is similar to the experience of losing a loved one (Fagin, 2006).

The death of a loved one is an event that creates a lot of distress. Though the initial period of intense grief gets better with time, it can be extremely difficult to adjust.

Losing a loved one is, indeed, another major source of stress. According to Holmes & Rahe (1967), the death of a spouse represents the most stressful crisis a person can experience. Once again, this is because it creates a massive change that must be adjusted to. Unlike other situations, like unemployment, which may be temporary, this is a permanent loss. In most cases, particularly with close family members like spouses or children, the loss can leave a void that little else can fill.

Divorce and separation also requires a great amount of change and adjustment. As with the loss of a loved one, people have to adjust to life without someone that they are accustomed to having in their lives. Aside from sadness, separation can also come with feelings of guilt, anger, and sometimes failure, as people ruminate about the reasons for the separation. The stress can be made worse in situations where the pair is fighting for assets or custody of the children. In fact, for children, divorce between parents is reported as being the number one stressor (Mullen & Costello, 1981).

Catastrophes can be another major source of stress. Whether it is a hurricane or a terrorist attack, the psychological consequences of experiencing a catastrophe can be far-reaching and long-lasting. One study conducted after the terrorist attacks on September 11 found that over 40% of people surveyed reported one or more substantial symptom of stress, even if they were not personally affected by the attack. Forty-seven percent of people reported being worried about their safety or the safety of loved ones (Schuster et al., 2001). Catastrophes can have even more devastating effects for people who lost a loved one or a home in a disaster.

STRESS-RELATED PSYCHOLOGICAL DISORDERS

Though not all stress leads to long-term psychological dysfunction, there are several disorders linked to stress or trauma. The category of disorders in the *DSM-5* that lists diagnostic criteria for several trauma and stress-related disorders includes one of the most well-known psychological disorders: **posttraumatic stress disorder,** or **PTSD.** PTSD may be diagnosed when an individual has been exposed, either directly, as a witness, or otherwise, to a traumatic experience such as actual or threatened death, injury, or sexual violence. After such an experience, sufferers may experience symptoms like recurring memories and dreams of the event. They may go out of their way to avoid stimuli that trigger memories of the stressful event. For example, a war veteran might link the sights and sounds of a fireworks display to what he experienced at war. It is very common for sufferers who have such triggers to avoid being around them for fear of experiencing a flashback, which causes sufferers to feel like they are back in the war zone. Though fireworks can logically resemble a war zone, triggers are unique to the person, and may only be tangentially related to the trauma. They can be anything from an image to a particular smell that they associate in their memories with that event. In many cases, this avoidance of certain triggers may impair one's ability to live a normal life. For example, someone who was in a serious car accident may develop a fear of driving or being in cars, leading her to avoid this common – often necessary – situation.

PTSD sufferers also experience mood changes, including increased sadness, fear, guilt, irritability, and can be easily startled or stressed. Certain traumas, like war or accidents that resulted in death, may leave a person feeling *survivor's guilt*. This is a condition in which a person feels guilty for surviving when others did not. Often, these conflicting feelings lead many sufferers of PTSD to withdraw from friends and family and stop taking part in enjoyable activities. This also occurs, in part, because when readjusting to life, the person might have trouble relating to loved ones, and he may feel like no one could possibly understand what he went through. Like many other psychological disorders, this one can be very isolating. To be diagnosed as PTSD, the symptoms must last more than one month. For similar symptoms that persist fewer than 30 days, one would be diagnosed with *Acute Stress Disorder*.

PTSD affects thousands of veterans every year.

COPING WITH STRESS

So how do we deal with all these major life stressors and hassles? All stresses, big or small, require people to adjust and manage the stress. The way in which we attempt to control the problems can vary widely and not all of them are positive, productive solutions.

DEFENSIVE COPING

One of the hardest challenges we experience as adults is admitting that we are faced with a stressful, negative situation that requires considerable coping and change. Many people simply cannot deal directly with their source of stress; others may not even be able to identify the true source of the stress. When this occurs, we employ **defense mechanisms** in order to cope (Freud, 1894). These are strategies used to manipulate the mind to deny or distort the nature of a problem. Simply put, these are ways in which we deceive ourselves, because doing so temporarily reduces stress and saves us the trouble of dealing with stressful problems or situations in life.

Typically the first defense mechanism to rear its ugly head is denial. *Denial* prevents us from having to acknowledge a painful reality. As we know from the research on death and dying, one of the first responses to our own impending demise is to deny that there is anything is wrong in the first place. Another common instance of denial occurs when people are in problematic relationships but do not want to admit it to themselves, usually because admitting it would require taking action, like separating from the person. As you saw in the study of social psychology, we can be quite skilled at convincing ourselves that something is true when it is not. In these situations, a person would convince himself that there is nothing wrong or problematic about his partner or relationship, when there clearly is.

Another defense mechanism according to Freud is *repression*, which is the exclusion of some reality from our consciousness altogether. For example, a child that was a victim of abuse might have blocked out memories and feelings about those events, so as to not have to cope with the psychological ramifications of those experiences.

Sometimes problems cannot be denied or repressed so we mentally alter the nature of the problem to make it easier for us to handle. One example of this is called *projection*, which is a way of rejecting our own unacceptable desires or behaviors by ascribing them to someone or something else. For example, thoughts of infidelity toward a partner, which produce guilt, may be turned into blame and lead to suspicion and accusations that the partner is being unfaithful, instead. Making oneself the victim and blaming the partner reduces the stress caused by the guilt of one's own unfaithful thoughts and motives.

When we experience guilt as a result of our own unfaithful thoughts or actions, we may project those onto our partners.

One may also employ a defense mechanism known as *identification* to deal with stress. Unlike projection in which one is projecting feelings onto others, identification involves assimilating desirable characteristics and attributes of others onto oneself in order to vicariously experience their successes. The stereotypical example of identification is parental identification with their children. A mother might suffer from feelings of inadequacy and failure because she was never able to become a famous ballet dancer like she always wanted, so she identifies with her child's dancing career in order to live vicariously through her and resolve these feelings.

Stressful situations can also lead to *displacement,* which shifts frustration from the object of stress to another, safer object. This "kick the dog" method of coping allows you to relieve stress by taking it out

Parents with unresolved conflicts related to failures sometimes push their children toward a goal they wanted to achieve. A father who never got to play in major league baseball may be very demanding of his son to achieve greater athletic ability.

on someone that has nothing to do with the stress, such as the family pet. Typically, displacement occurs when it is "safer" to take out your aggression onto someone or something than to address the root of the problem. For example, if your boss spent all day yelling at you, you might feel helpless to fight back for fear of losing your job. But you may go home and displace that anger onto your spouse and children, who had nothing to do with it in the first place.

Intellectualization is another defense mechanism which makes use of reasoning to block out certain painful truths or emotions. This method of coping uses thinking in order to avoid feeling and in doing so, allows us to detach partially from our problems. For example, having your identity stolen can be a very stressful situation and requires a lot of work to restore your finances, credit, loans, and other debts to order. Someone who is overwhelmed by all these procedures might intellectualize the situation by spending time researching the variety of methods and tactics that someone might use to steal your identity.

Freud believed certain defense mechanisms were socially acceptable because they represented signs of maturity. One such mechanism is *sublimation*, which allows us to redirect repressed and socially unacceptable impulses into more socially acceptable actions or behaviors. For example, an artist may transform painful experiences into beautiful paintings or songs. This sublimation allows him to function normally as these venues allow him to deal with and express these problems, without acting out in a way that is frowned upon.

DIRECT AND CONSTRUCTIVE COPING

When we do attempt to consciously resolve a problem in order to reduce the stress it causes, instead of masking it, we are engaging in *direct coping*. Direct coping tends to focus on the problem or situation in order to change it, in a way that is useful and constructive.

The first step in direct coping, similar to what one might hear at an addiction recovery meeting, is to admit that there is a problem. Once this is done, there are several different ways in which one can attempt to solve this problem.

One type of direct coping is *confrontation*. This is a common problem solving strategy that focuses on the problem and makes conscious efforts to reduce stress and accomplish a goal. This strategy may involve changing aspects about yourself, or finding ways to express anger and frustration, if that is what will solve the problem. Simply blowing off steam, like by going to the gym, can prevent you from blowing up in a rage when the stress becomes overwhelming. Sometimes confrontation merely requires persistence and effort, like when you fail an exam, for example. This may be frustrating, but if you study hard and do better next time, the stress caused by that situation will be largely alleviated.

Another effective way of coping with stress is *compromise*. Compromise, a hallmark of successful relationships, requires that we accept a give-and-take situation. As adults, we quickly learn that we do not always get our way, so we settle for the best possible scenario. For example, dividing up the chores in the household may be a source of stress for some. A compromise where one spouse agrees to do the dishes and another agrees to take out the trash can defuse that situation and make it less stressful in the future. Once these duties have been discussed and established, there is no reason to argue about it. People also compromise with themselves quite often. If you are doing a little shopping for yourself, you may be torn between buying a new pair of shoes or a new pair of jeans, knowing you cannot afford both (this would be an example of an approach-approach conflict). The reasonable thing to do would be to compromise and buy either the shoes or the jeans and save the other item for another shopping trip.

In certain situations, the most effective way of coping is to withdraw completely. Withdrawal might be associated with quitting or failure, but in certain instances, it can be the most productive, healthy course of action. As previously mentioned, being in an abusive relationship can cause a great deal of stress. This is a situation in which withdrawal is almost always the best solution, because no other method of coping can really solve the problem that causes stress: the abuse. Confronting or compromising with the batterer probably would not work, at least not in the long run. In fact, trying to compromise or confront the situation may actually put the victim in serious physical danger. The best thing to do, instead, is to remove herself from such a relationship. Despite the negative connotation of withdrawal, sometimes, in the eyes of many a person would be seen more negatively if she *does not* withdraw. This is precisely what happened to singer Rihanna when she continued to publicly date Chris Brown after the domestic violence incident that left her bloodied and bruised.

Public backlash grew after pop singer, Rihanna, was seen spending time with her abuser, Chris Brown.

Healthy ways of coping may require more effort, but they tend to be more effective in reducing stress in the long run. Constructive coping should also involve efforts to prevent stress, like not procrastinating and maintaining a healthy lifestyle, including exercise and adequate sleep as a way to keep stress at bay.

CHAPTER 13 REVIEW QUESTIONS

1. T/F. Stress can be good or bad.

2. Psychological stress that is motivating is called:

   a. Distress

   b. Eustress

   c. Pressure

   d. Frustration

3. Ernie only has one dollar and he cannot decide whether he wants to buy a candy bar or a can of soda. What type of conflict is he experiencing?

   a. Approach-approach conflict

   b. Avoidance-avoidance conflict

   c. Approach-avoidance conflict

   d. None of these; he is experiencing frustration

4. Jesse failed her final exam so she will not be able to pass her math course. What type of stress-causing experience is she facing?

   a. Conflict

b. Pressure

c. Frustration

d. A and C

5. During which stage of the General Adaptation Syndrome does the body become accustomed to the activity of the sympathetic nervous system until physical and psychological resources get used up? ______________________________

____

6. T/F. Stress is associated with major health problems like heart disease and diabetes.

7. Henry was just diagnosed with a sexually transmitted disease. He is convinced this could not possibly be true because he always uses a condom. What kind of defensive mechanism is he employing?

   a. Identification

   b. Intellectualization

   c. Sublimation

   d. Denial

8. Gabriel is really frustrated because his wife spends all their money on clothes and he does not have enough money for

the things he wants to do, like going to concerts. Which of the following would be a good example of a compromise?

a. He cancels her credit card and budgets everything she spends.

b. They agree to create a budget together that allots some funds for both of their interests.

c. They get divorced.

d. All of these are examples of effective compromise.

9. Maria feels really overwhelmed with school and work. She comes home in a bad mood and yells at her husband and reprimands the kids for playing too loudly. Which method of coping is she exhibiting?

a. Direct coping

b. Confrontation

c. Displacement

d. Sublimation

10. T/F. Withdrawal is a cowardly way of coping with a stressful situation and should only be considered as a last resort.

CHAPTER 14

PSYCHOLOGICAL THERAPIES

NOW THAT WE'VE LEARNED all about psychological disorders and stresses, let's turn our attention to the methods used to help alleviate these problems. There are two accepted types of therapies to treat psychological problems and help people function more effectively in their everyday lives. One of them is based on psychological techniques and involves a therapist helping a client overcome his problems. This type of therapy is called **psychotherapy**. Psychotherapy is not simply one established method, as you may be thinking. It is a variety of techniques ranging from behavioral to psychoanalytic, including styles that mix the different psychological perspectives, picking and choosing aspects from each one. Below we will discuss in detail, the specific techniques used by psychologists from these different psychological perspectives.

The other type of therapy, called **biomedical therapy,** uses medical methods to help treat psychological problems. Biomedical therapy can range from medication to surgery, as we will discuss below, and it has its advantages and disadvantages compared to psychotherapy. However, often both psychotherapy and medication are used together leading to successful outcomes.

HISTORICAL PERSPECTIVE

Treatment for psychological problems was not always so clear cut. As discussed in previous chapters, before psychology became its own discipline, there was widespread misinformation about mental illnesses and their causes.

In the sixteenth century, beginning in England, people began committing the mentally ill into asylums. There were no established treatments for psychological ills so patients were often beat or put in ice baths until they passed out as a spiritual cleanse (Hunt, 1993). Though asylums were created with good intentions as a place of refuge – as the definition suggests – these conditions were not conducive to improvement of mental health. Many patients, particularly those considered a danger to others, were chained and kept in dark rooms that were often dirty and not well-maintained.

In 1793, came the first effort to improve the treatment of the mentally ill by using guidance and kindness, a practice known as moral treatment, with the aim of improving their mental health. This movement was led by Frenchman Philippe Pinel (Brigham, 1844). By the mid-19th century, there were many mental hospitals in the United States that provided this type of humane treatment to the mentally ill. However, lack of funding led to the decline of conditions in such hospitals by the 1950s. It was also during this time that drug therapies began to surge in popularity, which led to the widespread release of people with severe psychological disorders, a practice called **deinstitutionalization**. This practice largely failed for several reasons. For one, follow-up care was not available, leading to a harsh transition from institutionalized life. Furthermore, many patients, having been committed for months or years, no longer had a support system outside of hospitals to fall back on. As a result, many of the displaced mentally ill became homeless, which is part of the reason why over 40% of the homeless population in the U.S. is mentally ill (Burt et al., 1999).

The other alternative to institutionalization and medication became psychotherapy, a move that was supported by research in the area. In a series of studies, mentally ill patients were assigned to either a hospital or to alternative programs including training to cope with stress, therapy, crisis intervention, and visits with mental health nurses (Kiesler, 1982). Though the hospitals provided adequate care, the alternative treatments were found to be more effective 9 out of 10 times. Studies like these provide support for the use of psychological techniques to improve mental health and reduce the number of people in inpatient institutions.

So what are the psychological techniques used by therapists, psychiatrists, and psychologists? The answer depends on the therapists' psychological perspective. You might have thought before reading this text that all therapy was the same thing and that all therapists are trained the same way. However, the techniques used in therapy can vary considerably depending on the perspective taken by the clinician and the way that perspective explains mental illness.

PSYCHOANALYSIS

Freud's **psychoanalysis** or psychodynamic therapy is based on the idea that mental illness is a way in which unconscious conflicts manifest themselves. As such, the treatment for these problems should be to uncover the unconscious conflicts, urges, and repressed memories that created the problem in the first place. Psychoanalysis is considered an *insight therapy* because it focuses on gaining an understanding of drives and motivations. Insight is very important for humanistic therapy, as well, but is de-emphasized in cognitive and behavioral therapies.

Though psychoanalysts often had patients lie down to discuss their concerns, modern therapists tend to prefer to have face-to-face conversations with their clients.

In traditional psychoanalysis, patients would lie down on a couch in order to be more relaxed and open, as a way to more easily access their childhood memories. The therapist would then employ a variety of different techniques to uncover what was in their unconscious, getting their patients to speak openly about their thoughts, feelings, and dreams.

Free association is one such technique, which is meant to get the patient to speak freely about whatever comes into their minds (Breuer & Freud, 1895). The idea is that in spontaneously speaking their minds, the patients reveal hidden, unconscious thoughts that present themselves as recurring themes or concerns. The psychoanalyst's job is to interpret the recurring themes and ideas that may underlie a patient's thinking. Similarly, Freud and his contemporaries use *dream interpretation* to analyze elements in dreams that could represent some unconscious wish or concern. As mentioned in Chapter 4, Freud analyzed not only the *manifest content* of the dream, which are the concrete events of the dream taken at face value, but also the *latent content*, the hidden symbolic meaning of the dream. By interpreting this content, he could unlock the secrets of their unconscious.

Another component of Freud's therapy is called **transference**, which is a process in which the therapist comes to symbolize an authority figure in the client's past. So if a patient had an abusive or neglectful parent, for example, he could unleash his repressed emotions about that parent to the therapist. According to Freud, this process brings about a catharsis that would theoretically resolve the person's concerns. This is known as "working through" conflicts. Naturally, the first step to resolving these conflicts is to gain insight into what they are.

Though groundbreaking for its time, traditional psychoanalysis has largely fallen out of favor compared to other therapeutic interventions. Neo-Freudian psychologists that carry on Freud's legacy tend to use modified versions of the original therapy, favoring face-to-face discussions instead of having the client lie down. They also encourage patients to face their current problems, as opposed to spending months or years trying to gain an understanding of the past. These modifications are more popular, as they leave less room for subjective interpretations from the therapist of past events, and they lead to faster psychological improvement. This is helpful because most people in contemporary society find it difficult to commit to therapy unless they see immediate gains.

HUMANISTIC THERAPY

Humanistic therapists take a slightly different approach to therapy. Instead of focusing on unconscious, hidden conflicts, they deal with the conscious, emotional experiences of their clients and their daily lives (Cain & Seeman, 2001). They emphasize the potential for change and improvement, as well as how conscious choices shape our lives. Within the umbrella of humanistic therapy, there are a variety of specific types, two of which are described below.

ROGER'S CLIENT-CENTERED THERAPY

If you recall, Carl Rogers had a theory of personality that states that the better a person's real self matches with his ideal self, the happier and more well-adjusted he becomes – a state Rogers defined as fully functioning. The goal of **client-centered therapy** is to help people become fully functional by helping them more accurately identify discrepancies between the real and ideal self and to help them work towards a realistic ideal. A central part of the therapy is to provide the client with unconditional positive regard that may have been missing from his life. According to Rogers, this total acceptance allows the client to get closer to his ideal self.

Though this is also a type of insight therapy – as is psychoanalysis – it is largely nondirective, meaning that the client does most of the work in uncovering his own motivations while the therapist acts as a guide. The therapist would not suggest reasons as to why the client may have certain feelings or what he should do about it. Instead, the therapy focuses on *reflection*, which allows the client to think about his own feelings and motivations, without the therapists' interjections, as they may be flawed or biased. To this end, the therapist generally restates what the client says to encourage the client to reach his own conclusions.

Client-centered therapists also demonstrate empathy and authenticity in their interactions with clients. Empathy requires that the therapist understand what the client is going through and authenticity refers to genuine, open responses to the client. In other words, the therapist is able to put herself in the client's shoes to be able to clearly see what the client is thinking and feeling, and to honestly and openly discuss her perspective with the client.

GESTALT THERAPY

Another humanistic therapy, called **Gestalt therapy,** takes a more directive approach involving leading questions and role playing. The goal of Gestalt therapy and these role playing exercises is for the therapist to help the client accept himself. Fritz Perls (1951), who developed Gestalt therapy, believed that a person experiences distress when his inner self does not match the person he projects to the world – a concept similar to Roger's theory.

Unlike client-centered therapy, Gestalt therapists take an active role in the therapeutic process, asking leading questions and confronting clients about their statements. Like other insight therapies, this technique helps people become more aware of their feelings, making them more responsible for their choices. They may also engage in planned role play, including discussions with an empty chair, used to represent someone in their lives. Empty chair therapy allows clients to redirect their unexpressed feelings toward someone in a safe environment alongside the therapist. Using techniques like this, therapists push clients to take responsibility for their lives, their feelings, and their actions in order to become more genuine in their lives, with the aim of being able to project their true inner selves to the outside world.

During the 2012 Republican National Convention, actor Clint Eastwood memorably delivered a speech to an empty chair in place of President Obama. This came across as silly to some, but this is actually very similar to empty chair therapy, which allows clients to vent their feelings toward a person that is not physically present.

BEHAVIOR THERAPIES

Behavior therapies use the basic principles of learning and reinforcement to change maladaptive behavior. These are not based on insight into feelings and motivations, but based on action. Since behaviorists believe that psychological disorders are a result of learning maladaptive ways to behaving, they developed techniques based on classical and operant conditioning to help clients unlearn these behaviors and to learn new, healthier behaviors.

THERAPIES BASED ON CLASSICAL CONDITIONING

As you know by now, classical conditioning is the process of learning involuntary responses by pairing a stimulus that causes a certain automatic response with a new stimulus. This leads to the conditioning of an otherwise unlearned automatic response in tandem with the paired stimulus. Using the same principle, therapists are able to help clients overcome many psychological disorders including phobias, obsessive-compulsive disorders, and similar anxiety disorders. The following represent three different behavioral therapies based on classical conditioning.

EXPOSURE THERAPIES

One behavioral therapy based on classical conditioning is **exposure therapy**, which forces the client to experience situations that he finds anxiety-provoking. Exposure can be done live or *in vivo*, thrusting a person into a situation he most fears. For example, a person with a fear of public speaking might be asked to deliver a speech in front of a large crowd. Exposure therapy can also be done virtually, using computer technology or using the client's imagination. For example, someone seeking treatment for fear of flying may be placed in a flight simulator to get him used to the sensations.

When a person has a phobia of something, he often makes efforts to avoid that object or situation and in some cases, even the thought of it can be distressing. The emphasis of exposure therapy is on getting the client to do something that he finds distressing, until he learns that the situation or object is not to be feared.

Exposure can be done gradually, using a fear hierarchy in a step-by-step procedure called systematic desensitization (which is described below), or all at once, using a technique called *flooding*. Flooding must be done in very controlled conditions to avoid something going wrong. The rationale is that the exposure to the feared stimulus without the possibility of escape would produce extinction of the conditioned fear when the person sees that his worst fears surrounding that situation do not come to light. Though quite anxiety-provoking at first, the experience of being plunged fully into an uncomfortable situation, only to find that nothing bad resulted from it, helps people become accustomed to that feared object or situation.

SYSTEMATIC DESENSITIZATION

Systematic desensitization is a process by which anxiety and fear are reduced by *gradually* exposing the client to increasingly anxiety-provoking situations (Wolpe, 1990). For example, imagine a person who is deathly afraid of spiders undergoing treatment for her phobia. Systematic desensitization begins with learning relaxation techniques, which allows the person to bring her anxiety response under control. After the person has mastered these techniques, she would be asked to construct a list, or hierarchy, of situations involving the feared object or situation from those that cause the least fear to those that cause the most fear.

Finally, using the relaxation techniques and under the supervision and guidance of a therapist, the person must confront every situation in the hierarchy. So this person might have listed seeing a picture of a spider as the lowest on her list, which means it would be the first thing that she does as part of the therapy. Pairing the relaxation techniques with the picture of a spider would lead the anxiety to gradually subside. Once looking at a picture of a spider no longer produces a fear response, the person moves up in the list to the next most stressful task, until eventually she is able to overcome the most stressful situation

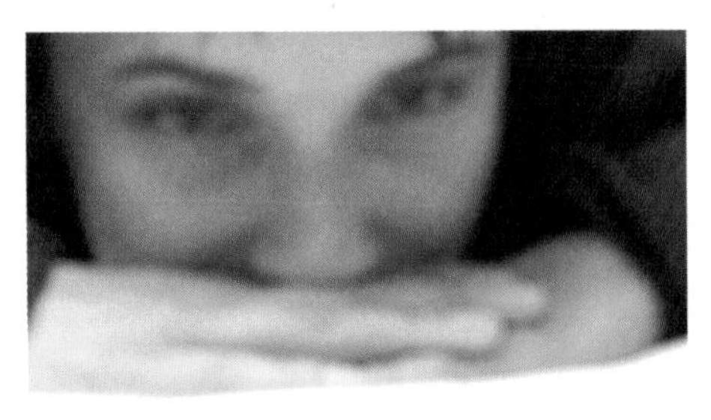

A person with a diagnosed phobia of spiders would never be able to calmly stare at one as it walks on his desk. With a lot of effort and gradual exposure to the spider, this may be possible.

on the list. By the end of systematic desensitization therapy, she may be able to hold a spider without significant anxiety.

This therapy works by replacing the fear response to a certain stimulus with a conditioned relaxation response to that stimulus. Since the two are incompatible, eventually the idea of calm and relaxation comes to be associated with the object instead of panic and fear.

AVERSION THERAPY

While systematic desensitization and exposure therapies attempt to make people feel more comfortable with a feared situation or stimulus, **aversion therapy** does the exact opposite. In this therapy, an undesirable or dangerous behavior, like smoking, is paired with something aversive in order to reduce the desire to smoke.

Think about the last time you got too drunk and got sick the next day. The experience of a serious hangover probably discouraged your drinking for some time afterward. This is the exact same principle behind aversion therapy. Basically, if you continuously link feeling very ill with drinking, over time you would probably stop drinking or drink less to avoid feeling ill. One type of aversion therapy is called the rapid-smoking technique in which a smoker is instructed to take a puff every 5 or 6 seconds, which creates nausea and dizziness – unpleasant

A hangover essentially acts as an aversive force which will make you less likely to want to drink again.

effects intended to deter the smoker from craving a cigarette again.

This therapy also uses elements of operant conditioning. Remember, behaviorists believe that we behave in certain ways because that behavior is reinforced somehow. Aversion therapy creates negative consequences for a specific behavior in the hopes that when the negative consequences outweigh the rewards, you will no longer engage in that behavior.

THERAPIES BASED ON OPERANT CONDITIONING

As mentioned above, operant conditioning suggests that we respond to incentives and reinforcers. Therapies based on this idea make use of these principles to change maladaptive behavior. One technique is to use *modeling*, a practice by which the therapist gives a client step-by-step instructions on how carry out a task, like breathing exercises for stress relief. The client can observe a model and copy his behavior in order to learn it. As we saw when discussing learning, this is one of the most common ways in which we learn in everyday life.

Reinforcement is an important tool in therapy, as well. When a desirable consequence follows a behavior, people are more likely to repeat the behavior. This is the idea behind *token economies* and *contingency contracting*. In a token economy, which can be used in hospitals or mental institutions, people are rewarded using some treat or privilege for behavior that is adaptive and appropriate. For example, patients in an institution may get a token every time they take their medication when directed or visit their therapist. Once they have gained enough tokens, they can redeem them for some reward, like a day trip out of the hospital or other privileges. This technique can also incorporate punishment, with patients losing tokens for bad behavior.

In contingency contracting, a formal agreement is established in which behavioral change, reinforcements, and penalties are all agreed upon. The client, thus, is aware of how he should act and what the consequences are for not adhering to the terms of the contract. This can be useful in treating drug addictions, where drug use can be specifically monitored and the client can come to expect certain penalties or consequences for drug use that violates the contract (Talbott & Crosby, 2001).

COGNITIVE THERAPIES

Cognitive psychologists believe that our psychopathology is a result of distorted thinking, so the resulting **cognitive therapies** aim to change these maladaptive ways of thinking. The rationale behind cognitive therapy is that if you can change your thinking, you can achieve psychological improvement (Beck, 1979). The basic goal is to help clients objectively analyze the truth about their negative beliefs and assumptions, and their faulty attributions about their own and others' behaviors.

Beck's original cognitive therapy for treating depression was focused on distortions of thinking. For example, he believed that people often jump to conclusions without evidence. This might be exemplified by someone whose friend did not call her back leading her to assume that her friend hates her. Beck also believed that depressed people are guilty of selective thinking, in which they focus only on the negative aspects of a situation and ignore the positive. Blowing things out of proportion and shouldering the blame for events that have nothing to do with them are also characteristic of depressive thinking.

Beck would probably say that if you think of the glass as half empty, what you need to do is change that perception.

The therapist attempts to get the client to objectively look at her beliefs to determine how accurate they are. For instance, a therapist might ask the girl described above what evidence she really has to support the assumption that her friend dislikes her. By discussing these beliefs and determining how logical or illogical they are, the client can learn to think more constructively.

This cognitive therapy also led to the creation of *cognitive behavioral therapy (CBT),* which in addition to attempting to change irrational, maladaptive cognition, helps clients develop behavioral strategies that can be used to cope with problems. Couched within the changing patterns of thinking, the client's actions are changed, as well.

RATIONAL-EMOTIVE BEHAVIOR THERAPY (REBT)

As with any type of therapy, Beck's cognitive therapy spurned the creation of a host of other cognitive therapies. Albert Ellis (1997) developed a therapy he called **rational-emotive behavior therapy**, which directly challenges clients' irrational beliefs and replaces them with more helpful statements. According to Ellis, many of the erroneous beliefs we hold about the world are black-and-white or all-or-none. For example: "If everyone does not love me, I am awful and unlovable." This statement implies that everyone you meet must be loving and affectionate, and is blind to the reality that some people simply do not get along and that does not necessarily reflect anything about you personally. REBT therapists are extremely directive and can come across as challenging when they confront the client. If you have ever watched television's Dr. Phil, you probably have a pretty good idea of how REBT is conducted.

If it has not occurred to you already, this therapy is not as warm and accommodating as other therapies that take a gentler approach to communicating with their clients. This would be more effective for people who prefer a no-nonsense approach to psychotherapy, even if it is harsher. The truth may be a tough pill to swallow but sometimes, we need to hear it.

STRESS-INOCULATION THERAPY

Another cognitive therapy is *stress-inoculation therapy*, which helps people improve their coping skills (Meichenbaum, 1996). In stressful situations, clients are urged to use self-talk to guide themselves through the crisis. For instance, if you are nervous about giving a speech, you are probably having racing thoughts about messing up, having people laugh at you, or falling on stage. This is precisely the kind of thinking that makes anxiety worse.

Using stress-inoculation training, a client would be taught to replace those negative thoughts with more adaptive, helpful thoughts, like: "It'll be over soon. I'm going to do great. I'm very prepared for this." This therapy is advantageous because it prepares a person to deal with the distressing situations that occur in real life without the help of the therapist, who is often not around when they occur. In this way, a person's stress response is refocused as a way to solve problems.

GROUP THERAPIES

All of the aforementioned therapies are traditionally individual therapies, meaning the client talks with the therapist alone. An alternative to these are *group therapies*, which are therapeutic methods that involve people other than the client and the therapist.

There are several different types of group therapies, including self-help groups, family therapy, and couple therapy. In each of these variations of group therapy, problems may be discussed or treated slightly differently.

In **self-help,** or **support groups**, people meet with others, who typically suffer from similar problems. This is not necessarily the case; sometimes, general counseling groups attract people from all walks of life with varying concerns. These groups may or may not function under the direction of one or more therapists. One of the most well-known examples of a support group is Alcoholics Anonymous, or AA.

In AA and support groups like it, everyone has a chance to speak about his situation and obtain input from others suffering from the same problem. This is advantageous in that it can help members of the group gain better insight into their problem, particularly from people at more advanced stages of recovery. The emotional support from others can be very helpful on the road to recovery. Studies have shown that breast cancer patients tended to have higher rates of survival if they participated in group therapy compared to those in individual therapy (Fawzy et al., 1993). Group therapy also tends to be very cost effective, sometimes even free of charge. The downside is that people must compete for the therapist's time. One must also be comfortable being completely open in front of strangers, so it is not a preferred method for people that are particularly shy.

Family therapy is also classified as a group therapy because it involves more than a one-on-one session with a therapist. This type of therapy brings all members of the family together, often when they are experiencing some problem at home. Divorce, which was previously discussed as a source of enormous stress, can often motivate families to attend therapy together. Behavioral problems in children or conflict in the home are other issues that can bring families to therapy. Family therapy can be helpful because not everyone necessarily sees the same side of a problem, so the therapist can help reconcile what is really going on and how to work through it as a unit. The ultimate goal is to discover and change any unhealthy or maladaptive ways in which the family members interact. Opening up lines of communication and learning how to work through disagreements tend to be skills learned in therapy.

Couple therapy has similar aims, except that it focuses on the people in a relationship instead of the whole family. Many couples fight or go through rough patches because they have different expectations of the relationship or the role of each person in the relationship. This can be very hard to express and can easily lead to problems. Couple therapy can help increase the frequency of productive communication between partners. It can also help partners develop mutual expectations and reach compromises for the benefit of the relationship.

Couple therapy can be very helpful, particularly when both people in the relationship want to put forth the effort to stay together. It may be less effective in cases where one person is not interested in confronting the problem or is not willing to compromise.

DOES THERAPY WORK?

Research has demonstrated that none of the psychotherapies differed in their effectiveness (Luborsky et al., 1975). You may be thinking to yourself: Does that mean that they were all equally effective or equally ineffective? The answer to that question is complex. Studying the effectiveness of therapy involves assuming that all therapies take the same amount of time to work, which is usually not the case. It is also difficult to compare therapies because it requires that a group of people suffering from psychological distress is withheld treatment in order to serve as a baseline for comparison to those in experimental therapy. They may end up suffering a great deal from not having access to treatment. To prevent this, researchers sometimes compare new therapies to established methods that are consistently effective, in place of having to place participants in a no-therapy condition. If a group of participants in a therapy effectiveness study improves, there may be other factors that influence their improvement. Without a no-treatment baseline, that can be hard to determine.

Nonetheless, people who have undergone therapy report feeling like it has helped more often than not, regardless of the type of therapy (Kotkin et al., 1996). As you have seen, different therapies are often a better fit for certain problems over others. A dissociative disorder, which is widely believed to be caused by traumatic childhood events, would probably be well treated by a psychodynamic psychologist. Whereas phobias are probably best handled by therapists with a behavioral perspective who will use exposure and desensitization techniques until the fear is gone.

Recent emphasis on common effective factors that transcend all psychological perspectives have identified several that have been shown to be correlated with success in therapy, regardless of discipline (Norcross, 2005). One of the most important common factors is the **therapeutic alliance**, which is the relationship between the client and the therapist. Warm, caring, respectful, and understanding relationships tend to lead to more effective outcomes. The setting should also feel safe in order for the client to be open to sharing emotions and revealing private thoughts. Positive experiences and the opportunity for catharsis are other notable common factors related to therapy's effectiveness. Personal preference also plays a major role. Therapy is something that requires effort on the part of the client in order to work. If you believe that the treatment you are receiving will not work, you probably won't put very much effort into trying to make it work, which means it probably won't. A social psychologist would call this a classic case of the self-fulfilling prophecy.

BIOMEDICAL THERAPIES

Aside from all these methods of psychotherapy, biomedical therapies such as medication, are readily available for the treatment of psychological problems. Therapists whose perspective is biological or psychiatrists who went to medical school are much more likely to prefer these methods to psychotherapy; they believe that the cause is biological so the treatment should match.

DRUG THERAPIES

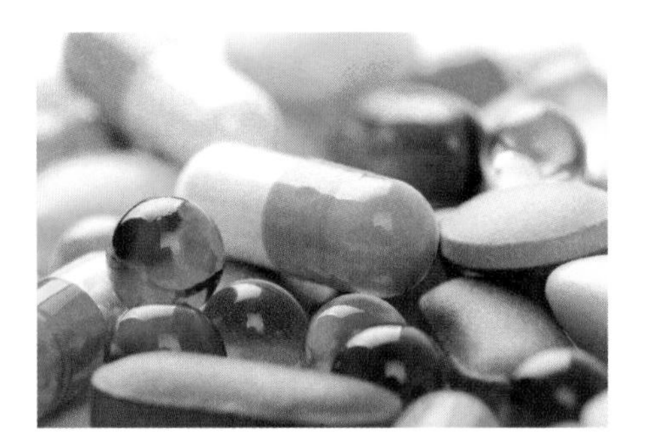

Psychopharmacology refers the use of medication and drugs to control or relieve the symptoms of psychological disorders, and it is increasingly common. Sometimes drugs are used alone and sometimes they are combined with psychotherapy, a practice that tends to yield greater success (Kearney & Silverman, 1998).

There are different categories of drugs that are used to treat specific psychological symptoms. *Antipsychotic drugs* are those that are used to treat psychotic symptoms, such as those present in schizophrenia like hallucinations and delusions. *Anti-anxiety drugs* are minor tranquilizers that are used to reduce symptoms of anxiety. These drugs, like Xanax and Valium, tend to have sedative effects because they reduce the activity of the nervous system. In recent years, some therapists have begun using antidepressant drugs to treat anxiety disorders such as panic disorder, OCD, and PTSD.

Antidepressant drugs are typically used in the treatment of depression because they have a positive effect on mood. *Monoamine oxidase inhibitors* (MAOIs) are antidepressants that block the enzyme monoamine oxidase from breaking down neurotransmitters that are involved in controlling mood, like norepinephrine, serotonin, and dopamine. *Tricyclic antidepressants* increase serotonin and norepinephrine activity in the nervous system, thus having similar effects as MAOIs. Both MAOIs and tricyclics tend to have severe side effects including weight gain, dizziness, insomnia, and sexual dysfunction (Geddes & Butler, 2002). In the search for an antidepressant with fewer side effects, *selective serotonin reuptake inhibitors* (SSRIs), like Prozac and Zoloft, were developed. These inhibit the reuptake of serotonin, making it more available in the nervous system and leading to feelings of well-being. The side effects of SSRIs are much less severe and thus, are preferred in the treatment of depression.

The use of drugs to treat psychological problems has been criticized by those who believe that medication simply reduces the symptoms of a disorder without actually solving the problem. In addition, the side effects of some medications can be so severe that people argue that the original psychological disorder may not be as bad as the problems brought on by the treatment. Despite these criticisms, many people prefer medication because it brings immediate relief compared to psychotherapy, and it does not require the kind of effort that therapy does before a disorder improves. Luckily, depending on your perspective, if you have the need for psychotherapy, the choice is yours.

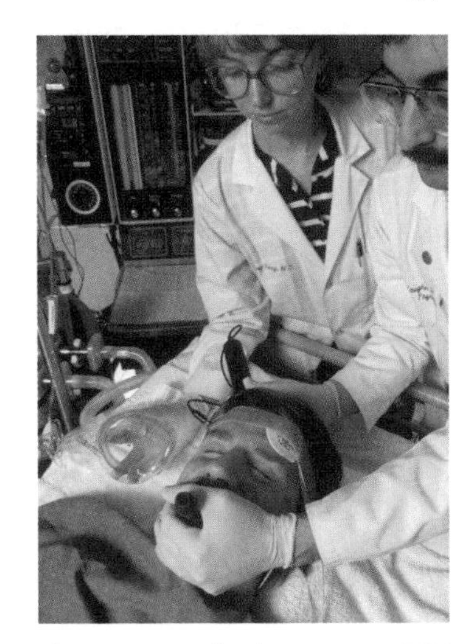

The process of administering ECT has evolved to reduce discomfort for the patient. A mouth guard is placed in the patient's mouth to avoid injury.

OTHER BIOMEDICAL THERAPIES

Biomedical therapies are not limited to medication. Other forms of biological therapies like electroconvulsive therapy (ECT) and psychosurgery are still used in some cases. **Electroconvulsive therapy (ECT)**, or shock therapy, is a therapy in which electrodes that deliver an electric current are placed on a person's head causing a seizure in the brain. This results in an immediate improvement in mood. Usually, ECT is used as a last resort in cases of severe depression that do not respond to other treatments like drugs or psychotherapy.

In the early days, ECT was used to treat all kinds of mental disorders with no anesthesia, sometimes resulting in serious physical side effects like broken bones and fractured teeth. The practice has evolved to be a lot more controlled and therapists must obtain written informed consent from the patient who is agreeing to undergo ECT.

Psychosurgery is another biomedical treatment that involves – you guessed it – brain surgery. This procedure involves removing or destroying brain tissue in order to alleviate psychological symptoms. Like ECT, the practice was a lot more brutal and inhumane decades ago when unruly and aggressive patients were lobotomized – meaning they had their frontal lobes severed – in order to reduce psychotic behavior. As you can probably imagine, this led to a host of unexpected consequences including major changes in personality, lack of emotional response, and cognitive and intellectual disabilities.

Contemporary versions of this practice include *bilateral anterior cingulotomy*, which involves using an electrode to destroy cells in a specific area of the brain, resulting in improvements for patients suffering from major depression, bipolar disorder, and OCD. As with ECT, these procedures are a drastic step that is usually taken only when other potential treatments have failed.

CHAPTER 14 REVIEW QUESTIONS

1. Psychological therapies involving exposure to a feared object or situation would be considered:

   a. Humanistic

   b. Behavioral

   c. Psychodynamic

   d. Cognitive

2. ______________________________ aims to change maladaptive and irrational patterns of thinking.

3. Which cognitive therapy involves challenging all-or-none thoughts in a highly directive and confrontational way?

   a. Beck's cognitive therapy

   b. Client-centered therapy

   c. Cognitive-behavior therapy

   d. Rational-emotive behavior therapy

4. T/F. Most people who have tried therapy believe it was not very helpful and opt to switch to medication.

5. MAOIs, SSRIs, and tricyclics are all examples of:

    a. Antidepressants

    b. Antipsychotics

    c. Antianxiety medications

    d. Surgical procedures

6. T/F. Electroconvulsive therapy and psychosurgery are still used in severe cases.

7. Which of these are advantages of self-help or support groups?

    a. People have unlimited time with the therapist.

    b. People benefit from a support group.

    c. The cost is lower.

    d. B and C

8. Miguel is trying to control his drinking problem. He is participating in a therapy that requires him to take a medication that makes him really sick whenever he has a drop of alcohol. What kind of therapy is he probably involved in?

    a. Stress-inoculation therapy

    b. Cognitive behavioral therapy

c. Flooding

d. Aversive conditioning

9. Brain surgery for the purpose of fixing a psychological problem is called ______________________________.

10. Which of the following therapies is meant to help clients become fully functioning by analyzing the differences between their real and ideal selves?

    a. Psychodynamic therapy

    b. Client-centered therapy

    c. Cognitive therapy

    d. B and C

GLOSSARY

Absolute threshold: The smallest amount of energy that one will sense.

Action potential: An electrochemical impulse that travels the length of a neuron's axon and activates other surrounding cells.

Adaptation: The process by which each of our senses adjusts to sensory stimuli so as to not overload our senses.

Adoption studies: Studies that involve comparing the traits of children that were adopted at birth and brought up by parents that are not genetically related to see if they are more similar to their biological parents or their adoptive parents.

Adrenal glands: The endocrine glands responsible for releasing hormones in response to stress that cause the changes in the body that we need to react quickly to an emergency or possible injury.

Agoraphobia: A disorder that causes individuals to avoid certain situations where they might not receive help if they develop panic symptoms.

Algorithm: In problem solving, a step-by-step process that guarantees the correct response.

Altered state of consciousness (ASC): A mental state that differs significantly from normal wakefulness.

Altruism: When we help someone with no expectation of reward.

Alzheimer's disease: A neurocognitive disorder that causes changes to the brain resulting in a dramatic loss of cognitive abilities.

Anal stage: The psychosexual stage which lasts from 18 months to 3 years, during which the anus is the primary source of pleasure.

Anorexia nervosa : An eating disorder in which individuals go to extreme lengths to lose weight and feel they are overweight even though they are underweight.

Anterograde amnesia: An inability to create new memories after the event that caused the amnesia.

Archetypes: Shared memories that make up the collective unconscious.

Attachment: An emotional bond.

Attention: Selectively concentrating on one aspect of your surroundings, while other aspects fade into the background.

Attitudes: Learned tendencies to respond in certain ways to ideas, objects, situations, or people.

Attributions: Explanations about the cause of behavior.

Auditory nerve: A bundle of neurons that carries information from each of the ears to different parts of your brain.

Autonomic nervous system: The part of the peripheral nervous system that controls essential internal life functions such as heart rate, digestion, respiratory rate, salivation, perspiration, and sexual arousal.

Availability heuristic: The tendency to estimate the likelihood of an event based on how easily it can be recalled.

Aversion therapy: In this type of therapy, an undesirable behavior is paired with something aversive or unpleasant in order to reduce its frequency.

Axon: A long fiber extending out from the cell body of a neuron that carries messages to other neurons or glands in the body.

Behavior therapies: Therapy that uses principles of learning and reinforcement to change maladaptive behavior.

Behavioral genetics: The study of the way our inherited genes affect our behavior.

Behaviorism: An approach to psychology, whose primary principle is that psychology is the study of observable behavior in people and animals, and not the unobservable behavior that takes place in our minds.

Big Five: Model of personality that suggests personality can be explained by five trait dimensions.

Binge-eating disorder: An eating disorder that involves recurring episodes of binge eating and distress associated with how much one is eating.

Binocular cues: Cues of depth perception that require the use of both eyes.

Biological psychology: see, **psychobiology**

Biomedical therapy: Therapy that uses medical methods to help treat psychological problems.

Bipolar disorders: A disorder that involves periods of both depression and mania.

Brightness constancy: The fact that the perceived brightness of familiar objects remains constant despite the fact that the amount of light they are seen under might vary from moment to moment.

Bulimia nervosa: An eating disorder that involves episodes of binge eating and purging to prevent weight gain.

Bystander effect: The greater the number of observed bystanders, the less likely people are to help.

Cannon-Bard theory: A theory of emotion that argues that any event that could produce an emotion triggers both a physiological response and the conscious experience of emotion simultaneously.

Case study: A research method that involves in-depth study of one person or a small group.

Central executive: In Baddeley and Hitch's model of short-term memory, it regulates and coordinates the activity of the other two parts of the system and decides what to selectively attend to and process.

Central nervous system (CNS): Consists of the brain and spinal cord, the parts of the nervous system that coordinate activity.

Cerebellum: A part of the hindbrain that plays an important part in motor control and has been found to have some involvement in cognitive functions such as attention and language.

Cerebral cortex: A layer of thin tissue surrounding the cerebrum.

Cerebrum: The part of the forebrain that controls all voluntary actions in the body and processes our thoughts, sensory information, produces language and emotion, and houses our memories.

Chromosomes: Organized structures of genetic material that we inherit from our parents which are found in every cell of the body.

Chunking: A technique that helps reduce the pieces of information one has to remember by grouping them into more meaningful pieces.

Circadian rhythm: The 24 hour cycle that controls when we sleep that follows the day-night cycle.

Classical conditioning: A behavioral modification technique in which a subject learns to respond a certain way to a conditioned stimulus after that stimulus is paired repeatedly with an unconditioned stimulus that naturally elicits the same reaction.

Client-centered therapy: A humanistic therapy that helps people become fully functional by helping them more accurately identify discrepancies between the real and ideal self.

Cognition: A representation of all types of thinking including the processes of attention, memory, communicating, reasoning, problem solving, and decision making.

Cognitive dissonance: The tension caused when attitudes clash with behavior.

Cognitive learning: The mental processes that take place in our brains when we learn.

Cognitive map: A type of mental representation of a spatial environment that we use to navigate that environment.

Cognitive therapies: Therapies that aim to change maladaptive ways of thinking that cause psychological distress.

Collective unconscious: Memories that are shared by all humans.

Color constancy: A perceptual constancy that allows us to perceive familiar objects as maintaining their color despite changing conditions under which they might be viewed.

Compensation: Attempts to overcome physical weaknesses and feelings of inferiority.

Compliance: When people change their behavior when asked to do so by others.

Concepts: Categories used to organize and classify new information.

Conditioned response (CR): In classical conditioning, a learned response to a conditioned stimulus.

Conditioned stimulus (CS): In classical conditioning, a stimulus that is originally neutral that when paired enough times with the unconditioned stimulus comes to be associated with it.

Confirmation bias: A tendency to favor our own beliefs in thinking.

Conflict: A major source of stress that occurs when one has different incompatible goals from which to choose.

Conformity: Changing your own behavior to match that of those around you.

Control group: In an experiment, the group that does not experience a change in the independent variable, acting as a baseline, or a base for comparison against the experimental group.

Cornea: The transparent outer layer of the eye.

Corpus callosum: The nerve fibers that connect the left and right hemispheres of the cerebrum.

Correlation: An existing relationship between two statistical variables.

Critical period: A period in which environmental influence can have major impacts on a baby's development.

Cross-sectional study: A research design that allows researchers to observe different people in varying age groups all at the same time.

Dark adaptation: The process by which our rods and cones become more sensitive to light in response to darkness.

Defense mechanisms: Strategies used to manipulate the mind to deny or distort the nature of a problem.

Deinstitutionalization: Widespread release of people with severe psychological disorders back into the community.

Delusions: False beliefs that a person holds, while refusing to accept conflicting evidence.

Dendrites: Short, thin structures that branch out from the cell body of a neuron that receive messages from other neurons to the cell body.

Dependent variable: In an experiment, the variable that is observed for change in response to manipulation of the independent variable.

Depressants: Substances that reduce, or depress, the activity of the nervous system.

Depressive disorders: Illnesses that involve depression, or overwhelming sadness, as their prevalent symptom.

Developmental psychology: The area of psychology focused on the changes we undergo throughout life.

Difference threshold: The smallest amount of change in the strength of a stimulus that one would be able to notice.

Direct observation: A behavioral assessment of personality that involves observing someone's behavior in the setting in which it naturally occurs, like school or work.

Discrimination: When prejudices result in unequal treatment of a person simply because they belong to a particular group.

Display rules: Cultural guidelines about when and how to express emotion.

Dissociative disorders: Disorders characterized by disintegration, or separation, of consciousness, memory, identity, emotion, perception, or behavior.

Dissociative identity disorder: A disorder in which a person experiences several distinct identities, each with their own unique characteristics, including different genders, preferences, talents, and mannerisms.

Dreams: A series of auditory and visual experiences occurring involuntarily in the mind during sleep.

Drive reduction theory: An approach that suggests that behavior is a result of attempting to relieve tension caused by needs.

Dualism: The idea that the mental world of thoughts and feelings is separate from the physical world of our bodies and objects.

Ego: The part of personality that is logical, rational, and responsible for interacting with reality.

Egocentrism: When children believe that everyone knows, thinks, and feels the same way they do.

Elaborative rehearsal: A way to commit information into LTM by relating new material to information already stored in long-term memory.

Electroconvulsive therapy (ECT): A therapy in which electrodes that deliver an electric current are placed on a person's head causing a seizure or convulsions.

Emotion: A conscious experience of a feeling that is characterized by physical arousal, behaviors that reveal feeling to the outside world, and an inner awareness of the feeling.

Emotional memory: A specific learned emotion.

Endocrine glands: Organs in the body that are responsible for releasing specific hormones into the bloodstream.

Episodic memories: Memories for events in time.

Experimental group: In an experiment, the group that experiences a change of the independent variable.

Experimenter bias: The subjective biases and expectations of a researcher which may influence the way the results of an experiment are interpreted.

Explicit memories: Memories that are consciously available to us.

Exposure therapy: A behavioral therapy that forces the client to experience situations that he finds anxiety-provoking.

Extinction: When a classical or operant learned response disappears.

Family studies: The study of psychological traits in family members.

Family therapy: A type of therapy that is performed with all members of a family present.

Fetal alcohol syndrome (FAS): A condition that causes physical and cognitive defects associated with alcohol consumption during pregnancy.

Fight-or-flight response: The physiological reaction that we experience in response to anything that we perceive to be a threat to survival.

Flashbulb memory: A very clear and detailed memory of an event that is surprising and emotionally impactful.

Forebrain: The largest and top-most part of the brain, containing the cerebrum, as well as other important structures like the thalamus and the limbic system.

Fovea: A point on the retina that represents our visual focus.

Framing effect: A decision making heuristic that can bias decisions depending on how information is presented.

Frontal lobe: The part of the cerebral cortex right behind the forehead that is involved in planning and execution of goal-oriented tasks.

Frustration: The experience produced by the inability to meet a desired goal.

Frustration-aggression theory: Theory that suggests that prejudices are the result of people's frustrations over their own negative circumstances.

Fully functioning person: A person who accurately perceives himself and the world and is open to experience.

Functionalism: A theory that considers our mental processes in terms of their role in adapting to the environment.

Fundamental attribution error: The tendency to attribute the behavior of others to internal causes, without considering the potential situational factors influencing their actions.

Gender Dysphoria: The distress accompanying incongruence between one's assigned gender and one's expressed gender.

Gene: The unit of heredity that is passed from a parent to their children.

General adaptation syndrome (GAS): The sequence of physiological reactions that occurs when one experiences stress.

Genetics: The study of how different traits are passed down in living organisms.

Genital stage: The last psychosexual stage when repressed sexual feelings emerge once again, and they are directed toward peers.

Gestalt therapy: A directive therapy involving leading questions and role playing, in which the therapist attempts to help the client accept himself.

Ghrelin: A hormone released by the empty stomach which signals hunger and stimulates appetite.

Gonads: Endocrine glands that secrete masculine and feminine hormones that are responsible for our sex characteristics. In males, they are the testes and in females, the ovaries.

Grammar: The rules that determine how words and phrases can be combined and the meaning of these combinations.

Gustatory perception: The sense of taste.

Hair cells: The receptor cells for hearing.

Hallucinations: False sensory perceptions.

Hallucinogens: A group of substances that cause changes in perception, thought, emotion, and consciousness.

Heuristics: Mental shortcuts in problem solving and decision making.

Hierarchy of needs: A theory proposed by Abraham Maslow which organizes motives from the most basic to the most complex.

Hindbrain: The division of the brain closest to the spinal cord that supports vital bodily functions such as breathing, heart rate, and blood pressure.

Hindsight bias: A tendency to see events that already occurred as being more predictable than they were before they happened.

Holophrases: One-word utterances that have meaning and are used in early language development.

Homeostasis: A level of internal stability and balance.

Hormones: Chemical substances released by endocrine glands that regulate various functions in the body.

Human sexual response cycle: An organization of the phases that comprise the sexual act: excitement, plateau, orgasm, and resolution.

Hyperthymesia: A superior form of autobiographical memory, or a person's life stories.

Hypnosis: A state in which a person is in a trance and is functioning at a level of awareness other than ordinary wakefulness.

Hypothesis: A testable explanation for a phenomenon.

Id: According to Freud's personality theory, the primitive part of personality that constantly seeks pleasure.

Ideal self: An idea of the person we strive to be.

Images: Mental representations of sensations.

Implicit memories: Non-declarative memories that we may not be aware we have and that we cannot clearly verbalize.

Incentives: Rewards for behaviors that motivate the behavior.

Inclusion: An educational practice in which children with mental disabilities are educated alongside non-disabled students.

Independent variable: In an experiment, the variable that is manipulated by researchers to see how it affects the dependent variable.

Inferiority complex: An internalization of feelings of inferiority which can be paralyzing.

Information processing theory: A theory of memory which divides the process into three major components: sensory registers, short-term memory, and long-term memory.

Informed consent: A research participant's agreement to be part of a study once he understands the possible risks of a procedure or treatment.

Insight learning: A kind of learning that takes place all of a sudden by understanding different aspects of a problem to get the solution.

Insomnia: The inability to fall asleep or to sleep as long as desired.

Instincts: Innate behaviors that exist in both humans and animals.

Insulin: The hormone that converts glucose into energy that the body can use.

Intelligence quotient (IQ): A numerical score of intelligence, for which the average score is 100.

Interneurons: Neurons that transmit messages from one neuron to another.

Ion: A negatively charged atom or molecule.

James-Lange theory: A theory of emotion that suggests that our emotional experience is an interpretation of physiological changes in the body.

Kinesthetic sense: The sensory system responsible for the sensation of the positions of the body.

Language acquisition device (LAD): According this theory, humans are hardwired in a way that facilitates language learning.

Language: The complex system humans use to communicate.

Latency stage: When children lose interest in sexual behavior and mostly play with others of the same gender.

Law of effect: The basic principle of operant conditioning states that when behavior has positive consequences, we are more likely to repeat it, and when it has negative consequences, we are less likely to repeat it.

Learning set: A predisposition to learn based on previous learning experiences.

Learning: The process of acquiring new knowledge, skills, and synthesizing information.

Lens: A clear structure in the eye that helps focus the light onto the retina.

Leptin: A hormone secreted by fat cells when there are adequate fat stores in order to decrease hunger.

Light adaptation: The process by which our rods and cones become less sensitive to light when there is a lot of light available in the environment.

Limbic system: A set of structures in the forebrain including the hypothalamus, amygdala, and hippocampus that is responsible for a variety of different functions.

Linguistic relativity hypothesis: The theory that the language people speak can affect the way in which they conceptualize the world.

Locus of control: The degree of control people perceive to have over what happens to them.

Longitudinal study: A developmental research method in which age-related changes are measured in the same group of people at different ages.

Long-term memory (LTM): The memory store where information becomes relatively permanent, allowing us to retrieve it to work with it in short term memory.

Maladaptive: Something that does not allow a person to function normally in his daily life.

Meditation: A state of consciousness in which a person purposefully alters his consciousness.

Medulla: The long, narrow structure directly above the spinal cord that is involved in functions such as breathing, heart rate, and blood pressure.

Memory: The process by which information is encoded, stored, and retrieved.

Menopause: The cessation of the menstrual cycle and ovulation in middle age.

Mental set: A tendency to approach problems a certain way, preventing the use of novel approaches.

Mere exposure effect: The idea that repeated exposure to a stimuli breeds liking.

Metabolism: The process that converts the food we ingest to energy that our body can use.

Midbrain: The part of the brain above the hindbrain associated with vision and hearing.

Midlife crisis: A period in middle adulthood where one feels ready for a change due to feeling stagnant and unfulfilled.

Mnemonics: Techniques like jingles or acronyms that transform to-be-remembered information into something that is easier to remember.

Monocular cues: Cues for distance and depth perception that come from the information only one eye provides.

Motivation: A process that moves people to behave in a way directed at meeting some need or desire.

Motor neurons: Neurons that transmit information from the brain and spinal cord to control muscles.

Narcolepsy: A chronic disorder in which the brain is unable to regulate sleep-wake cycles normally, leading to episodes where a sufferer falls asleep involuntarily.

Natural selection: Darwin's theory that posits that organisms that are best adapted to the environment are more likely to survive and reproduce, thus passing on those evolutionary adaptations to other generations.

Naturalistic observation: A descriptive research method that allows one to study behavior in a natural setting.

Neurodevelopmental disorders: Disorders that tend to have an onset in childhood, though many of them continue into adulthood.

Neurons: Cells that make up the nervous system that transmit information through electrical and chemical signals.

Neurotransmitters: Chemicals that cross the synaptic gap between neurons and transmit signals to other neurons.

Night terror: A sleep disorder that involves waking inconsolable in a panic.

Obedience: A behavioral response to a direct order from an authority figure.

Object permanence: The knowledge that an object exists even if it is out of sight.

Observational learning: Learned behavior that results from observing others' behavior.

Observer bias: In research, the prior expectations or biases of the observer that may influence their observations and may lead to misinterpretation of the findings.

Obsessive-Compulsive Disorder (OCD): A disorder which is marked by obsessions, or persistent thoughts, that cause extreme anxiety and compulsive behaviors.

Occipital lobe: Lobe of the cerebral cortex that processes visual information.

Oedipus complex: When boys develop a strong jealousy of their fathers because of their sexual attraction to their mothers.

Olfaction: The sense of smell.

Olfactory bulb: The part of the brain that perceives different odors.

Operant conditioning: A type of learning in which behavior is changed based on the consequences of that behavior.

Opponent-process theory: This theory supposes that we have three pairs of color receptors: yellow-blue, red-green – that are responsible for the hues we see – and black-white that determine the brightness of the colors we see.

Optic nerve: A thick collection of neural fibers that transmits information from the retina of the eye to the brain.

Oral stage: During this stage of psychosexual development, the mouth is the erogenous zone and children relieve sexual tension by sucking and swallowing.

Overjustification effect: The subsequent reduction in intrinsic motivation when external rewards are given.

Panic attack: A brief period of intense fear, resulting in extreme physical and psychological discomfort, without any reasonable cause.

Panic Disorder: A disorder that develops when people who are prone to panic attacks develop a fear of having another one.

Paraphilic disorders: Sexual behaviors and interests that are persistent, intense and cause distress to an individual or risk of harm to them or others.

Parasympathetic division of the nervous system: Responsible for the activities that occur when the body is at rest like digestion and sexual arousal.

Parietal lobe: The lobe of the cerebral cortex that integrates sensory information from all over the body and oversees spatial abilities.

Perception: The way one's brain interprets and organizes incoming sensory information.

Perceptual constancy: The tendency to perceive objects in our environment as unchanging even when the sensory information we receive changes.

Perceptual expectancy: A predisposition to perceive things a certain way.

Peripheral nervous system (PNS): Connects the central nervous system to the rest of the body, gathering information from the senses and carrying out motor actions.

Personality disorders: Patterns of thinking, feeling, and behaving that are rigid and maladaptive, interfering with normal social interaction.

Personality traits: The specific ways in which people differ from one another.

Personality: The way individuals think, act, and feel throughout life.

Persuasion: The process through which our attitudes can be changed purposefully by other people.

Phallic stage: The stage of psychosexual development lasting from 3 to 6 years of age that is marked by curiosity and interest in the genitals.

Pheromones: Chemicals that can affect behavior.

Phobias: Unreasonable and excessive fears of specific objects or situations.

Phonological loop: In Baddeley and Hitch's model of short term memory, it is responsible for processing auditory information.

Photographic memory: The ability to recall images, sounds, and objects with extreme precision. Also known as **eidetic memory**.

Pituitary gland: An endocrine gland which sits at the base of the brain and controls the activities of the other glands in the endocrine system.

Pleasure principle: The need for immediate satisfaction regardless of the cost or consequences, by which the id functions.

Pons: A structure located on the brain stem that carries signals from the cerebellum and medulla to and from the forebrain and is involved in the control of sleep, respiration, and equilibrium, among others.

Posttraumatic stress disorder (PTSD): A disorder that may develop when an individual has been exposed, either directly, as a witness or otherwise, to a traumatic experience, such as actual or threatened death, injury, or sexual violence.

Prejudice: An unfairly negative stereotyped attitude about members of a social group.

Pressure: Stressful feeling that can come from an internal or external demand or expectation for behavior.

Priming: A process in which prior exposure to one stimulus affects a response to a later stimulus.

Proactive interference: When old material interferes with new material we are trying to learn.

Procedural memories: Our learned skills.

Psychoanalysis: Therapy which seeks to uncover the unconscious aspects behind our thoughts and behavior that characterizes Sigmund Freud's psychodynamic perspective.

Psychoanalytic theory: See **Psychoanalysis.**

Psychobiology: The study of how mental processes and behavior are related to biological processes.

Psychodynamic theory: See **Psychoanalysis**.

Psychological disorder: A pattern of behavior that causes distress and affects one's ability to function in daily life.

Psychology: An applied discipline involving the scientific study of mental processes and behavior.

Psychopathology: The study of abnormal behavior.

Psychopharmacology: The use of medication and drugs to control or relieve the symptoms of psychological disorders.

Psychosexual stages: According to psychoanalytic psychology, stages of development during which children focus their sexual energy on a different erogenous zone, leading to the development of personality.

Psychosurgery: Brain surgery.

Psychotherapy: Therapy that is based on psychological techniques and involve a therapist listening to and helping the client work through his problems.

Punishment: In behavioral conditioning, it is a consequence that leads to a decrease in behavior.

Pupil: The opening in the center of the colored part of the eye.

Random sample: A sample of a larger population in which every member of the population has an equal chance of being chosen.

Rational-emotive behavior therapy: A cognitive therapy which directly challenges clients' irrational beliefs.

Reality principle: Principle by which the ego operates as it attempts to satisfy the demands of the id in a way that is realistic and does not have negative consequences.

Receptor cell: A specialized cell in the sense organs that responds to a specific type of energy.

Reciprocal determinism: The idea that behavior is influenced by three distinct factors: the environment, the behavior itself, and personal or cognitive factors that one learns from their experiences.

Recovered memories: Memories of an experienced wherein all memory had been lost until the event was later suddenly recalled.

Reinforcement: In operant conditioning, a consequence that makes it more likely that behavior will be repeated.

Reliability: A test's dependability and consistency.

REM (rapid-eye movement) sleep: A stage of sleep during which our brain waves return to the high-frequency short waves of *NREM stage 1*, and our eyes move rapidly back and forth under our eyelids.

Representative sample: A sample of the population that closely represents the population it is drawn from.

Representativeness heuristic: A tendency to make decisions about something based on how much it looks like a prototypical case.

Response generalization: In operant conditioning, this occurs when the conditioned response is repeated under conditions other than the one originally in which it was learned.

Retina: The layer that lines the back part of the eye and contains the receptor cells for vision.

Retroactive interference: When new material to be learned interferes with material already stored in long-term memory.

Retrograde amnesia: A condition in which patients are unable to remember information learned before the accident or disease that caused the amnesia.

Rote rehearsal: The process of keeping information in short-term memory by repeating it.

Sample: A portion of the population that research is conducted on.

Schema: The way in which we organize our expectations and beliefs about people and things.

Schizophrenia: A severe disorder that renders an individual unable to distinguish what is real and what is not due to hallucinations and bizarre or delusional thoughts and behaviors.

Scientific method: The variety of techniques used by psychologists to research various topics that involves collecting and analyzing observable and measurable data.

Selection studies: A genetic study in which animals with certain desirable traits are inbred to produce offspring with more of that trait.

Self-actualization: The principal belief of humanistic psychologists that humans have an inherent drive to become everything that one is capable of becoming.

Self-actualizing tendency: The tendency to strive to fulfill a person's innate capabilities to his full extent.

Self-concept: An image we have of ourselves based on what we know and what other people say about us.

Self-efficacy: Our expectancies about how likely we are to succeed in a task.

Self-fulfilling prophecy: When impressions and expectations of peple bring about the behavior we expects from them.

Self-help groups: Therapy in which persons meet with others, typically who share similar problems.

Semantic memories: Our knowledge of factual information.

Sensation: The neurological process that occurs when energy from the environment stimulates our sensory organs.

Sensory neurons: Neurons that transmit information from the senses to the brain and spinal cord.

Sensory register: A memory store that receives and holds the stimuli it receives for a very short time.

Serial position effect: The finding that recall of an item varies depending on the position of the item in a list.

Sexual dysfunctions: Disorders marked by some impairment or loss of function in the sexual response.

Sexual orientation: The gender a person prefers for romantic and sexual intimacy.

Shape constancy: The tendency for familiar objects to maintain a constant shape in our minds, even when our vantage point affects the image our eyes see.

Short-term memory (STM): The memory store in which all the information one is currently attending to is held.

Size constancy: The tendency to perceive objects as maintaining their known size despite changing sensory information to the contrary.

Sleep apnea: A sleep disorder characterized by difficulties breathing or low breathing during sleep.

Sleeptalking: See **Sleepwalking.**

Sleepwalking: Along with sleeptalking, sleep disorders that occur in NREM stage 3, slow wave sleep, and involve performing activities that one usually does when awake.

Social anxiety disorder (Social Phobia): An anxiety disorder that is marked by excessive fear surrounding social situations.

Social cognition: The way in which people think about other people and how that thinking influences interactions with those people.

Social influence: The process by which other people affect our thoughts, feelings and behavior.

Social learning: See **Observational Learning**.

Social psychology: The scientific study of how we are influenced by the presence of others.

Somatic nervous system: The part of the peripheral nervous system that has to do with voluntary control of body movements and the transmission of information from the senses to the central nervous system.

Somatic symptom disorders: Disorders characterized by symptoms of physical illness that cause significant distress or disruption of daily life.

Somatosensory system: A broad sensory system that processes the sensation of touch, temperature, body position, and pain.

Sound waves: Oscillating changes in air pressure that are transmitted through air or water and are interpreted by the brain as sound.

Spinal cord: Part of the central nervous system that is made up of long axons and connects the brain to the rest of the body.

Spontaneous recovery: When a previously extinguished response re-emerges with no training.

Stereotypes: The belief that all members of a particular social category share the same characteristics.

Stimulants: Substances that give energy and induce temporary improvement in mental and physical capacities.

Stimulus discrimination: In conditioning, a process by which a learner is taught to discriminate between similar stimuli.

Stimulus generalization: In conditioning, a tendency to respond to similar cues, even if they are not identical to the ones present during learning.

Strain study: A study performed on animals that allows researchers to see the kinds of differences that appear as a result of genetic differences when the environment is the same.

Stranger anxiety: Fearful responses of babies when they are approached by an unfamiliar person.

Stress: The emotional, cognitive, and physical response to situations that are challenging or threatening.

Stressor: A situation or stimulus that provokes a stress reaction.

Substance dependence: Addiction to a substance marked by tolerance and withdrawal symptoms when the use of the substance is discontinued.

Superego: The part of personality that functions as a moral center.

Support groups: See **Self-help groups**.

Sympathetic division of the nervous system: Division of the autonomic nervous system that mobilizes the body for an emergency.

Synapse: The area between neurons that allows neurons to form electrochemical connections to communicate with one another.

Systematic desensitization: A process that reduces anxiety and fear by gradually exposing the client to increasingly anxiety-provoking situations.

Tactile perception: Sense of touch.

Taste buds: Sensory organs on the tongue that contain receptor cells for taste.

Temperament: Different patterns of reactions to stimulation exhibited by newborns.

Temporal lobe: The lobe of the cerebral cortex that processes auditory information, including the comprehension of language, balance and equilibrium, the regulation of emotion and motivation, and some complex visual tasks such as facial recognition.

Thalamus: A structure in the brain that relays information to and from the cerebral cortex and regulates consciousness, sleep, and alertness.

Theory of multiple intelligences: The idea that intelligence is made up of at least eight distinct abilities that are independent from others.

Theory: A well-substantiated explanation of a phenomenon that organizes known facts based on careful empirical observations of the phenomenon.

Therapeutic alliance: The relationship between the client and the therapist.

Thyroid gland: An endocrine gland located in the neck that is responsible for regulating the body's metabolism.

Tip-of the tongue (TOT) phenomenon: A failure to retrieve a word from LTM.

Transduction: The process by which physical energy is converted to electrochemical signals that are then interpreted by the brain and allows us to interpret the information.

Transference: A technique in which the therapist symbolizes an authority figure in the client's past.

Trial and error strategy: A method of problem solving that is used to randomly create solutions and test them to see if they work.

Triarchic theory of intelligence: A theory that proposes that intelligence is composed of three broad skills: analytical skill, creative skill, and practical skill.

Trichromatic theory of color: This theory holds that three types of receptors, or cones, are responsible for the perception of color: one sensitive to red light, one sensitive to green light, and one sensitive to blue-violet light.

Twin studies: Genetic studies done on twins to determine what kinds of traits are genetically influenced and which are unchanged by genetics.

Unconditional positive regard: Love and respect that is not linked to or dependent on specific behavior.

Unconditioned response (UR): In classical conditioning, it is one's automatic response to a certain stimulus.

Unconditioned stimulus (US): In classical conditioning, it is a stimulus, or event that automatically elicits a certain reflexive response.

Vestibular sense: The sense of balance.

Visuospatial sketchpad: In Baddeley and Hitch's model of short term memory, it is responsible for holding visual information and spatial movements.

Wakefulness: A state of consciousness during which a person is conscious, awake, and reasonably aware and coherent.

REFERENCES

Adams, R. J. (1987). An evaluation of colour preferences in early infancy. *Infant Behaviour and Development, 10,* 143-150.

Adler, A. (1954). *Understanding human nature.* New York: Greenburg Publisher.

Aiken, L. R. & Groth-Marnat, G. (2005). *Psychological testing and assessment* (12th ed.). Boston: Allyn & Bacon.

Ainsworth, M. D. S., & Bell, S. M. (1970). Attachment, exploration, and separation: Illustrated by the behavior of one-year-olds in a strange situation. *Child Development, 41*(1), 49-67.

Allport, G. W. (1954). *The nature of prejudice.* New York: Anchor.

Altabe, M. N. & Thompson, J. K. (1994). Body image. In *Encyclopedia of human behavior* (Vol. 1, pp. 407-414). San Diego, CA: Academic Press.

Altemeyer, B. (2004). Highly dominating, highly authoritarian personalities. Journal of Social Psychology, 144,

American Psychiatric Association. (2013). *Diagnostic and statistical manual of mental disorders.* (5th ed.). Washington, DC: American Psychiatric Publishing, Incorporated.

American Psychological Association. (2003). *Ethical principles of psychologists and code of conduct.* Retrieved June 1, 2013, from http://www.apa.org/ethics/code/index.aspx.

Anderson, J. R. (1983). A spreading activation theory of memory. *Journal of Verbal Learning and Verbal Behavior, 22,* 261-295.

Arborelius, L., Owens, M.J., Plotsky, P.M., Nemeroff, C.B. (1999) The role of corticotrophin-releasing factor in depression and anxiety disorders. *Journal of Endocrinology, 160*, 1-12.

Aristotle & Smith, R. (1989). *Prior analytics*. Indianapolis: Hackett Pub. Co.

Aronson, E., Blaney, N., Stephan, C., Sikes, J., & Snapp, M. (1978). *The jigsaw classroom*. Beverly Hills, CA: Sage.

Arrigo, J. M. & Pezdek, K. (1997). Lessons from the study of psychogenic amnesia. *Current Directions in Psychological Science, 6*, 148-152.

Asch, S. E. (1956). Studies of independence and conformity: I. A minority of one against a unanimous majority. *Psychological Monographs, 70*(9, Whole No. 416.)

Asch, S.E. (1951). Effects of group pressure on the modification and distortion of judgments. In H. Guetzkow (Ed.), *Groups, leadership and men* (pp. 177–190). Pittsburgh, PA:Carnegie Press.

Atkinson, R. C. & Shiffrin, R. M. (1968). Human memory: A proposed system and its control processes. In K. W. Spence & J. T. Spence (Eds.), *The psychology of learning and motivation, 2*, 89-195. New York, NY: Academic Press.

Baddeley, A. (2000). The episodic buffer: a new component of working memory? *Trends in Cognitive Science, 4*(11), 417-423.

Baddeley, A. D. & Hitch, G. J. (1974). Working memory. *The psychology of learning and motivation, 8*, 47-89.

Baddeley, A. D. (1966). Short-term memory for word sequences as a function of acoustic, semantic and formal similarity. *Quarterly Journal of Experimental Psychology, 18*(4), 363-365.

Bailey, J. M. & Pillard, R. C (1991). A genetic study of male sexual orientation. *Archives of General Psychiatry, 48*, 1089-1096.

Ball, K., Berch, D. B., Helmers, K. F., Jobe, J. B., Leveck, M. D., Marsiske, M., Morris, J. N., Rebok, G. W., Smith, D. M., Tennstedt, S. L., Unverzagt, F. W., & Willis, S. L. (2002). Advanced Cognitive Training for Independent and Vital Elderly Study Group. Effects of cognitive training interventions with older adults. A randomized controlled trial. *Journal of American Medical Association, 288*, 2271-2281.

Bandura, A. (1965). Influence of models' reinforcement contingencies on the acquisition of imitative responses. *Journal of Personality and Social Psychology, 1*, 589-595.

Bandura, A. (1986). *Social foundations of thought and action: A social cognitive theory*. Englewood Cliffs, NJ: Prentice Hall.

Bandura, A. (1998). Exploration of fortuitous determinants of life paths. *Psychological Inquiry, 9*, 95-99.

Bandura, A., Ross, D., Ross, S. A. (1961). Transmission of aggression through the imitation of aggressive models. *Journal of Abnormal and Social Psychology, 63*(3), 575–582.

Bartlett, F. (1932). *Remembering: A study in Experimental and Social Psychology*. Cambridge: Cambridge University Press.

Bator, R. J. & Cialdini, R. B. (2006). The nature of consistency motivation: Consistency, aconsistency, and anticonsistency in a dissonance paradigm. *Social Influence, 1*, 208-233.

Baumesiter, R. F. (1991). The need to belong: Desire for interpersonal attachments as a fundamental human motivation. *Psychological Bulletin, 113*(3), 497-529.

Beck, A. T. (1979). *Cognitive therapy and the emotional disorders*. New York: International University Press.

Bengston, V. L., Cuellar, J. B., & Ragan, P. K. (1977). Stratum contrasts and similarities in attitudes toward death. *Journal of Gerontology, 32*(1), 76-88.

Berman S.M., Kuczenski, R., McCracken, J. T., London, E.D. (2009). Potential adverse effects of amphetamine treatment on brain and behavior: a review. *Molecular Psychiatry, 14*(2), 123–142.

Blake, T. (Ed.). (1995). *Enduring issues in psychology: Opposing viewpoints.* San Diego, CA: Greenhaven Press.

Blass, T. (1991). Understanding behavior in the Milgram obedience experiment: The role of personality, situations, and their interactions. *Journal of Personality and Social Psychology, 60*, 398-413.

Blass, T. (1999). The Milgram paradigm after 35 tears: Some things we know now about obedience to authority. *Journal of Applied Social Psychology, 25*, 955-978.

Botwin, M. D. & Buss, D. M. (1989). The structure of act data: Is the Five-Factor Model of personality recaptured? *Journal of Personality and Social Psychology, 56*, 988-1001.

Bouchard, T. J. Jr. (1984). Twins reared together and apart: What they tell us about human diversity. In S. W. Fox (Ed.), *Individality and determination.* New York: Plenum.

Bouchard, T. J. Jr. (1996). IQ similarity in twins reared apart: Findings and responses to critics. In R. J. Sternberg & E. Griogorenko (Eds.), *Intelligence: Heredity and environment.* New York: Combridge University Press.

Bowden, E. M. & Jung-Beeman, M. (2003). Aha! Insight experience correlates with solution activation in the right hemisphere. *Psychonomic Bulletin and Review, 10*, 730-737.

Bowlby, J. (1969). *Attachment and loss: Vol. I. Attachment.* New York: Basic Books.

Bowlby, J. (1973). *Attachment and loss: Vol. 2. Separation: Anxiety and anger.* New York: Basic Books.

Bowlby, J. (1980). *Attachment and loss: Vol. 3. Separation: Loss.* New York: Basic Books.

Brackbill, Y. & O'hara, J. (1958). The relative effectiveness of reward and punishment for discrimination learning in children. *Journal of Comparative and Physiological Psychology, 51*(6), 747-751.

Brener, N. D., Kann, L., McManus, T., Kinchen, S. A., Sundberg, E. C., & Ross, J. G. (2002). Reliability of the 1999 Youth Risk Behavior Questionnaire. *Journal of Adolescent Health, 31*(4), 336-342.

Breuer, J., & Freud, S. (1895). *Studies on hysteria (cathartic method). Special Edition, 2*, 1-309.

Brewer, M. B. (2001). Ingroup identification and intergroup conflict: When does in-group love become outgroup hate? In R. D. Ashmore, L. Jussim, & D. Wilder (Eds.), *Social identity, intergroup conflict, and conflict resolution.* New York: Oxford University press.

Brigham, A. (1844). Asylums exclusively for the incurably insane. The *American Journal of Psychiatry, 151*, 50-70.

Brody, L., & Hall, J. (2000). Gender, emotion, and expression. In M. Lewis & J. Haviland-Jones (Eds.), *Handbook of emotions* (2nd Ed., pp. 338-349). New York: Guilford.

Brooks, D.N. & Baddeley, A.D. (1976). What can amnesic patients learn? *Neuropsychologia, 14*, 111-129.

Bruchmüller, K., Margraf, J. Schneider, S. (2012). Is ADHD diagnosed in accord with diagnostic criteria? Overdiagnosis and influence of client gender on diagnosis. *Journal of Consulting and Clinical Psychology, 80*(1), 128.

Brunner, E. J., Hemingway, H., Walker, B., Page, M., Clarke, P., Juneja, M., Shipley, M. J., Kumari, M., Andrew, R., Seckl, J. R., Papadopoulus, A., Checkley, S., Rumley, A., Lowe, G. D., Stansfeld, S. A., & Marmot, M. G. (2002). Adrenocortical, autonomic and inflammatory causes of the metabolic syndrome: Nested case-control study. *Circulation, 106*, 2659-2665.

Burke, R. S., & Stephens, R. S. (1999). Social anxiety and drinking on college students: A social cognitive theory analysis. *Clinical Psychology Review, 19*, 513-530.

Burnham, C. A. & Davis, K. G. (1969). The nine dot problem: Beyond perceptual organization. *Psychonomic Science, 17* (6), 321-323.

Burt, M. R., Aron, L. Y., Douglas, T., Valente, J. Lee, E., & Iwen, B. (1999). Homelessness: Programs and the people they serve. Retrieved from http://www.urban.org/UploadedPDF/homelessness.pdf

Bushman, B. J. & Baumeister, R. F. (1998). Threatened egotism, narcissism, self-esteem, and direct and displaced aggression: Does self-love or self-hate lead to violence? *Journal of Personality & Social Psychology, 75*, 219-229.

Butcher, J. N. & Rouse, S. V. (1996). Personality: Individual differences and clinical assessment. *Annual Review of Psychology, 47*, 87-111.

Buxbaum, J.D. (2009) Multiple rare variants in the etiology of autism spectrum disorders. *Dialogues Clinical Neuroscience, 11*(1),35–43.

Cahill, L., & McGaugh, J. L. (1998). Mechanisms of emotional arousal and lasting declarative memory. *Trends in Neurosciences, 21*, 294-299.

Cain, D., & Seeman, J. (Eds.). (2001). *Humanistic psychotherapies: Handbook of research and practice*. Washington, DC: APA Publications.

Campbell, H.F. (1851) "Injuries of the Cranium—Treppaning". *Ohio Medical & Surgical* Journal, 4(1), 31–5, crediting the *Southern Med & Surgical Journal.*

Cannon, W. B. & Washburn, A. L. (1912). An explanation of hunger. *American Journal of Psychology, 29*, 441-454.

Cannon, W. B. (1929). Organization for Physiological Homeostasis. *Physiological Revie,w 9*(3), 399–421.

Caplan, R. D. & Kenneth, J. W. (1975). Effects of work load, role ambiguity, and Type A personality on anxiety, depression, and heart rate. *Journal of Applied Psychology, 60*(6), 713-719.

Carroll, M. E., Anker, J. J. & Perry, J. L. (2009). Modeling risk factors for nicotine and other drug abuse in the preclinical laboratory. *Drug and Alcohol Dependence, 104*, 132-135.

Cattell, R. B. (1990). Advances in Cattellian personality theory. In L. A. Pervin (Ed.), *Handbook of personality: Theory and research* (pp. 101-110). New York: Guilford Press.

Chen, J-Q. & Gardner, H. (2005). Assessment based on multiple-intelligences theory. In D.P. Flanagan & P. L. Harrison (Eds.), *Contemporary intellectual assessment: Theories, tests and issues* (77-102). New York: Guilford.

Chomsky, N. (1972). *Language and mind.* New York: Harcourt, Brace, Jovanovich.

Chwalisz, K. Diener, E., & Gallagher, D. (1988). Autonomic arousal feedback and emotional experience: Evidence from the spinal cord injured. *Journal of Personality and Social Psychology, 54*, 820-828.

Cialdini, R. B. (2001). The science of persuasion. *Scientific American, 284*, 76-81.

Cialdini, R. B., Trost, M. R., & Newsom, J. T. (1995). Preference for consistency: The development of a valid measure and the discovery of surprising behavioral implications. *Journal of Personality and Social Psychology, 69*, 318-328.

Cialdini, R., Vincent, J., Lewis, S., Catalan, J., Wheeler, D., & Darby, B. (1975). Reciprocal concessions procedure for inducing compliance: The door-in-the-face technique. *Journal of Personality and Social Psychology, 31*, 206-215.

Cohen, L. J. (1997). Rational drug use in the treatment of depression. *Pharmacotherapy, 47*, 113-142.

Colapinto, J. (2001). *As nature made him: The boy who was raised as a girl.* New York, NY: Harper Perennial.

Costa, P. T. Jr., & McCrae, R. R. (1992). *Revised NEO Personality Inventory (NEO-PI-R) and NEO Five-Factor Inventory (NEO-FFI) professional manual.* Odessa, FL: Psychological Assessment Resources.

Crowley, A. E. & Hoyer, W. D. (1994). An integrative framework for understanding two-sided persuasion. *Journal of Consumer Research, 20*, 561-574.

Curtis, R. C., & Miller, K. (1986). Believing another likes or dislikes you: Behaviors making the beliefs come true. *Journal of Personality and Social Psychology, 51*, 284-290.

Dalbert, C. (2001). *The justice motive as a personal resource: Dealing with challenges and critical life events.* New York: Kluwer Academic/Plenum.

Darley, J. M., & Latane, B. (1968). Bystander intervention in emergencies: Diffusion of responsibility. *Journal of Personality and Social Psychology, 8*, 377-383.

Darwin, C. R. (1859). *On the origin of species.* London: John Murray.

Dearborn, M. J., & Hastings, J. E. (1987). Type A personality as a mediator of stress and strain in employed women. Journal of Human Stress, 13(2), 53-60.

Deci, E. L. (1971). Effects of externally mediated rewards on intrinsic motivation. *Journal of Personality and Social Psychology, 18*(1), 105-115.

Deinzer, R., Kleineidam, C. H., Winkler, R., Idel, H., & Bahg, D. (2000). Prolonged reduction of salivary immunoglobulin A (slgA) after a major academic exam. *International Journal of Psychophysiology, 37*, 219-232.

DeWall, C. N. & Bushman, B. J. (2009). Hot under the collar in a lukewarm environment: Words associated with hot temperature increase aggressive thoughts and hostile perceptions. *Journal of Experimental Social Psychology, 45*(4), 1045-1047.

Dollard, J., & Miller, N. F. (1950). *Personality and psychotherapy.* New

York:McGraw-Hill.

Dorathy, M. J. (2001). Dissociate identity disorder and memory dysfunction: The current state of experimental research and its future directions. *Clinical Psychology Review, 21*(5), 771-795.

Dronkers, N. F., Plaisant, O., Ibazizen, M. T., and Cabanis, E. A. (2007). Paul Broca's historic cases: High resolution MR Imaging of the brains of Leborgne and Lelong. Brain, 130(5), 1432-1441.

Duncker, K. (1945). *On problem solving.* Psychological Monographs, 58(270).

Eagly, A. H. & Chaiken, S. (1993). *The psychology of attitudes.* Forth Worth, TX: Harcourt Brace.

Eagly, A. H., Ashmore, R. D., Makjijani, M. G., & Lango, L. C. (1991). What is beautiful is good, but…: A meta-analytic review of the physical attractiveness stereotype. *Psychological Bulletin, 110*, 109-128.

Ebbinghaus, H. (1913). *On memory: A contribution to experimental psychology.* New York: Teachers College.

Eichenbaum,H. & Fortin, N. (2003). Episodic memory and the hippocampus: It is about time. *Current Directions in Psychological Science, 12*, 53-57.

Eisenberger, N. I., Lieberman, M. D., & Williams, K. D. (2003). Does rejection hurt? An fMRI study of social exclusion. *Science, 302*, 290-292.

Ekman, P. (1999), Basic Emotions, in Dalgleish, T; Power, M, *Handbook of Cognition and Emotion*, Sussex, UK: John Wiley & Sons.

Ekman, P., & Friesen, W. V. (1975). *Unmasking the face.* Englewood Cliffs, NJ: Prentice Hall.

Ekman, P., Friesen, W. V., O'Sullivan, M., Chan, A., Diacoyanni-Tarlatzis, I., Heider, K., et al. (1987), Universals and cultural differences in the judgments of facial expressions of emotion. *Journal of Personality and Social Psychology, 53*, 712-717.

Ellis, A. (1997). *The practice of rational emotive behavior therapy*. New York: Springer.

Epel, E., Lapidus, R., McEwen, B., & Brownell, K. (2001). Stress may add note to appetite in women: A laboratory study of stress-induced cortisol and eating behavior. *Psychoneuroendocrinology, 26*(1), 37-49.

Erienmeyer-Kimling, L. & Jarvik, L. F. (1963). Genetics and intelligence: A review. *Science, 142*, 1477-1479.

Erikson, E. H. (1959). Growth and crises of the healthy personality. *Psychological Issues, 1*, 50-100.

Erikson, E.H. (1968). *Identity: Youth and crisis*. New York: Norton.

Fagin, L. (2006). Stress and Unemployment. *Stress & Health, 1*(1), 27-36.

Fantz, R. L. (1961). The origin of form perception. *Scientific American, 204*, 66-72.

Faraone, S. V., Perlis, R. H., Doyle, A. E., Smoller, J. W., Goralnick, J. J., Holmgren, M. A. & Skylar, P. (2005). Molecular genetics of attention-deficit/hyperactivity disorder. *Biological Psychiatry, 57*(11), 1313-1323.

Farber, B. A. & Lane, J. S. (2001). Positive regard. *Psychotherapy: Theory, Research, Practice, Training, 38*(4), 390-395.

Fawzy, F. I., Fawzy, N. W., Hyun, C. S., Elashoff, R., Guthrie, D., Fahey, J. L., & Morton, D. L. (1993). Malignant malenoma effects of an early structured psychiatric intervention, coping, and affective state on recurrence and survival 6 years later. *Archives of General Psychiatry, 50*(9), 681-689.

Feingold, A. (1988). Matching for attractiveness in romantic partners and same-sex friends: A meta-analysis and theoretical critique. *Psychological Bulletin, 104*(2), 226–235.

Festinger, L. & Carlsmith, J. (1959). $1/$20 experiment: Cognitive consequences of forced compliance. Journal of Abnormal and Social Psychologu, 58(2), 203-210.

Festinger, L. (1957). *A theory of cognitive dissonance*. Stanford, CA: Stanford University Press.

Fischer, A. H., Rodriguez-Mosquera, P. M., van-Bianen, A. E. M. & Manstead, A. S. R. (2004). Gender and culture differences in emotion. *Emotion, 4*, 87-94.

Freud, S. & Bonaparte, M. (ed.) (2009). *The Origins of Psychoanalysis. Letters to Wilhelm Fliess: Drafts and Notes 1887-1902*. Kessinger Publishing.

Freud, S. & Brill A. A. (ed.) (1913). *Interpretation of Dreams*. New York: The Macmillan Company.

Freud, S. (1894). *The neuro-psychoses of defence*. SE, 3: 41-61.

Freud, S. (1900). *The interpretation of dreams*. SE, 4-5, (cf. J. Crick, Trans. 1999). London: Oxford University Press.

Freud, S. (1911). The handling of dream interpretation in psychoanalysis. In J. Strachey (Ed. and Trans.), The standard edition of the complete psychological works of Sigmund Freud (Vol. 12, 89-96). London: Hogarth Press.

Freud, S. (1954). *The origins of psychoanalysis*. New York: Basic Books. (Original work published 1904)

Gabrieli, J. D. E. (1998). Cognitive neuroscience of human memory. *Annual Review of Psychology, 49*, 87-115.

Galanter, M., & Kleber, H. D. (2008). *The American Psychiatric Publishing Textbook of Substance Abuse Treatment* (4th ed.). United States of America: American Psychiatric Publishing Inc.

Gamwell, L. & Tomes, N. (1995). *Madness in America: Cultural and medical perspectives of mental illness before 1914*. Ithica, NY: Cornell University Press.

Ganchrow, J. R., Steiner, J. E., & Munif, D. (1983). Neonatal facial expressions in response to different qualities and intensities of gustatory stimuli. *Infant Behavior Development, 6*, 473-478.

Garbarino, J. (1999). *Lost boys: Why our sons turn violent and how we can save them*. New York, NY: The Free Press.

Geddes, J., & Butler, R. (2002). Depressive Disorders. *Clinical Evidence, 7*, 867-882.

Gopnik, A. (1996). The post-Piaget era. *Psychological Science, 7*, 221-225.

Gross, C. G. (1999). A hole in the head. *The Neuroscientist, 5*, 263-269.

Gumustekin, K.; Seven, B.; Karabulut, N.; Aktas, O.; Gursan, N.; Aslan, S.; Keles, M.; Varoglu, E.; Dane, S. (2004). Effects of sleep deprivation, nicotine, and selenium on wound healing in rats". *International Journal of Neuroscience,* 114 (11), 1433–1442.

Haidt, J. & Keltner, D. (1999). Culture and Facial Expression: Open-ended Methods Find More Expressions and a Gradient of Recognition. *Cognition & Emotion, 13*(3), 225–266.

Harlow, H. F. (1949). The formation of learning sets. *Psychological Review, 56*, 51-65.

Harlow, H. F. (1958). The nature of love. *American Psychologist, 13*, 673-685.

Harrell, R. F., Woodyard, E., & Gates, A. I. (1955).*The effect of mother's diet on the intelligence of the offspring.* New York: Teacher's College, Columbia Bureau of Publications.

Harris, M. & Rosenthal, R. (1985). Mediation of the interpersonal expectancy effect: A taxonomy of expectancy situations. In P. Blanck (Ed.), *Interpersonal expectations: Theory, research, and application* (pp. 350-378). New York: Cambridge University Press.

Harrison, P. J. (1999). The neuropathology of schizophrenia: A critical review of the data and their interpretation. *Brain, 122*, 593-624.

Hartfield, E. & Rapson, R. L. (1992). Similarity and attraction in intimate relationships. *Communication Monographs, 59*, 209-212.

Hazan, C., & Shaver, P. (1987). Romantic love conceptualized as an attachment process. *Journal of Personality and Social Psychology, 52*(3), 511-524.

Heider, F. (1958). *The psychology of interpersonal relations*. New York: Wiley.

Hering, E. (1964). *Outlines of a Theory of the Light Sense*. Cambridge: Harvard University Press.

Hermann, B. P., Seidenberg, M., Sears, L., Hansen, R., Bayless, K., Rutecki, P., et al. (2004) Cerebellar atrophy in temporal lobe epilepsy affects procedural memory. *Neurology, 63*, 2129-2131.

Heylens, G., De Cuypere, G., Zucker, K., Schelfaut, C., Elaut, E., Vanden Bossche, H., De Baere, E., & T'Sjoen, G. (2012). Gender Identity Disorder in Twins: A Review of the Case Report Literature. *The Journal of Sexual Medicine, 8*, 751–757.

Holmes, T. H. & Rahe, R. H. (1967). The Social Readjustment Rating Scale. *Journal of Psychosomatic Research, 11*(2), 213-218.

Hull, C. L. (1943). Principles of behavior. New York: Appleton-Century-Crofts.

Hunt, M. (1993). *The story of psychology*. New York: Anchor Books.

ISAD 2013 Worldwide Shark Attach Summary. International Shark Attack File. 2014. Retrieved 22 April 2014.

James, W. (1890). *The principles of psychology*. New York: Holt.

James, W. (1948). What is emotion 1884. In W. Dennis (Ed.), *Readings in the history of psychology* (290-303). East Norwalk, CT: Appleton-Century-Crofts.

Johnson, W., Bouchard, J. T. Jr., Segal N. L., & Samuel, J. (2005). General intelligence and reading performance in adults: is the genetic factor structure the same as for children? *Personality and Individual Differences,*

38, 1413-1428.

Johnston, L. D., O'Malley, P. M., Bachman, J. G., & Schulenberg, J. E. (2011). *Monitoring the Future national results on adolescent drug use: Overview of key findings, 2010*. Ann Arbor: Institute for Social Research, The University of Michigan.

Jones, E. E., & Harris, V. A. (1967). The attribution of attitudes. *Journal of Experimental Social Psychology, 3*, 1-24.

Jung, C. (1933). *Modern man in search of a soul*. New York: Harcourt Brace.

Kastenbaum, R. & Costa, P. T. Jr. (1977). Psychological perspective on death. *Annual Review of Psychology, 28*, 225-249.

Kearney, C. A., & Silverman, W. K. (1998). A critical review of pharmacotherapy for youth with anxiety disorders: Things are not as they seem. *Journal of Anxiety Disorders, 12*, 83-102.

Kenrick, D. T. & Keefe, R. C. (1992). Age preferences in mates reflect sex differences in reproductive strategies. *Behavioral and Brain Sciences, 15*, 75-133.

Kiesler, C. A. (1982). Mental hospitals and alternative care: Noninstitutionalization as a potential public policy for mental patients. *Psychologist, 37*, 349-360.

Kingstone, A., Enns, J. T., Mangun, G. R., & Gazzaniga, M. S. (1995). Right hemisphere memory superiority: Studies of a split-brain patient. *Psychological Science, 73*, 389-410.

Kinsey, A. C., Pomeroy, W. B., & Martin, C. E. (1948). *Sexual behavior in the human male. Philadelphia*: Saunders.

Kinsey, A. C., Pomeroy, W. B., Martin, C. E., & Gebhard, P. H. (1953). *Sexual behavior in the human female. Philadelphia*: Saunders.

Klinesmith, J., Kasser, T., & McAndrew, F. T. (2006). Guns, testosterone and aggression: An experiemental test of a meditational hypothesis.

Psychological Science, 17(7), 568-571.

Kohlberg, L. (1973). Continuities in childhood and adult moral development revisited. In P. Bates & K. W. Schaie (Eds.), *Life-span development psychology: Personality and socialization*. San Diego, CA: Academic Press.

Kohler, W. *The mentality of apes*. Oxford, England: Harcourt, Brace.

Kotkin, M., Daviet, C., & Gurin, J. (1996). The Consumer Reports mental health survey, *American Psychologist, 51*(10), 1080-1082.

Kubler-Ross, E. (1969). *On death and dying*. New York: Macmillan.

Leport, A. K., Anson, H., Stark, C., McGaugh, J, & Cahill, L. (2011). Highly superior autobiographical memory (HSAM): An investigation of the behavioral and neuroanatomical components. Paper presented at Washington, DC: Society for Neuroscience. Abstract retrieved from http://www.abstractsonline.com/Plan/ViewAbstract.aspx?sKey=474f1dc2-cb67-4a11-841e-838e360f9d4a&cKey=ece5ba79-6e52-464f-b6a0-7f95ba548d59&mKey={8334BE29-8911-4991-8C31-32B32DD5E6C8}#

Lerner, M. J. (1980). *The belief in a just world: A fundamental delusion*. New York: Plenum.

Levin, J. R. & Nordwall, M. B. (1992). Mnemonic vocabulary instruction: Additional effectiveness evidence. *Contemporary Educational Psychology, 17* (2), 156–174.

Levy, S. E., Mandell, D.S,, & Schultz, R.T. (2009). Autism. *Lancet, 374*(9701),1627–1638.

Lewis, J. R. (1995). *Encyclopedia of afterlife beliefs and phenomenon*. Detroit, MI: Visible Ink Press.

Liebel, R. L., Rosenbaum, M., & Hirsch, J. (1995). Changes in energy expenditure resulting from altered body weight. *New England Journal of Medicine, 332,*

621-628.

Lim U., Subar A.F., Mouw T., et al. (2006). Consumption of aspartame-containing beverages and incidence of hematopoietic and brain malignancies. *Cancer Epidemiology, Biomarkers and Prevention, 15*(9):1654–1659.

Loehlin, J. C., Horn, J. M., & Willerman, L. (1997). Heredity, environment and IQ in the Texas adoption study. In R. J. Sternberg & E/ Grigorenko (Eds.), *Intelligence: Heredity and environment* (105-125). New York: Cambridge University Press.

Loftus, E. F. and Palmer, J. C. (1974) Reconstruction of automobile destruction: An example of the interaction between language and memory. *Journal of Verbal Learning and Verbal Behavior, 13*, 585-589.

Loftus, E. F. and Pickrell, J. E. (1995). The formation of false memories. *Psychiatric Annuals, 25*, 720-725.

Luborsky, L., Singer, B., & Luborsky, L. (1975). Comparative studies of psychotherapies: Is it true that "everyone has won and all must have prizes"? *Archives of General Psychiatry, 32*, 995-1008.

Maccoby, E.E. (1992). The role of parents in the socialization of children: An historical overview. *Developmental Psychology, 28*, 1006-1017.

MacKinnon, D. F., Jamison, K. R., & DePaulo, J. R. (1997). Genetics of manic depressive illness. *Annual review of neuroscience, 20*(1), 355-373.

Maier, S. F. & Watkins, L. R. (1998). Cytokines for psychologists: Implications of bidirectional immune-to-brain communication for understanding behavior, mood, and cognition. *Psychological Review, 105*, 83-107.

Majnemer, A., Brownstien, A., Kadanoff, R., & Shevell, M. I. (1992). A comparison of neurobehavioral performance of healthy term and low-risk preterm infants at term. *Developmental Medicine & Child Neurology, 34*(5), 417-424.

Maloney, M. P. & Ward, M. P. (1976). *Psychological assessment: A conceptual approach*. New York: Academic Press.

Manns, J. R., Hopkins, R. O., & Squire, L. R. (2003). Semantic memory and the human hippocampus. *Neuron, 38*, 127-133.

Martin, J.A., Hamilton, B.E., Sutton, P.D., Ventura, S.J., Matthews, T.J., Kirmeyer, S. & Osterman, M.J.K.. (2010). Births: Final data for 2007. *National Vital Statistics Reports, 58*(24).

Maslow, A.H. (1943). A theory of human motivation. *Psychological Review, 50*(4), 370–96.

Masters, W. H. and Johnson, V. E. (1966). *Human sexual response*. Oxford, UK: Little, Brown.

Matsumoto, D. (1990). Cultural similarities and differences in display rules. *Motivation and Emotion, 14*(3), 195–214.

McClelland, D. C., Arkinson, J. W., Clark, R. A., & Lowell, E. L. (1953). *The achievement motive*. New York: Appleton-Century.

McDougall, W. (1908). *An introduction to social psychology*. London: Methuen & Co.

Meichenbaum, D. (1996). Stress inoculation training for coping with stressors. *The Clinical Psychologist, 49*, 4-7.

Meier, C. A., Ruef, H., Ziegler, A., & Hall, C. S. (1968). Forgetting of dreams in the laboratory. *Perceptual and Motor Skills, 26*, 551-557.

Melzack, R. & Katz, J. (2004). The gate control theory: Reaching for the brain. In T. Hadjisavropoulos & K. Craig (Eds.), *Pain: Psychological perspectives*. Mahwah, NJ: Erlbaum.

Mental Health America. (2013). Child and adolescent suicide. Alexandria, VA: Mental Health America. (2013). Retrieved July, 2013, from http://www.

mentalhealthamerica.net/go/information/get-info/children-s-mental-health/child-and-adolescent-suicide.

Meston, C. M. & Frohlich, P. F. (2000). The neurobiology of sexual function. *Archives of General Psychology, 57*, 1012-1030.

Milgram, S. (1964). Behavioral study of obedience. *Journal of Abnormal and Social Psychology, 67*, 371-378.

Miller, A. G. (2004). What can the Milgram obedience experiments tells us about the Holocaust? Generalizing from the social psychology laboratory. In *The Social Psychology of Good and Evil.* (pp 193-239). The Guilford Press: New York, NY.

Miller, G. A. (1956). The magical number seven, plus or minus two: Some limits on our capacity for processing information. *Psychological Review, 63*, 81–97.

Morgan, C. D. & Murray, H. A. (1935). A method for investigating fantasies: The Thematic Apperception test. *Archives of Neurology and Psychiatry, 34*, 298-306.

Mullen, K. D., & Costello, G. (1981). *Health awareness through self-discovery: A workbook.* Minneapolis: Burgess Publishing.

Murray, H. A. (1938). *Explorations in personality.* New York: Oxford University Press.

Nansel, T.R., Overpeck, M., Pilla, R.S., Ruan, W.J., Simons-Morton, B., and Scheidt, P. (2001). Bullying behaviors among U.S. youth: Prevalence and association with psychosocial adjustment. *Journal of the American Medical Association, 285*(16), 2094-2100.

National Institute of Mental Health. (2010). The numbers count: Mental disorders in America. Retrieved from http://www.nimh.nih.gov/health/publications/the-numbers-count-mental-disorders-in-america/index.shtml

Neimeyer, R. A. & Chapman, K. M. (1980/1981). Self-ideal discrepancy and fear of death: The test of an existential hypothesis. *Omega, 11*, 233-239.

Nelson, D. E., Jarman, D. W., Rehm, J. R., Greenfield, T. K., Rey, G., Kerr, W. C., Miller, P., Shielf, K. D. Ye, Y., & Naimi, T. S. (2013). Alcohol-attributable cancer deaths and years of potential life lost in the United States. *American Journal of Public Health, 103*(4), 641-648.

Nichino, S., Ripley, B., Overeem, S., Lammers, G. J., & Mignot, E. (2000). Hypocretin (orexin) deficiency in human narcolepsy. *The Lancet, 225*(9197), 39-40.

Nickerson, R. S. (1998). Confirmation bias: A ubiquitous phenomenon in many guises. *Review of General Psychology, 2*(2), 175-220.

Nieto, F. J., Peppard, P.E., Young, T., Finn, L., Hla K. M., Farré, R. (2012). Sleep disordered breathing and cancer mortality: results from the Wisconsin Sleep Cohort Study. *American Journal Respiratory Critical Care Medicine, 186*, 190–194.

Norcross, J. C. (2005). A primer on psychotherapy integration. In J. C. Norcross & M. Goldfried (Eds.), *Handbook of psychotherapy integration* (2nd ed., pp. 3-23). New York, NY: Oxford University Press.

Parker E.S., Cahill L & McGaugh J.L. (2006). A case of unusual autobiographical remembering. *Neurocase,* 12 (1), 35–49.

Pastor, D. (1981). The quality of mother-infant attachment and its relationship to toddlers' initial sociability with peers. *Developmental Psychology, 17*(3), 326-335.

Pavlov, I. P. (1927). *Conditional reflexes* (G.V. Anrep, trans.) London: Oxford University Press.

Perls, F. (1951). *Gestalt therapy*. New York: Julian Press.

Piaget, J. (1952). *The origins of intelligence in children*. New York: Norton.

Piaget, J. (1983). Pieaget's theory. In W. Kessen (Ed.), *Handbook of child psychology: Volume 1. Theoretical models of human development* (pp. 103-128). New York: Wiley.

Plato. (2002). Phaedo. Five Dialogues. (G.M.A. Grube, Trans.). Indianapolis: Hackett Publishing Co.

Plomin, R. (1997). Identifying genes for cognitive abilities and disabilities. In R. J. Sternberg & E. Griogerenko (Eds.), *Intelligence: Heredity and Environment* (89-104). New York: Cambridge University Press.

Plomin, R., DeFries, J. C., McClearn, G. E., & McGuffin, P. (2000). *Behavioral genetics* (4th ed.). New York: Worth Publishers.

Quiles, M. Y., Quiles, Sebastian, M. J., Pamines, A. L., Botella, A. J. & Treasure, J. (2013). Peer and family influence in eating disorders: a meta-analysis. *European Psychiatry, 28*(4), 199-206.

Renzulli, J. S. (1978). What makes giftedness? Reexamining a definition. *Phi Delta Kappan*, 60, 180-184, 261.

Robbins, J. (2013) GPS: A turn by turn case-in point. In *Cases on Emerging Information Technology Research and Applications.* (pp. 88-111). Hershey, PA: IGI Global.

Roehling, M. V., Roehling, P. V., & Pichler, S. (2007). The relationship between body weight and perceived weight-related employment discrimination: The role of sex and race. *Journal of Vocational Behavior, 71*(2), 300-318.

Rogers, C. R. (1961). *On Becoming a Person: a Therapist's View of Psychotherapy.* Boston: Houghton Mifflin.

Rosenthal, A. M. (1964). *Thirty-eight witnesses: The Kitty Genovese case*. New York: McGraw-Hill.

Rotter, J. B. (1954). *Social learning and clinical psychology*. Englewood Cliffs, NJ: Prentice Hall.

Savic, I. & Lindstrom, P. (2008). PET and MRI show differences in cerebral asymmetry and functional connectivity between homo- and heterosexual subjects. *Proceedings of the National Academy of Sciences, USA, 105*(27), 9403-9408.

Schacter, D. L., Gilbert, D. L. & Wegner, D. M. (2009). *Psychology*. (2nd ed.). New Work (NY): Worth Publishers.

Schacter, S., & Singer, J. (1962). Cognitive, social, and physiological determination of emotional state. *Psychological Review, 69*, 379-399.

Schneier, F. R., Martin, L. Y., Liebowitz, M. R., Gorman, J. M., and Fyer, A. J. (1989). Alcohol abuse in social phobia. *Journal of Anxiety Disorders, 3*(1), 15-23.

Schuster, M. A., Stein, B. D., Jaycox, L. H., Collins, R. L., Marshall, G. N., Elliott, M. N., Zhou, A. J., Kanouse, D. E., Morrison, J. L., & Berry, S. H. (2001). A national survey of stress reactions after the September 11, 2001, terrorist attacks. *New England Journal of Medicine, 345*, 1507-1512.

Segerstrom, S. C. & Miller, G. E. (2004). Psychological stress and the human immune system: A meta-analytic study of 30 years of inquiry. *Psychological Bulletin, 130*(4), 601-630.

Seligman, M. (1975). *Helplessness: Depression, development and death.* New York: W. H. Freeman.

Seligman, M.E.P., & Maier, S.F. (1967). Failure to escape traumatic shock. *Journal of Experimental Psychology, 74*, 1–9.

Selye, H. (1956). *The stress of life.* New York: McGraw-Hill.

Sentyrz, S. M. & Bushman, B. J. (1998). Mirror, mirror on the wall, who's the thinnest one of all? Effects of self-awareness on consumption of full-fat, reduced-fat, and no-fat products. *Journal of Applied Psychology, 83*, 944-

949.

Sharot, T., Delgado, M. R. & Phelps. E. A. (2004). How emotion enhances the feeling of remembering. *Nature Neuroscience 7* (12), 1376–1380.

Sher, L. (2005). Type D personality: the heart, stress, and cortisol. *Q J Med, 98*, 323-329.

Sherif, M., Harvey, O.J., White, B.J., Hood, W., & Sherif, C.W. (1961). *Intergroup Conflict and Cooperation: The Robbers Cave Experiment*. Norman, OK: The University Book Exchange.

Shteingart, H. Neiman, T. & Loewenstein, Y. (2013). The role of first impression in operant learning. *Journal of Experimental Psychology: General, 142*(2), 476-488.

Silber, MH; Ancoli-Israel, S; Bonnet, MH; Chokroverty, S; Grigg-Damberger, MM; Hirshkowitz, M; Kapen, S; Keenan, SA et al. (2007). The visual scoring of sleep in adults. *Journal of Clinical Sleep Medicine, 3*(2), 121–31.

Skeels, H.M. (1942). The study of the effects of differential stimulation on mentally retarded children: A follow up report. *American Journal of Mental Deficiencies, 46*, 340-350.

Skinner, B. F. (1938). *The Behavior of Organisms: An Experimental Analysis*. New York: Appleton-Century.

Skinner, B. F. (1948). 'Superstition' in the pigeon. *Journal of Experimental Psychology, 38*, 168-172.

Skinner, B. F. (1957). *Verbal behavior*. Englewood Cliffs, NJ: Macmillan.

Skinner, B. F. (1971). *Beyond freedom and dignity*. New York: Knopf.

Smith, C.T., Nixon, M.R., & Nader, R. S. (2004). Posttraining increases in REM sleep intensity implicate REM sleep in memory processing and provide a biological marker of learning potential. *Learning & Memory, 11*, 714-719.

Smith, E. R., & Mackie, D. M. (2005). Applying social psychology in everyday life. In F. W. Schneider, J. A. Gruman, & L. M. Coutts (Eds.), *Applied social psychology: Understanding and addressing social and practical problems* (pp. 75-99). Thousand Oaks, CA: Sage.

Smith, R. A., Kirby, R. R., Gooding, J. M., Civetta, J. M. (1980). Continuous positive air pressure mask (CPAP) by face mask. *Critical Care Medicine, 8*(9), 483-485.

Snyder, M., & Swann, W. B. Jr. (1978). Behavioral confirmation in social interaction: From social perception to social reality. *Journal of Experimental Social Psychology, 14*, 148-162.

Spaniol, J., Madden, D. J., Voss, A. (2006). A Diffusion Model Analysis of Adult Age Differences in Episodic and Semantic Long–Term Memory Retrieval. *Journal of Experimental Psychology: Learning, Memory, and Cognition, 32*(1), 101–117.

Sternberg, R. J. (2003). Intelligence. In D. K. Freedheim (Ed.). *Handbook of psychology: History of psychology* (Vol. 1, 135-136), New York: John Wiley & Sons.

Sternberg, R. J. (April 1982). Who's intelligent? *Psychology Today*, 30-39.

Stirling, L. J. & Yeomans, M. R. (2004). Effect of exposure to a forbidden food on eating in restrained and unrestrained women. *International Journal of Eating Disorders, 35*(1), 59-68.

Sue, S. & Okazaki, S. (1990). Asian-American educational achievements: A phenomenon in search of an explanation. *American Psychologist, 45*(8), 913-920.

Surwit, R. S., Schneider, M. S., & Feinglos, M. N. (1992). Stress and diabetes mellitus. *Diabetes Care, 15*(10), 1413-1422.

Sutherland, P. (1992). *Cognitive development today: Piaget and his critics*. London: Paul Chapman.

Talarico, J. M. & Rubin, D. C. (2003). Confidence, not consistency, characterizes flashbulb memories. *Psychological Science, 14* (5), 455–461.

Talbott, G. D., & Crosby, L. R. (2001). Recovery contracts: Seven key elements. In R. H. Coombs (Eds.). *Addiction recovery tools* (pp. 127-144). Thousand Oaks, CA: Sage.

Tamminga, C. A., & Vogel, M. (2005). Images in neuroscience: The cerebellum. *American Journal of Psychiatry, 162*, 1253.

Teitelbaum, P. & Epstein, A. N. (1962). The lateral hypothalamus syndrome: Recovery of feeding and drinking after lateral hypothalamic lesions. *Psychological Review, 69*(2), 74-79.

Terman, L. M., Lyman, G., Ordahl, G., Ordahl, L., Galbreath, N., Talbert, W. (1915). The Stanford revision of the Binet-Simon scale and some results from its application to 1000 non-selected children. *Journal of Educational Psychology, 6* (9), 551–62.

Theunissen, M. J. M., Polet, I. A., Kroeze, J.H.A., & Schifferstein, H. N. J. (2000) Taste asaptation during the eating of sweetened yogurt. *Appetite, 34*(1), 21-27.

Thomas, A., & Chess, S. (1977). *Temperament and development*. New York: Brunner/Mazel.

Thorndike, E. L. (1898) Animal intelligence. *Psychological Review Monograph, 2* (4, whole No. 8).

Thorndike, E. L. (1914) *The psychology of learning*, New York, Teachers College.

Tolman, E. C. & Honzik, C. H. (1930). Introduction and removal of reward, and maze performance in rats. *University of California Publications in Psychology, 4*, 257-275.

Tramer, M. R., Carroll, D., Campbell, F. A., Reynolds, D. J. M., Moore, R. A., & McQuay, H. J. (2001) Cannabinoids for control of chemotherapy induced nausea and vomiting: quantitative systematic review. *BMJ, 323*(16).

Treisman, A. M. (1960). Contextual cues in selective listening. *Quarterly Journal of Experimental Psychology, 12*, 242-248.

Tsuang, M.T., Lyons, M. J., Meyer, J. M., Doyle, T. (1998). Co-occurrence of abuse of different drugs in men: The role of drug-specific and shared vulnerabilities. *Archives of General Psychiatry*, 55, 967–972.

Turner, T.H.; Drummond, S.P.A.; Salamat, J.S.; Brown, G.G. (2007). Effects of 42 hr sleep deprivation on component processes of verbal working memory. *Neuropsychology, 21* (6), 787–795.

Tversky, A. and Kahneman, D. (1981). The Framing of Decisions and the Psychology of Choice. *Science, 211* (4481), 453–458.

Vanyukov, M. M., Tarter, R. E., Kirillova, G. P., Kirisci, L., Reynolds, M. D., Kreek, M. J., Conway, K. P., Maher B. S., Iacono, W. G., Bierut, L., Neale, M. C., Clark, D. B., & Ridenour, T. A. (2012). Common liability to addiction and "gateway hypothesis": Theoretical, empirical and evolutionary perspective. *Drug and Alcohol Dependence, 123*(Supp 1), S3-S17.

Visser, P. S. & Krosnick, J. A. (1998). Development of attitude strength over the life cycle: Surge and decline. *Journal of Personality and Social Psychology, 75*(6), 1389-1410.

Walden, B. McGue, M., Iacono, W. G., Burt, S. A., & Elkins, I. (2004). Identifying shared environmental contributions to early substance use: The respective roles of peers and parents. Journal of *Abnormal Psychology, 113*(3), 440-450.

Watson, J. B. & Rayner, R. (1920). Conditioned emotional reactions. *Journal of Experimental Psychology, 3*, 1-14.

Weschler, D. (1955). *Manual for the Weschler Adult Intelligence Scale*. Oxford, England: Psychological Corp.

Whorf, B. L. (1956). *Language, thought, and reality*. New York: MIT Press-Wiley.

Wicker, A. W. (1971). An examination of the "other variables" explanation of attitude-behavior inconsistency. *Journal of Personality and Social Psychology, 19*, 18-30.

Wilcox, W. B. & Marquardt, E. (2011).*The state of our unions: Marriage in America 2011*. University of Virginia, National Marriage Project.

Wilding, J.M., & Valentine, E.R. (1997). *Superior Memory*. Hove, England: Psychology Press.

Wilson B. A., & Wearing D. (1995). Prisoner of consciousness: a state of just awakening following herpes simplex encephalitis. In: Campbell R, Conway M.A., (Eds). *Broken memories*. Oxford: Blackwell.

Wolpe, J. (1990). *The practice of behavior therapy*. New York: Pergamon Press.

Woodward, S. A., Markman, E. M., & Fitzsimmons, C. (1994). Rapid word learning in 13- to 18- month olds. *Developmental Psychology, 30*, 538-553.

Wooten, B. and Miller, D.L. (1997) The psychophysics of color. In *Color Categories in Thought and Language* (Hardin, C.L. and Maffi, L., eds), pp. 59–88, Cambridge University Press.

Wundt , W. (1904). *Principles of physiological psychology. Vol. 1.* (5th ed.) EB Titchener (Trans.)
New York: Macmillan, 1904.

Yaggi, H. K., Concato, J., Kernan, W. N., Lichtman, J. H., Brass, L. M., & Mohsenin, V. (2005). Obstructive sleep apnea as a risk factor for stroke and death. *New England Journal of Medicine, 353*, 2034-2041.

Zager, A.; Andersen, M.L.; Ruiz, F.S.; Antunes, I.B. and Tufik, S. (2007). Effects of acute and chronic sleep loss on immune modulation of rats. *Regulatory, Integrative and Comparative Physiology* **293**: R504–R509.

Zajonc, R. B. (2001). Mere exposure: A gateway to the subliminal. *Current Directions in Psychological Science, 10*(6), 224-228.

Zuckerman, M. (1994). *Behavioral expression and biosocial bases of sensation seeking*. New York: Cambridge University Press.

INDEX

A

Aaron Beck 1, 289, 342, 343, 351, 386
abnormality 282
  models of 284
Abraham Maslow 7, 181, 365
absolute threshold 56, 57
accommodation 206
achievement 190
action potential 30, 31, 56
actor-observer bias 269
adaptation 58, 59, 60, 316, 317, 360, 364, 368
  dark adaptation 59
  light adaptation 60
addiction 93, 94, 96, 97, 98, 325
ADHD. *See* attention-deficit hyperactivity disorder
adolescence 214
  social development in 215
adoption studies 50, 160, 355
adrenal glands 46, 316
adulthood 217
agoraphobia 291
agreeableness 245
Albert Bandura 123, 128, 237
Albert Ellis 343

alcohol 91, 92, 101, 389, 403, 406
Alfred Adler 236, 250
algorithm 166, 174
altered state of consciousness (ASC) 80
altruism 7, 274
Alzheimer's disease 142, 220, 356
American Psychological Association (APA) 22
amphetamines 94, 101
amplitude 62, 77
amygdala 37, 141, 368
anal stage 233
Anorexia Nervosa 184, 356
anterograde amnesia 143
anti-anxiety drugs 348
antipsychotic drugs 348
antisocial personality disorder 302
anxiety disorders 290
approach-approach conflict 312
approach-avoidance conflict 313
archetypes 235
Asperger's syndrome 304
assimilation 206
asylums 284, 332
attachment 209, 210, 211, 212, 224, 233, 396, 404
  ambivalent/anxious 211
  avoidant 211
  disorganized 211
  secure 211
attention 131, 304, 356
attention-deficit hyperactivity disorder (ADHD) 304
attitudes 261, 262, 264, 270, 273, 359, 372, 386, 392, 398
attraction 8, 233, 272, 273, 371, 396

proximity in 273
similarity in 273, 274, 301, 385, 386
attributions 267, 268, 342
auditory nerve 63
autistic spectrum disorder 304
autonomic nervous system 33
availability heuristic 170, 175
aversion therapy 340
avoidance-avoidance conflict 312
avoidant personality disorder 303
axon 28, 31

B

Baddeley's model of short term memory 132
barbiturates 91, 92, 101
basic emotions 194, 199
basilar membrane 63
behavioral and social cognitive perspective 228
behavioral assessments 246
behavior genetics 47
behaviorism 5, 6
behavior therapies 337, 357
B. F. Skinner 5, 24, 111, 128, 164
Big Five 243, 248, 357
bilateral anterior cingulotomy 350
binge-eating disorder 185, 357
binocular cues 71
biological perspective 3
biological psychology 27, 47
biomedical therapies 347
biomedical therapy 332
bipolar disorders 289

bipolar I 289
bipolar II 289
Bobo doll study 123
brain 4, 6, 16, 29, 32, 35, 36, 37, 38, 39, 40, 41, 43, 46, 53, 56, 59, 61, 62, 63, 64, 65, 66, 67, 68, 71, 72, 73, 78, 80, 82, 83, 87, 88, 91, 95, 135, 142, 148, 182, 190, 192, 220, 225, 289, 299, 301, 350, 356, 358, 363, 365, 369, 371, 372, 373, 375, 377, 378, 380, 381, 386, 398, 400, 401, 402
forebrain 35, 36, 38, 358, 368, 373
hindbrain 35, 36, 358, 369
midbrain 35, 36
Bulimia Nervosa 184, 358
bystander effect 275

C

caffeine 19, 94
Cannon-Bard theory 192, 199, 358
Carl Jung 235, 250
Carl Rogers 7, 24, 241, 250, 251, 335
case studies 16
catastrophes 320
CBT. *See* cognitive behavioral therapy
central executive 132
central nervous system 32, 33, 35, 41, 43, 372, 378
central nervous system (CNS) 32
cerebellum 36, 141, 373, 409
cerebral cortex 37, 38, 39, 53, 79, 364, 371, 372, 380
cerebrum 36, 38, 358, 360, 363
chromosomes 48
chunking 133, 358
circadian rhythm 81
classical conditioning 104, 105, 116, 118, 119, 126, 338, 360, 381
client-centered therapy 336, 337

cocaine 95
cochlea 63
cocktail party phenomenon 131
cognition 161, 220, 261, 359, 392, 396, 408
cognitive behavioral therapy 343
cognitive dissonance 263, 277, 394
cognitive learning 120
cognitive map 121
cognitive perspective 6
cognitive therapies 342
collective unconscious 235, 250, 356
color vision 60
compensation 236
compensatory decision 168
compliance 256, 277, 359
compromise 325, 329
computerized axial tomography (CAT) scans 41
concepts 165, 360
concrete Operational Stage 207
conditioned response (CR) 106
conditioned stimulus (CS) 106
cones 58
confirmation bias 170, 174, 175
conflict 312, 327, 360
conformity 254, 255, 256, 384
confrontation 325
conscientiousness 244
contingencies 119, 385
contingency contracting 341
conventional 217
convergence 74
conversion disorder 296

cornea 57
corpus callosum 38
correlational research 18
correlations 18
cortisol 34, 46, 314, 316, 318, 393, 406
couple therapy 345
critical period 204
cross-sectional studies 202
culture-fair tests 160

D

Darwin 7, 50, 370, 391
daydreams 90
death
  stages of facing death 221
death 221
decay theory 142
decision making 168
defense mechanisms 231, 322, 324
deinstitutionalization 333
delusions 300, 361
dendrites 28, 31
denial 225, 322, 328
dependent variable 20, 366
depressants 91, 361
depressive disorders 287, 361
development
  infancy and childhood 204
developmental psychology 201
Diagnostic and Statistical Manual of Mental Disorders. *See* DSM
difference threshold 57
direct coping 325

direct observation 246
discrimination 186, 270, 271, 379, 387, 405
displacement 323
display rules 197, 401
dissociative amnesia 296
dissociative disorders 296, 361
dissociative fugue 296
dissociative identity disorder 297, 362
distance and depth perception 71
diversity-universality 10
divorce 319, 345
door-in-the-face 257, 390
dopamine 95, 289, 301, 348
dream interpretation 334
dreams 87, 88, 362, 394
drive reduction theory 178, 179
drug-altered states of consciousness 90
DSM 84, 96, 185, 286, 287, 289, 290, 298, 299, 301, 320
dualism 2

E

eardrum 63
eating disorders 184
ego 219, 230, 231, 375
egocentrism 207
eidetic memory. *See* photographic memory
elaborative rehearsal 135, 150, 362
electroconvulsive therapy (ECT) 349, 362
electroencephalograph (EEG) 40, 80
emotion
  cultural differences in 197
emotion 191

communication of 195
gender differences in 196
theories of 191
emotional memory 140, 142
endocrine system 27, 44, 45, 46, 52, 67, 316, 373
endocrine glands 45, 46, 47, 355, 365
enduring Issues 9
epinephrine 46, 94
episodic buffer 133, 384
episodic memories 139, 363
erectile disorder 298
Erik Erikson 212
evolutionary perspective 7
experimental research
control group 19
experimental group 19
experimental research 19
explicit memories 138, 363
exposure therapy 338
extinction 116, 117, 339
extraversion 244, 250
extroversion 243
eyewitness memory 144

F

factitious disorder 296
family studies 49, 363
family therapy 345, 363
female sexual interest/arousal disorder 298
fetal alcohol syndrome (FAS) 204
fetishism 298
fight-or-flight 34, 44

flashbulb memory 146
flooding 149, 339
fMRI 41, 392
foot-in-the-door 257
formal operational stage 209
fovea 58
framing effect 171
free association 334
frequency 62, 77, 83, 340, 357, 375
frontal lobe 39, 91
frotteurism 298, 299
frustration 271, 310, 311, 323, 325, 327
frustration-aggression theory 271
fully functioning person 241
functional fixedness 168
functionalism 3
fundamental attribution error 268

G

gate control theory 67, 402
gender dysphoria 299, 364
general adaptation syndrome (GAS) 316
generalized anxiety disorder (GAD) 12, 290
genes 47, 48, 49, 357, 404
genetics 47, 364, 393, 400
genital stage 234
Gestalt therapy 336, 364, 404
ghrelin 182
glucose 182, 367
gonads 47
grammar 162
group therapies 344

gustatory perception 64

H

hair cells 63
hallucinations 300, 365
harry harlow 189
heuristics 166, 169, 172
hierarchy of needs 180, 181, 198
hindsight bias 171
hippocampus 37, 141, 368, 392, 401
hoarding disorder 294
holophrases 164
homeostasis 178, 183
hormones 44, 45, 46, 47, 182, 219, 316, 317, 318, 355, 362, 365
humanistic perspective 228
humanistic perspective 6
human sexual response cycle 187
hunger 37, 178, 179, 181, 182, 183, 230, 365, 368, 389
hyperthymesia 147
hypnosis 98, 148
hypothalamus 37, 79, 81, 182, 368, 409
hypothesis 12

I

id 230, 231, 250, 373, 375
ideal self 241, 336, 359
identification 84, 187, 323, 387
illness anxiety disorder 295
images 165, 366, 409
implicit memories 139, 140
Impressions 266
incentive theory 179

inclusion 157

independent variable 19, 20, 360, 361, 363

inferiority complex 236

information processing theory 130

informed consent 22

insight learning 122

insomnia 84, 367

instincts 178, 198, 367

insulin 182, 367

intellectual disability 49, 156, 157, 174, 282, 304

intellectualization 324, 328

intelligence 10, 12, 25, 26, 48, 50, 95, 153, 154, 155, 157, 158, 159, 160, 161, 173, 201, 273, 282, 367, 380, 381, 393, 396, 397, 404, 409

intelligence quotient. *See* IQ

intelligence testing 155

interposition 71

interviews 246

IQ 155, 156, 158, 159, 160, 161, 174, 282, 367, 386, 400

Ivan Pavlov 5

J

James-Lange theory 191, 192, 199, 367

Jean Piaget 206

John B. Watson 5, 128

Julian Rotter 239

just world hypothesis 269

K

kinesthetic sense 67, 68

Kitty Genovese 275, 405

Kubler-Ross 221, 222, 225, 399

L

language 162, 163, 367, 390, 411
language acquisition device (LAD) 164
late adulthood 219
latency stage 234
latent content 334
latent learning 120
law of effect 109
learned helplessness 115, 116, 240, 288
learning 6, 35, 41, 81, 89, 103, 105, 106, 107, 108, 109, 111, 113, 114, 115, 117, 119, 120, 121, 122, 123, 125, 128, 137, 143, 163, 164, 168, 174, 189, 236, 259, 285, 337, 338, 339, 345, 357, 359, 367, 370, 371, 378, 379, 384, 387, 396, 405, 407, 409, 411
learning set 122
lens 8, 58
leptin 182, 368
limbic system 36, 37, 52, 65, 363
linear perspective 72
linguistic relativity hypothesis 163
locus of control 240
longitudinal study 202
long term memory (LTM) 134
lowball technique 258
lysergic acid diethylamide (LSD) 95

M

magnetic resonance imaging (MRI) 41
major depressive disorder 288
mania 289
manifest content 334
manoamine oxidase inhibitors (MAOIs) 348

marijuana 96
medication 12, 284, 332, 333, 341, 348, 349, 351, 352, 374
meditation 98, 368
medulla 36, 64, 373
memory 3, 129, 130, 132, 134, 135, 138, 144, 146, 151, 369, 407, 408, 411
forgetting 137, 142, 143, 296, 297
menopause 219
mental disorders
classification of 286
mental set 167
mere exposure effect 273
metabolism 46, 81, 183, 186, 380
middle adulthood 218
midlife crisis 218
mind-body 11
Minnesota Multiphasic Personality Inventory (MMPI-2) 248
mnemonics 136, 150, 369
monocular cues 71
moral development 217
motion parallax 72
motivation 177, 178, 181, 186, 369, 401

N

narcissistic personality disorder 303
narcolepsy 87, 100, 369
naturalistic observation 14
natural selection 50
nature-nurture 10
neo-Freudian psychodynamic theorists 235
nervous system
divisions of 31, 32, 37

neurodevelopmental disorders 303, 370
neurons 28, 29, 31, 35, 42, 43, 52, 56, 64, 67, 80, 81, 356, 357, 361, 369, 370, 377, 380
  interneurons 42, 43
  motor neurons 42, 43
  sensory neurons 42, 43, 56
neuroticism 245
neurotransmitters 31, 289, 348
nicotine 94
nightmares 86
night terror 86
non-REM 82, 83
norepinephrine 289, 348
NREM stage 1 82, 83, 375
NREM stage 2 82
NREM stage 3 82, 84, 86, 378

O

obedience 254, 258, 260, 386, 402
obesity 185, 186, 318
object permanence 206
observational learning 123
observer bias 15, 370
obsessive-compulsive disorder (OCD) 294, 370
occipital lobe 39, 40, 59
oedipus complex 233, 371
olfaction 64, 371
olfactory bulb 64
openness 243
operant conditioning 104, 109, 110, 111, 113, 116, 117, 119, 120, 126, 338, 341, 367, 371, 375

opiates 93
opponent-process theory 61
optic nerve 59
oral stage 232
organ of Corti 63
orgasmic disorders 298
overjustification effect 180
oxytocin 187

P

panic attack 291
panic disorder 290, 291, 306, 371
paranoid personality disorder 301, 302
paraphilic disorders 298
parasympathetic 34, 44
parietal lobe 39, 65, 68
pedophilia 299
perception 6, 25, 56, 57, 60, 67, 68, 69, 70, 71, 73, 74, 76, 78, 95, 170, 296, 357, 361, 365, 369, 380, 381, 393, 408
perceptual constancy 70, 359
brightness constancy 71
color constancy 70, 78, 359
shape constancy 70
size constancy 70, 78, 377
perceptual expectancy 75
performance tests 159
peripheral nervous system (PNS 32, 43
peripheral nervous system (PNS). 32
persistent depressive disorder (dysthymia) 288
personality 227, 229, 232, 236, 246, 247, 248, 250, 252, 297, 301, 302, 372, 385, 386, 388, 389, 390, 391, 392, 393, 396, 397, 399, 410, 411

assessment of 246
personality traits 228
persuasion 264, 265, 266, 390, 391
elements of 264
phallic stage 233
pheromones 64, 187
phobias 292, 293, 338, 339, 347
phonological loop 132, 134
photographic memory 147
physical attractiveness 188, 272, 392
pituitary gland 46
Plato 1, 2, 404
pleasure principle 230
pons 36
postconventional 217
posttraumatic stress disorder 290, 320
preconventional 217
prejudice 270, 271, 383
premature ejaculation 298
prenatal development 203
preoperational stage 207
pressure 311, 327, 328, 373
primacy effect 137, 266
primary emotions 193
priming 140
proactive interference 143
problem solving 165
methods of 166
problem solving barriers 167
procedural memories 140
projective tests 248
psychoanalysis 229, 236, 333, 334, 335

psychoanalytic theory 228
psychobiology. *See* biological psychology; *See* biological psychology
psychodynamic perspective 4, 228, 374
psychological disorder 283, 349
psychology
  contemporary theories of 3
  definition of 1
psychopathology 281, 282, 342
psychopharmacology 348, 374
psychosurgery 350, 374
psychotherapy 7, 229, 242, 331, 333, 347, 348, 349, 392, 404
PTSD. *See* posttraumatic stress disorder
punishment 109, 110, 113, 115, 116, 117, 120, 125, 127, 179, 236, 259, 341, 387
pupil 57

R

rational-emotive behavior therapy 343
reality principle 230
recency effect 137
receptor cell 56
reciprocal determinism 237
reciprocity of liking 274
recovered memories 148, 375
reflection 75, 100, 336
reinforcement 109, 115, 125, 127, 164, 239, 263, 285, 294, 337, 357, 385
reliability 158, 173, 375, 387
REM 82, 83, 84, 87, 88, 89, 375, 407
replication 21
representativeness heuristic 169
repression 322
response generalization 119
retina 58, 61, 81, 363, 368, 371

retinal disparity 73
retroactive interference 143
retrograde amnesia 143
rods 58
Rorschach inkblot test 75, 248
rote rehearsal 133, 135, 150, 376

S

sampling
  random sample 13
  representative sample 13
sampling 12
schema 266
schemas 206
schizoid personality disorder 303
schizophrenia 300, 307, 376
scientific method 11
selection studies 48
selective serotonin reuptake inhibitors (SSRIs) 349
self-actualization 7, 181, 198
self-actualizing tendency 241
self-concept 241
self-efficacy 238, 239
self-fulfilling prophecy 267, 274
self-help 344
semantic memories 139, 377
sensation 28, 36, 55, 56, 57, 64, 65, 66, 67, 77, 187, 367, 378, 412
sensorimotor stage 206
sensory register 130
serial position effect 137
serotonin 289, 348
set point theory 186

sexual dysfunctions 298
sexual masochism 298
sexual orientation 188, 189, 270, 385
sexual sadism 298
short term memory (STM) 132
Sigmund Freud 2, 4, 24, 88, 100
Skinner box 111
sleep 80
  sleep deprivation 81
sleep apnea 85, 377
sleep disorders 84
sleeptalking 86, 378
sleepwalking 86, 378
social anxiety disorder 290, 293, 378
social cognition 261
social development 209
social influence 254, 256, 277, 378
social learning 123
social phobia. *See* social anxiety disorder
social psychology 253, 378
sociocultural perspective 8
Socrates 1, 2, 24
Solomon Asch 255
somatic nervous system 33
somatic symptom disorders 295, 378
somatosensory system 66
sound waves 62, 378
spinal cord 32, 35, 36, 42, 43, 52, 67, 192, 358, 368, 369, 377, 390
spontaneous recovery 117
spreading activation theory of memory 136, 384
stability-change 10
stages of psychosocial development 212

Stanley Milgram 259
stereotypes 186, 267, 268
stimulants 93, 94
stimulus discrimination 119
stimulus generalization 117, 118, 119
strain study 48
stranger anxiety 210
strange situation procedure 210
stress 309, 310, 315, 318, 319, 320, 321, 327, 328, 343, 352, 379, 393, 402, 408
stress-inoculation therapy 343
stressor 310, 316, 320
sublimation 324
substance dependence 96
substance use
  cause of 97
superego 230, 231
support groups 344, 352
surveys 17
sympathetic 34
synapse 29
systematic desensitization 339, 380

T

tactile perception 66
taste buds 64, 65
temperament 48, 205
temporal lobe 39, 40, 64, 397
testosterone 187, 219
thalamus 36, 37, 363
Thematic Apperception Test (TAT) 249
theory 12
theory of evolution. *See* Darwin

theory of multiple intelligences 154
therapeutic alliance 347
therapy
  common effective factors of 347
  effectiveness of 346
thyroid gland 46, 183
tip-of the tongue (TOT) phenomenon 137
token economies 341
trait perspective 228, 243
transduction 56, 59
transference 334
transvestic disorder 299
trepanning 283
trial and error strategy 166
triarchic theory of intelligence 154
trichotillomania 295
trichromatic theory 60
tricyclic antidepressants 348
twin studies 50, 305, 381
two-factor theory 193
type A personality 314, 389, 391
type B personality 314
type D personality 314, 406

U

umami 64
unconditional positive regard 242, 336
  versus conditional positive regard 242
unconditioned response (UR) 106
unconditioned stimulus (US). 105
unconscious. *See* psychodynamic perspective
unconscious mind 229, 235

V

validity 159, 173

vestibular sense 68

visuospatial sketchpad 133

W

wakefulness 79, 80, 82, 98, 355, 366

Weschler Intelligence Scale-Fourth Edition (WAIS-IV) 155

Wilhelm Wundt 2, 3, 24

William James 3

Y

young adulthood 218

Z

zygote 203

IMAGE CREDITS

Cover

Jaxanna Martinez

About the Author

Bill Cruz

Chapter 1

Page 1: ra2studio/Shutterstock, Inc. Page 2: mishabender/Shutterstock, Inc.; Page 4: Levent Konuk/Shutterstock, Inc. Page 5: Novosti/Science Source; Page 7: kuznetcov_konstantin/Shutterstock, Inc.; Page 8: Everett Collection/Shutterstock, Inc.; Page 9: Deklofenak/Shutterstock, Inc.; Page 14: zentilia/Shutterstock, Inc.; Page 16: Tyler Olson/Shutterstock, Inc.; Page 17: Andrey_Popov/Shutterstock, Inc.; Page 22: hakafot/Shutterstock, Inc.; Page 23: Vit Kovalcik/Shutterstock, Inc.

Chapter 2

Page 27: Yakobchuk Vasyl/Shutterstock, Inc.; Page 28: DTKUTOO/Shutterstock, Inc.; Page 29: Designua/Shutterstock, Inc.; Page 30: Designua/Shutterstock, Inc.; Page 32: Jaxanna Martinez; Page 33: Alila Medical Media/Shutterstock, Inc.; Page 34: Alila Medical Media/Shutterstock, Inc.; Page 35: ducu59us/Shutterstock, Inc.; Page 37: BlueSkyImage/Shutterstock, Inc.; Jaxanna Martinez; Page 38: Doggygraph/Shutterstock, Inc.; Page 39: BlueRingMedia/Shutterstock, Inc.; Page 41: Steve Buckley/Shutterstock, Inc.; Allison Herreid/Shutterstock, Inc.; Page 42: Blamb/Shutterstock, Inc.; Page 45: Alila Medical Media/Shutterstock, Inc.; Page 48: Andrea Danti/Shutterstock, Inc.; Page 49: Picture-Pets/Shutterstock, Inc.; mrkornflakes/Shutterstock, Inc.

Chapter 3

Page 55: Little_Desire/Shutterstock, Inc.; Page 57: Kzenon/Shutterstock, Inc.; Page 58: Matthew Cole/Shutterstock, Inc.; Page 59: Designua/Shutterstock, Inc.; Page 60: Foto-Ruhrgebiet/Shutterstock, Inc.; Anna Ismagilova/Shutterstock, Inc.; Page 62: Bill Cruz.; Page 63: Alila Medical Media/Shutterstock, Inc.; Page 65: Luna2631/ Shutterstock, Inc. Page 66: DJTaylor/Shutterstock, Inc.; Page 67: Maridav/ Shutterstock, Inc.; Page 68: Vita Khorzhevska/Shutterstock, Inc.; Page 69: Ye Liew/ Shutterstock, Inc.; Page 70: benchart/Shutterstock, Inc.; Page 72: Nithid Memanee/ Shutterstock, Inc.; Sergey Filin/Shutterstock, Inc.; Page 73: Alila Medical Media/ Shutterstock, Inc.; Page 76: zizar/Shutterstock, Inc.

Chapter 4

Page 79: Bruce Rolff/Shutterstock, Inc.; Page 80: Andrey_Kuzmin/Shutterstock, Inc.; Page 83: Alila Medical Media/Shutterstock, Inc.; Page 86: Circlephoto/ Shutterstock, Inc.; Page 88: Carlos Caetano/Shutterstock, Inc.; Page 91: Kamira/ Shutterstock, Inc.; Page 93: joannawnuk/Shutterstock, Inc.; Page 94: Ehab Edward/ Shutterstock, Inc.; Page 96: William Casey/Shutterstock, Inc.

Chapter 5

Page 103: VLADGRIN/Shutterstock, Inc.; Page 105: Ruffles Art Studio/ Shutterstock, Inc.; Page 106: Jaxanna Martinez; Page 109: Andrei Shumskiy/ Shutterstock, Inc.; Page 110: Jaxanna Martinez; Page 111: Photo Researchers, Inc.; Page 114: Suzi Nelson/Shutterstock, Inc.; Page 116: Igor.stevanovic; Shutterstock, Inc.; Page 118: Bill Cruz.; Page 121: Iculig/Shutterstock, Inc.; Page 123: Bonita R. Cheshier/Shutterstock, Inc.; Page 124: Albert Bandura.

Chapter 6

Page 129: StockImageGroup/Shutterstock, Inc.; Ken Tannenbaum/Shutterstock, Inc.; Page 130: Jaxanna Martinez; Page 131: Kzenon/Shutterstock, Inc.; Page 135: LoloStock/Shutterstock, Inc.; Page 137: s-bukley/Shutterstock, Inc.; Page 139: Andresr/Shutterstock, Inc.; Page 140: BlueSkyImage/Shutterstock, Inc.; Page 141: Sebastian Kaulitzki/Shutterstock, Inc.; Page 144: Blend Images/Shutterstock, Inc.; Page 145: Wavebreakmedia/Shutterstock, Inc.; Page 146: ©Bettman/CORBIS; Page

148: Olesya Feketa/Shutterstock, Inc.

Chapter 7

Page 153: Serget Nivens/Shutterstock, Inc.; Page 155: Rob Byron/Shutterstock, Inc.; Page 156: Bill Cruz; Oage 157: Denis Kuvaev/Shutterstock, Inc.; Page 158: Alila Medical Media/Shutterstock, Inc.; Page 160: MJTH/Shutterstock, Inc.; Page 164: Aletia/Shutterstock, Inc.; Page 166: Pavel Ignatov/Shutterstock, Inc.; Page 167: Jaxanna Martinez; Page 169: Marcel Jancovic/Shutterstock, Inc.; Page 172: Jenn Mackenzie/Shutterstock, Inc.

Chapter 8

Page 177: ArtFamily/Shutterstock, Inc.; Page 179: Kjakimullin Aleksandr/Shutterstock, Inc.; Page 181: Jaxanna Martinez; Page 183: CandyBox Images/Shutterstock, Inc.; Page 184: Sylvie Bouchard/Shutterstock, Inc.; Ryan R Fox/Shutterstock, Inc.; Page 185: Marish/Shutterstock, Inc.; Page 186: Olga Dogadina/Shutterstock, Inc.; Page 188: Curioso/Shutterstock, Inc.; Page 190: Photo Researchers, Inc.; Photo Researchers, Inc.; Page 192: Jaxanna Martinez; Page 193: Jaxanna Martinez; Page 194: Pekic/Shutterstock, Inc.; Page 195: auremar/Shutterstock, Inc.; Page 196: Blend Images/Shutterstock, Inc.; Page 197: Diego Cervo/Shutterstock, Inc.

Chapter 9

Page 201: Mopic/Shutterstock, Inc.; Page 203: udaix/Shutterstock, Inc.; Page 205: Tony Wear/Shutterstock, Inc.; Page 207: Sunny Studio-Igor Yaruta/Shutterstock, Inc.; Page 208: Spencer Grant/Photo Researchers, Inc.; Page 210: Jaxanna Martinez; Page 213: Jaxanna Martinez; Page 215: Rido/Shutterstock, Inc.; Page 216: runzelkorn/Shutterstock, Inc.; Sascha Burkard/Shutterstock, Inc.; Page 219: Diego Cervo/Shutterstock, Inc.; Page 220: auremar/Shutterstock, Inc.; Page 221: Blamb/Shutterstock, Inc.; Page 222: CandyBox Images/Shutterstock, Inc.

Chapter 10

Page 227: Straight 8 Photography/Shutterstock, Inc.; Page 229: Photo Researchers; T and Z/Shutterstock, Inc.; Page 231: Marcin Sylwia Ciesielski/Shutterstock, Inc.;

Page 233: Oksana Kuzmina/Shutterstock, Inc.; Page 235: ollyy/Shutterstock, Inc.; Page 238: Jaxanna Martinez; Page 240: Solphoto/Shutterstock, Inc.; Page 241: Gts/Shutterstock, Inc.; Page 244: Corepics VOF/Shutterstock, Inc.; Page 247: Sinseeho/Shutterstock, Inc.; Page 249: Olimpik/Shutterstock, Inc.

Chapter 11

Page 253: bikeriderlondon/Shutterstock, Inc.; Page 254: originalpunkt/Shutterstock, Inc.; Page 255: Bill Cruz; Page 256: James Lazos/Shutterstock, Inc.; Page 258: La Vieja Sirena/Shutterstock, Inc.; bikeriderlondon/Shutterstock, Inc.; Page 262: Hdc Photo/Shutterstock, Inc.; Page 264: Syda Productions/Shutterstock, Inc.; Page 265: StockLite/Shutterstock, Inc.; Page 269: Tyler McKay/Shutterstock, Inc.; Page 271: cubm/Shutterstock, Inc.; Page 272: Rido/Shutterstock, Inc.; Page 274: Ralf Maassen (DTEruope)/Shutterstock, Inc.; Monkey Business Images/Shutterstock, Inc.; Page 275: William Perugini/Shutterstock, Inc.

Chapter 12

Page 281: RomanRuzicka/Shutterstock, Inc.; Page 282: Bill Cruz; Page 287: Bill Cruz; Page 288: luxorphoto/Shutterstock, Inc.; Page 289: ArtFamily/Shutterstock, Inc.; Page 291: Creatista/Shutterstock, Inc.; Page 292: Andrew Lever/Shutterstock, Inc.; Cartoonresource/Shutterstock, Inc.; Page 293: hxdbzxy/Shutterstock, Inc.; Page 294: Wollertz/Shutterstock, Inc.; Page 297: Corepics VOF/Shutterstock, Inc.; Page 300: Cranach/Shutterstock, Inc.; Page 302: Jaxanna Martinez; Page 303: Eugenio Marongiu/Shutterstock, Inc.; Page 305: Synchronista/Shutterstock, Inc.

Chapter 13

Page 309: Roberto Kneschke/Shutterstock, Inc.; Page 311: Edw/Shutterstock, Inc.; Vladimir Gjorgiev/Shutterstock, Inc.; Page 315: Liewluck/Shutterstock, Inc.; Page 318: Dmitry Lobanov/Shutterstock, Inc.; Page 319: Kzenon/Shutterstock, Inc.; Page 321: Straight 8 Photography/Shutterstock, Inc.; Page 323: gosphotodesign/Shutterstock, Inc.; Page 324: aceshot1/Shutterstock, Inc.; Page 326: © Danny Moloshok/Reuters/Corbis

Chapter 14:

Page 331: wavebreakmedia/Shutterstock, Inc.; Page 334: Adam Gregor/ Shutterstock, Inc.; Page 337: © Justin Lane/epa/Corbis; Page 340: Peter Gudella/ Shutterstock, Inc.; Marcos Mesa Sam Wordley/Shutterstock, Inc.; Page 347: ollyy/ Shutterstock, Inc.; Page 344: Monkey Business Images/Shutterstock, Inc.; Page 346: Olimpik/Shutterstock, Inc.; Page 348: Thirteen/Shutterstock, Inc.; Page 349: Will & Deni McIntyre/Science Source.